The German Aces Speak II

Quarto.com

First published in 2014 by Zenith Press, an imprint of The Quarto Group,
100 Cummings Center, Suite 265-D, Beverly, MA 01915, USA.
T (978) 282-9590 F (978) 283-2742

The Quarto Group titles are also available at discount for retail, wholesale, promotional, and bulk purchase. For details, contact the Special Sales Manager by email at specialsales@quarto.com or by mail at The Quarto Group, Attn: Special Sales Manager, 100 Cummings Center, Suite 265-D, Beverly, MA 01915, USA.

ISBN: 978-0-7603-6155-9

Digital edition published in 2018
eISBN: 978-0-7603-6156-6

The Library of Congress has cataloged the previous edition of this book as follows:

Heaton, Colin D.
The German aces speak II : World War II through the eyes of four more of the Luftwaffe's most important commanders / Colin D. Heaton and Anne-Marie Lewis.
pages cm
Includes bibliographical references.
ISBN 978-0-4603-4590-0 (hbk.)
1. World War, 1939-1945—Aerial operations, German. 2. Germany. Luftwaffe—Officers—Biography. 3. Fighter pilots—Germany—Biography. 4. Fighter pilots—Germany—Interviews. I. Lewis, Anne-Marie. II. Title.
D787.H32163 2011
940.54'4943—dc23
2013035994

Editor: Elizabeth Demers
Design Manager: James Kegley
Layout: Helena Shimizu

The German Aces Speak II

World War II Through the Eyes of Four More of the Luftwaffe's Most Important Commanders

Colin D. Heaton and
Anne-Marie Lewis

Zenith Press

This book is dedicated to the men who flew fighters in World War II, and especially to our late friends, Col. Edward R. "Buddy" Haydon, USAF, who flew in the 352nd Fighter Group, and his wonderful late wife, the lovely Nelda. She waited for him to return despite the odds. They are missed very much and always remembered.

Maj. Urban L. "Ben" Drew, USAF, also left us for his final sortie, and his friendship and assistance over the years are a part of the lasting legacy of the history we produce.

"The warrior merely carries the sword on behalf of others. His task is a lordly one, because the warrior still agrees to die for the mistakes of others."

— *Alexandre Sanguinetti*

Contents

Acknowledgments

WE WISH TO THANK all of the *Luftwaffe* men who assisted with this series of projects over the years, especially the men featured in this volume. We also wish to thank Norman Melton for his perpetual assistance and friendship as well as longtime friends Mike and Ursula Steinhoff Bird. They have been the most supportive people over the last two decades. We also thank Dr. Dennis Showalter and Trevor J. Constable for their assistance and interest in our works over the years, and for writing the forewords. Thanks also to former *Luftwaffe* pilots Jorg Czypionka and Kurt Schulze for proofreading the manuscript.

We also wish to thank the men mentioned in this book for their friendship and assistance, as well as granting the many interviews over the years before they left us: Erich Hartmann, Johannes Steinhoff, Dietrich Hrabak, and Günther Rall. They were fine men and good friends. Special thanks to our friends, the late Colonel Raymond F. Toliver and Trevor J. Constable, who brought the men of the *Luftwaffe* to the postwar world and created the great interest in the subject. It was they who created my interest, which persists to this day.

Special thanks to our agent, Dr. Gayle Wurst of Princeton International Agency for the Arts. Her dedication and diligence have been a key factor in the production of our projects, and for that we are eternally grateful. We would also like to mention Steven Daubenspeck, Elizabeth Demers, Scott Pearson, and Erik Gilg at Zenith Press and thank them for their support in bringing the voices and stories of these aces of World War II to life.

Introduction

LIKE THE FIRST VOLUME in this series, this book focuses on four German fighter pilots who were not only heroes to their nation but also brave men embroiled in a war beyond their control, dedicated to their code of honor as aviators. They were gentlemen of the old school, warriors in a violent conflict who believed in the code of chivalry and fair play. This may sound archaic now, given the devastation of the Second World War and the horrors of the Holocaust, which painted all wartime Germans with a demonic brush, especially after the world awoke to the scope of the almost unspeakable genocide that the Nazis had wrought.

Detractors will try to argue that the airmen of the *Luftwaffe* were no better than the *Einsatzgruppen*, the extermination squads that followed German forces and eliminated "undesirables" per the grand plan. This collective predisposition is, unfortunately, grounded upon misinformation and postwar perceptions. It is of utmost importance to present accurately the men behind the successes and tragedies of the war. We created this series of books to present the personal stories of German aviators in their own words. This oral history method provides a deeper understanding of the nature and evolution of aviation history as well as the agonies and victories these warriors endured. The four German pilots included in this series were like their fellow professional soldiers in that they were dedicated to the survival and protection of their country and their people. As authors, we have found many verified examples of Germans who acted with impeccable conduct and honorable intent; readers thus have the unique opportunity to examine the war from their perspectives.

Many of these men received high postwar security clearances and positions, and some—such as Johannes Steinhoff, Dietrich Hrabak, and Günther Rall—reached the apex of the command structure within the North Atlantic Treaty Organization (NATO). Steinhoff, Hrabak, Rall, and Erich Hartmann are just four representatives among the tens of thousands of young men who may not have wanted a war and may not have believed in their nation's political platform.

The recollections from these four aces are the expanded, unabridged versions of interviews we conducted over many years, as time allowed, with Hrabak, Hartmann, Steinhoff, and Rall, and which we have previously published in abridged format in various magazines such as *World War II*, *Aviation History*, and *Military History*. Whenever possible, we used relevant secondary and primary source material to corroborate and supplement the aces' oral testimony.

We present these aviators' thrilling stories of the war to educate and entertain readers, and to provide an insight into the German perspective on the greatest conflict in history.

Foreword

By Dr. Dennis Showalter

NEVER DID MEN FIGHT better in a worse cause than the soldiers of Nazi Germany. Among them, the fighter pilots stand out. And among the fighter pilots, pride of place goes to the *Experten*. "Ace" was a word the Germans did not use. The British and Americans averaged five victories. Over thirty *Luftwaffe* pilots scored 150, or more. *Experten* indeed. A surprising number of these extraordinary pilots survived the war. Four of them tell their stories here, and their reading takes me back to my collaboration with Johannes Steinhoff on *Voices from the Third Reich*. I can still hear the old-timers comparing missions and experiences, aircraft types and opponents—and, yes, even girls.

In these pages, Steinhoff describes going against American heavy bomber formations. Gunther Rall compares British and Russian fighter pilots. Hartmann recalls some of his epic dogfights—and his ten postwar years as a Soviet captive. And yet these men inspire a wider question: how to explain their participation in a system that is an enduring stench in humanity's nostrils? Their dismissive contempt for the

Reich's leaders, from Hitler and Göring to the functionaries and flunkies that buzzed around the air bases, is a consistent theme. So is their willingness to challenge the competence of the desk heroes who tried to tell them how to fight a war. But one looks in vain for systematic, principled questioning.

This gap can be explained on three levels. First, these pilots were constantly at the air war's cutting edge. There was no rotation to training schools, no war bond tours. Instead the *Experten* were moved from threat point to threat point until their luck ran out—and luck, as Hartmann says, was a big part of survival. But maintaining the complex skills of a fighter pilot was even more important. Survival in air-to-air combat was not a passive act. It ultimately depended on killing, man to man, an enemy no less skilled and determined than oneself. And particularly as stress and fatigue increased, that goal required, above all, focus: mobilizing will power to concentrate on the immediate.

A second crucial factor was the fighter-pilot culture. Owing something to the images of World War I in the air, much to the prewar youth movements, and even more to German romanticism, this mentality emphasized a free spirit that eschewed mundane considerations. It was a significant element of the *Luftwaffe's* ethos. And it discouraged anything resembling systematic introspection.

Third on the list comes the conviction, universal among the *Experten* in particular, that they were defending families and homes, a culture, a way of living. Nazism's success in conflating these with National Socialist ideology, in making them metaphors for the thousand-year Reich, does not render these ideals illegitimate. "You need to understand, Dennis," Johannes once said, "we pilots believed—no, we knew—that we were fighting for everything God gives men to fight for." This may not be a justification. It is an explanation.

Foreword

By Trevor J. Constable

THIS OLD WORLD HAS turned over a few times since the late Col. Raymond F. Toliver and I embarked upon the task of telling something of the German side of the fighter war. Prejudice still rules in many circles, and Ray should have been advanced to general. I recall with some humor the incredulity of German ace Heinz Bär, on learning that Ray had flown a stunning 750 different types of aircraft. Bär had 220 aerial victories to his credit, but Ray's achievements topped his in Bär's personal opinion.

When *The Blond Knight of Germany* eventually came out, it was with a minimum printing. It sold out quickly but was not renewed. The book was sold as a paperback version, which was done without any reference to either of us authors or Erich Hartmann, with whom we had a full agreement.

Then there was a call from Howard Hughes in the middle of the night to secure the film rights to *Blond Knight*. Hughes called it "the greatest book about a fighter pilot I ever read." Howard had the rights for about a year before giving up on it. There was too much opposition. However, today it is different, but there is still staunch opposition to any film regarding Erich, even now.

All four aces in this book are veterans of NATO. You can hear them speak to you as if they were still alive. Thanks to the enterprise of getting them to speak about their lives as they unfolded, you have their comments on a wide range of subjects, including the Nazi hierarchy. General Steinhoff's views on being grabbed by Göring is classic stuff. You will want to hear it more than once. You have in your hands a rare piece of history by four men who made it.

The Blond Knight of Germany

Oberst Erich Hartmann
April 19, 1922–September 19, 1993
1,456 missions, 832 combats, 352 kills
Ten years and seven months in Soviet captivity
Knight's Cross, Oak Leaves (Nr 420),
Swords (Nr 75), Diamonds (Nr 18)

I WAS BORN ON April 19, 1922, in Weissach. This is near Württemberg. My father was a respected physician who had been a doctor in the army in the First World War, and my mother was a licensed pilot. My father would never speak about the war. I know that he saw terrible things, and when Hitler came to power, he was very upset that we Germans could be so damned stupid. My brother also became a doctor after the war.

My father's cousin was a diplomat, the consul for the German embassy in China, and he convinced Father to move us there, since Germany was not exactly the best place to be economically. We had food shortages in Germany, and it was hard for doctors to survive. No one had money; there was nothing like a social health care system. There was very little income. That was why we had previously moved from Weissach to Stuttgart, a larger city with more opportunities.

We lived in Changsha province, and I was young and Alfred was [two years] younger, but I barely remember any of it. Most of what I remember were the things my father and mother told me later. Father had gone ahead for a couple of months, so that he could set up the house, his practice, you know; and we followed a few weeks after receiving the telegram that he was ready for us. We had a nanny, a *Kindermädchen*, and we spoke German and some Mandarin, but I remember very little of it. We were four hundred miles up the Yangtze River. I remember it being a pretty place for the most part.

Finally, things there became bad for foreigners. There had been deaths [of foreigners], and one of my father's friends—a British man, I think also a doctor, and three others—had their heads cut off and placed on fence posts. There had been some random violence against foreigners, mostly from the Communists, who were fighting their former allies, the Kuomintang Nationalists. They carried signs in various languages that read "Foreign Devils Out" and "Death to the Foreign Devils" and things like that.

It was the Nationalists who hated the West, especially the British, French, and Belgians—the primary colonial powers. Remember, after the Great War, Germany had lost all of its colonies, so we were no longer part of this collective group. Then they had the great battle between the two groups [Nationalists and Communists] in Shanghai in 1927. That was the last straw, and my father sent us home. My mother found an office for his practice, so when he came home, he could go straight to work.

I became a pilot for probably the same reason as most boys—to recapture the glory of the aces in the Great War—as well as the fact that my mother was a licensed pilot. She started flying once we came home and [already] had her light-plane license. My mother went into part ownership of a small plane with a family friend. They used to fly out of the airport at Bad Böblingen. After the Great Depression hit Germany, they had to sell the plane in 1930. Then Hitler came to power in 1933, and people could fly again within a year or so.

My mother used to take Alfred and me up and teach us things. My father wanted nothing to do with it, but he humored her. My father thought that I was a kind of daredevil, or an idiot. I knew I wanted to fly, as did Alfred, but my father was less than enthusiastic. Under Hitler, there could not be an open powered-aircraft flight program [official program due to the Treaty of Versailles], not at first. Then they allowed a commercial flight-training program, but the Treaty of Versailles was harsh to Germany. That was how Hitler came to power. He passed the order that every village, every town had to have a glider-training program. This was to be part of the Hitler Youth program, so I did not have to formally join the Hitler Youth, as did most kids [not in flying programs].

I became a licensed glider pilot at fourteen and flew as often as I could. We had this homemade glider, built well. It was placed on a sloping hill, fairly steep, perhaps a forty to fifty degree angle. This large, braided, rubber rope was used as a pulley, and as the pilot sat inside, maybe eight, ten, or twelve people would each grab an end, like using a slingshot. This launched the glider into the air, and we could sometimes get about six to twelve feet high and then gain some altitude on the way down. We used to keep the time, logging our seconds in the air for each flight.

These experiences really gave me a feel for the air, for control surfaces, and for later when you have to land without power. Later, our formal [*Luftwaffe*] training was also in gliders, so those of us with this previous experience did the best. When we were lucky, we launched into a headwind, which gave us lift, and you could really get some flight time. I did not have the longest flight, but I did have one that lasted about twenty seconds or so. The average was about eight to ten seconds.

We [glider club boys] had some problems with this one group—a gang, I think you would say. This sounds stupid, but we were the glider club; the real troublemakers were the bicycle gang. We sometimes had fights, but what about I cannot even remember. However, it became serious one night when one of our glider boys came and told us that the bicycle boys had taken my brother and another boy we knew. They had taken them to a barn nearby and were going to hurt them. We ran as fast as we could. It was not far. We went in, and I found this long tire jack and attacked them all. There were over a dozen of them, and they all ran. They never bothered us again.

I managed a lot of flying time in gliders, and I became an instructor at age fifteen. Alfred later became a Stuka gunner flying in North Africa, and he was captured in Tunisia. That was probably lucky for him and saved his life. My father was not pleased that I wanted to be a pilot, as he wanted us both to follow him into medicine, and this was also a dream that I had, but it was not to be. Then I met Uschi.

I was a typical German boy, I guess, as was my brother Alfred. We had some problems, due to mischief, but nothing really bad, although we did sink a kayak once. We used to ride it over this shallow, man-made dam at the lake nearby. We enjoyed that. But, another time I decided to take it over a higher dam, and it ripped on something, a nail in a board under water, and the kayak split down the middle. The kayak was finished, and both it and I washed over the dam wall. On another occasion, I entered into a ski jump event, a competition. The only problem was I had never been on skis before. I made the jump, but my father called me a clown. Once I made a homemade glider, wood and canvas. I took it to the roof and launched. It did not end well, but I was not hurt.

Uschi and I were in the same school, and finally I decided to track her down. I caught up with her and a girlfriend, stopped my bicycle, and introduced myself. I knew that she was the one for me, although I was only seventeen and she was two years younger. Our parents were none too thrilled about it, I can tell you, but they came around. At this time, Uschi had another admirer. I made a great mistake of taking her out on a date, to a film at the cinema, and I lost track of time. I brought her back very late, and her parents gave her a three-month restriction, and she could go no place but school and back. She was not to have any contact with me because I was a bad influence.

Uschi used to take dance lessons, and she went to this studio. Her father or mother would take her. I would wait around the corner, and then when they left I would go in. This was how we still met. The teacher finally became tired of seeing me there and asked me to leave. So, I paid and signed up for the dancing classes! We called ourselves Romeo and Juliet, but Uschi said that she was not going to kill herself over me, so I could forget about that. I told her that I would never let that happen. She was the love of my life. We were teenagers, but we knew even then that we were to be together forever.

Uschi kept telling me about this boy in school. He kept calling her for dates, coming to the house. She did not like him. I went to speak with him and told him to stay away from my girlfriend. He kept calling, so a week later I went to see him again. He was two years older, a bigger kid. He just looked down at me and laughed. I dropped him with two punches. He then agreed to leave her alone.

Uschi and I were destined to be together; that was fate. And she waited a long time, even after the war. We were married in 1944, after I had the Diamonds, and Gerd [Gerhard] Barkhorn was my best man with Willi [Wilhelm] Batz and Krupi [Walter Krupinski] as witnesses. However, we still had little time to spend together. We could not marry in a church due to the logistical problems [this was due to having to book a church in advance and Erich's combat schedule]. That would have to wait until 1956, when I returned [from Soviet captivity], so we married in the *Rathaus*, or town hall.

I started military flight training in October 1940 in East Prussia. This lasted until January 1942 when I went to Zerbst-Anhalt. I graduated as a *Leutnant* in March 1942. Later, I went to advanced aerial gunnery school and advanced fighter training at Berlin-Gatow, where I got into a little trouble. I was showing off, buzzing the airfield, and was sentenced to house arrest. They also made me pay two-thirds of my monthly salary for three months. Ironically, my roommate flew the same aircraft I had been in. It developed a technical problem, and he was killed in the crash. After completing my school, I received my orders.

My first scare was in this school, where I had just transitioned into the 109. We were to take a *Schwarm* of student pilots—solo flying, of course—and perform a timed event. We were to scramble, take off, and climb to four thousand meters, probably around thirteen thousand feet or so. Then we were to dive and land. This had to be done within a certain amount of time. I had to do it again because I fell behind. I was the last one to make it. I took off, reached the altitude, did the split-S [maneuver] to return when something went "bang," and I felt this fast rush of cold air. The plane started spinning, and I remember releasing the canopy and I was out, tumbling. I then felt the parachute open and I landed fine. It was a mechanical problem rather than anything I did, and I still graduated with top marks.

I arrived in Russia and reported to JG-52 just before the winter [1942], after a slight mishap. Well, I would not say crashed, because I never got off the ground. We were supposed to fly Stukas to Mariopol, but when I started the Stuka, I realized that it had no brakes, and it reacted differently from a Messerschmitt 109. Because I could not stop, I crashed into the operations shack, and another man flipped his Ju-87 up over on its nose. They decided to send us in a Ju-52, since it was safer both for the aircraft and for us.

Dieter Hrabak [Hartmann's commanding officer upon arriving] has been a good friend over the years, as has his wonderful wife, Marianne. Dieter was the first person to tell me to talk to you, since he and the others trust you. I like you also. Dieter was a very understanding yet disciplined commander, and his experience showed. When I first arrived, I was sent to his underground bunker at Maikop. He gave me the same talk that I would later have from Paule Rossmann. He explained how we fight the war here, and that new pilots had to rely upon the veterans. I would be taking orders in the air from men far below me in rank. It was experience that mattered in the air. Rank was left on the ground.

Hrabak taught us how not just to fly and fight but also how to work as a team and stay alive. That was his greatest gift. He was very open to discussing his own mistakes and how he learned from them, hoping we would learn also. Hrabak assigned me to 7./III./JG-52 [7th *Staffel* of the 3rd *Gruppe* from JG-52; each *Gruppe* had three to four *Staffeln*] under *Major* Hubertus von Bonin, an old eagle from the Spanish Civil War and the Battle of Britain. We learned a lot from him also.

My new wing commander [Hrabak] was addressing me when a fighter came in smoking and suddenly landed, flipped over, and exploded. We knew the pilot was dead. One of the men said, "It is Krupinski," and out of the blinding smoke this man walked from the wreckage with a singed uniform but no other damage. He was smiling and complained about the flak over the Caucasus, but without any real surprise on his face. This was my first meeting with "The Count." He had landed in a pile of bombs. Amazing. Well, he [Walter "Krupi" Krupinski] came in, introduced himself, demanded another plane, went up, was shot down, scored a victory, and was brought back by car. He then took another plane, scored two kills, and returned, then wanted dinner. The whole event was treated as casually as a card game. Batz looked at me and said, "That is *Graf* ["Count"] Krupinski, and he is not quite right in the head."

Another thing about Krupi, and I say this because he is still today one of my best friends, he was the biggest playboy I ever knew. This guy had girls everywhere. I mean, when he landed someplace, there was always a girl waiting for him, and still I do not know how he did it. When he met Uschi, he was very open and said that she was very beautiful and asked if she had any sisters. He is still a clown, but more settled now that he has been married for many years.

My first mission was on October 14, 1942. [*Feldwebel* Eduard] "Paule" Rossmann and I were in our flight, and Rossmann radioed that he spotted ten enemy aircraft below us. He was a seasoned combat veteran. I was told [by Hrabak], "Today you fly with Rossmann, and he is a good leader and never lost a wingman. He will teach you." That was important for the new man in a unit. I learned this and passed this concept down when I became a leader.

In being a fighter pilot, confidence is everything. If you do not have that and the hunter instinct, you should go to bombers. For example, even [Adolf "Dolfo"] Galland lost a lot of wingmen and a couple were killed, perhaps due to his hunting nature or bad luck. Even [Hans-Joachim] Marseille, whom I did not know personally, also had that type of reputation later in North Africa. Before that, he had lost several [wingmen]. In battle, I would break contact from the enemy if I lost sight or radio contact with my wingman. Keeping the unit integrity was the most important thing to me. You learn by good examples. My first mission with Rossmann would not be something that I would be proud of later. I was an idiot.

We were at twelve thousand feet, and the enemy was far below us. I could see nothing, but I followed Rossmann down and then we came upon them. I knew that I had to get my first kill, so I went full throttle and left Rossmann to shoot at a plane. My shots missed, and I almost collided and had to pull up. Suddenly I was surrounded by the Soviets, and I headed for low cloud cover to escape. All along, Rossmann kept talking to me, and I had a low-fuel warning. Then the engine went dead and I bellied in, destroying my fighter. I knew I was in trouble. I had violated every commandment [rule] a fighter pilot lives by, and I expected to be thrown out of the unit.

I was sentenced by [*Major* Hubertus] von Bonin to spend three days working with the ground crews. It gave me time to think about what I had done. I was lucky. I could have been given a court-martial. What I learned from Rossmann and later Krupinski I later taught to new pilots when I became a leader. I learned that being a good leader is more important than being a successful fighter pilot with a lot of victories.

After the incident, Rossmann and I had a long talk. He walked in and saluted me—I was the senior officer—and I felt like the schoolboy who forgot his homework. We called each other by first names, too. He was a good man, and he cared a lot about the new pilots and me. Just as Hrabak had told us not "to fly with the muscles, but fly with the head," Rossmann gave me words of great wisdom. "It is not necessary that you go straight at the enemy when you first see them. Look at their formation, their tactics. Look to see if there is a straggler falling behind. Maybe he has a problem or is not experienced. Take him down first. That has a psychological effect. The emotional fighter will lose the battle. The pilot who keeps his head and thinks will win."

I never forgot that. I remembered that when I scored my first kill and all the rest. In the beginning, I had little respect for [Soviet] pilots because of their way of fighting and the very primitive technology they had. I looked over a few of their aircraft. They did not have gun sights, and sometimes they had a circle painted inside the windscreen. However, I learned to respect their abilities later.

That was a day I will never forget, scoring my first kill, November 5, 1942. It was a Shturmovik IL-2, the toughest aircraft to bring down because of its heavy armor plate. You had to shoot out the oil cooler underneath; otherwise, it would not go down. I had learned from Krupinski to wait until I was about a hundred meters away from my target before I fired. Now, you are probably closing in fast. The angle of the attack is not as important as the distance from your target. Some pilots slow down, use the flaps, and match the enemy speed. I understood that Marseille did this. That is dangerous. Some pilots without much experience will close in and then be afraid of a collision, but that will not happen if you follow the basic rules. I always came in fast, closed, fired, and pulled away. I did not want to be hit by pieces flying off, but that did happen on several occasions and even on this one, actually.

That was also the day of my second forced landing, since I had flown into the debris of my kill. I learned two things that day: Get in close, shoot, and break away immediately after scoring the kill. We had flown in a large formation; Rall, Steinhoff, and all of us were in the air. Right after this mission, Rall and Steinhoff had to go receive their Oak Leaves. My next kill came in February the following year. This was when Krupinski came to Taman and was my new squadron leader. He replaced [*Hauptmann* Wilhelm] "Willi" Batz, who was an excellent fighter pilot and a good leader. I learned much from him, a fine gentleman.

My first winter in Russia and Ukraine was memorable, and I thought I would freeze to death. We hardly ever had buildings to stay in. We lived in tents over dugout bunkers and holes in the ground, like Boy Scouts. Steinhoff, Hrabak, and others who had already been through the previous winter reminded me that the winter of 1941 was the worst in living history, and they told me stories of how bad that was.

They were in the North Caucasus at that time, when the temperatures dropped to fifty degrees below zero as an average temperature. Sometimes it was even colder. Men froze to death and machines locked up. I could not imagine such an extreme, until I went into the gulags.

That first winter was still damned cold, and we had a lot of problems with the motors. We used to have the crew chiefs start them every hour and run them for about ten minutes around the clock to keep them operational. Then we got very lucky. We had a Russian prisoner, who was no fan of Stalin or the Communists, show us how to start our engines in the sub-zero cold by mixing gasoline into the oil crankcase. I thought it was crazy. This was unheard of to us, and we were sure we would lose a fighter in the explosion. It worked because the fuel thinned out the congealed oil and evaporated as the starter engaged. It was wonderful. Another guy showed us how to start a fire under the cowling, keeping the oil and coolant warm, and start the engine—another helpful hint. This same guy showed us how to keep the weapons firing by dipping them in boiling water, thus removing the lubricants that froze the mechanisms shut.

Without the oils, they worked fine in the freezing weather. I felt sad for these prisoners, who hated no one and were forced to fight a war they would rather have avoided. We took care of these men as long as we could, until they had to be handed over to the authorities and sent to prisoner of war camps. The Ukrainian man told us that the Russians came in twice and took his farm, all of his grain that he grew, and that they did this to everyone. He was a boy the first time, in the 1920s, a teenager I think. His father argued with the official, and they shot him on the spot. Then they came again just a few years before the war, and again they took everything.

We knew that millions of Ukrainians died from starvation. Stalin wanted their food for the Russians, and the rest he sold for money internationally. Stalin needed currency. The Ukrainians and many others were arrested and sent to mines and labor camps. We Germans have a bad reputation because of the Jews, and that is deserved, I will admit. However, we never hear anything about the Soviets, their crimes, killing their own people, the gulags and mass murder, what they did to other Europeans during and after the war.

Günther Rall had been badly wounded in a crash back in November 1941, a year before. The only good thing that came out of that was his marriage to his doctor, Hertha, a wonderful lady. Rall came back to flying with JG-52, and he replaced von Bonin as the new *Gruppenkommandeur*, and this is when I met him. That was the beginning of our friendship. In August 1943, Rall made me *Kommandeur* of the 9. *Staffel*, which had been Hermann Graf's command. This was when I flew with Krupi for a while. I think it was about this time I learned that my brother Alfred had been captured in Tunisia. I would not see him again for over a decade.

We had fights with every kind of aircraft you could imagine. We fought against the P-40, Yak, MiG, LaGG, Pe, and Il models, even Hurricanes, Spitfires, and Airacobras. In my opinion, only the Spitfire, which was a rare sight, and the Yak were a real danger in combat, as long as the 109 was flown by a good pilot. The LaGG was very fast and not as maneuverable, but it could catch us, especially from altitude. We jokingly called it the flying coffin, because it was made of wood and the dead man was already in it. The airframe was rather light with a powerful engine in later models, and heavy cannon. It was very dangerous.

However, it was our tactics that made the difference, as well as our communications. Many of these enemy aircraft did not have radios, or gun sights, except for the American and British fighters, and they were really flown by clowns [unskilled pilots]. The exceptions were the Red Banner units. It was because of our advantages in training, equipment, communications, tactics, and leadership that we amassed so many kills. Not to mention that we were always outnumbered, often ten or twenty to one on the average mission. We had a lot of targets.

We learned that the United States had sent something like ten thousand fighters to the Soviet Union. The Soviet pilots loved the Airacobra and King Cobra [two variants of the P-39 design], which by all accounts were inferior in fighter-against-fighter combat, but they were one hell of a great ground attack aircraft. The Soviets used their aircraft more like flying artillery. The weapons system on that beast [P-39] was impressive—machine gun and cannon and a rear-mounted engine, air-cooled. We ran into a lot of them in 1942 through 1943. Our ground troops and panzer men hated them, almost as much as they hated the IL-2.

The P-40 [Warhawk] was also outclassed by our 109 and especially the Fw-190. It was a good ground attack aircraft with six machine guns, but it could not duel with us. Those guys were always lost in battle. It is also interesting that, when I first arrived at the front in October 1942, we really did not see too many enemy aircraft in our sector, the southern front. Even so, we shot a lot of them down. With this new equipment from the United States [Lend Lease], the enemy also soon had better aircraft of their own; the Yak-7 and 9 and the LaGG-5 and 7 were aircraft that you had to be wary of by 1943. The MiG-3 was better than the MiG-1.

All these had heavy cannon, and the latest Yak was the one airplane that could turn and dive with a 109, but it could not out-climb the Gustav. This was especially true with emergency power boost [on the G model].

We never saw many cars, trucks, or anything like that until 1943—mostly T-34s and a few American-made [M4] Shermans and other lighter tanks. Nineteen forty-three was a very different year. We saw many automobiles—Buicks, Studebakers, jeeps—and of course aircraft, so many we could not really count them all. Very few ground vehicles were Russian made. The Russians had a strange attack method on the ground. I saw this myself, when we were flying over Stalingrad. In that area, they would attack in waves of five or six ranks. The first wave had weapons, and the following soldiers had nothing. They did not even have tank support—nothing. They had to pick up the weapons from the dead and wounded and keep going forward. Then the next wave did the same thing, and the next. It was incredible to us. Throwing away lives that way.

One memorable day was August 1, 1943. We had a large fight with a lot of Russians. Some of the men called out Yaks, which I did not see, as I was in a fight with nine LaGGs. I shot down five of these because I managed to hit them from above, shooting down two quickly, then I pulled up and killed another one. The two remaining in that group tried to climb, but I had more speed. I caught them. I shot one LaGG and he just broke apart—the pilot bailed out—while the other LaGG still thought he could outrun me. Then the craziest thing happened.

This guy dropped his landing gear and his engine. He stopped in midair, and I was almost going to collide into the back of him. I pushed the rudder and half rolled, pulling past him, still climbing. I did not want to get shot in the back, so I pulled the stick all the way back, got away, and then reversed, rolled back, and looked to the right. He had stalled and was falling, actually tumbling back to earth. I followed him down and was going to shoot, but I decided not to. He never recovered and struck the ground and burned.

All the time I kept hearing cries of "*Horrido!*" over the radio and knew that the guys were getting some good scores. I thought I knew where Barkhorn's *Staffel* was, so I flew there. I had just arrived when I heard someone call out a Yak, and then I heard Gerd call out one also. I looked up and saw this Yak smoking, coming through the clouds, followed by Gerd's 109. I knew this would be an easy kill to confirm.

Then, about August 5, 1943, we heard that some of our victories were being questioned. My name came up, as did those of [Hermann] Graf, Rall, Barkhorn, Steinhoff, [Alfred] Grislawski. Göring could not believe the staggering kills being recorded from 1941 on. By 1943, we were sweeping large numbers of the enemy out of the skies. I even had a man in my unit, Friedrich "Fritz" Obleser, who questioned my kills.

The first questions came from *Unteroffizier* Carl Junger, and the men [in the unit] were whispering that I had claimed more kills than I had. They did not bother to ask the men who flew with me, who had confirmed these victories. That made me angry. Later, Junger would be my wingman and see my method. Obleser and I knew each other, and we were in flight school together and arrived at JG-52 at the same time. He went to 8. *Staffel* and I was in 7. *Staffel*. He was a good pilot and had success, but I do not think that he was a great shot. I do not claim to be, either; I was an ambush hitter. But Obleser also questioned my kills.

So, I spoke with Hrabak, who knew better, and then I asked Rall to have Obleser transferred from the 8. *Staffel* to be my wingman for a while in 9. *Staffel.* Obleser had flown with Rall as his wingman many times and confirmed many of his 275 victories, and he flew leading his own *Rotte* with my flight so that he could observe. Rall was in the hospital, and that was how I overtook him in the scoring. Same with Barkhorn. He became a believer after a few missions and signed off on some kills as a witness, and we became friends after that.

Sometimes I flew with Krupinski, Graf, Grislawski, Steinhoff, Rall, and of course Barkhorn. All of these men were great fighter pilots—the best. Having a kill confirmed was not an easy thing. If you did not have a witness in the air, then you had to have one on the ground; if not a witness, then you had to have the crash site. We hardly ever had gun cameras in Russia, and that would have helped many men confirm kills that crashed on the enemy side of the line when there was no air witness. You also had to have the altitude of the attack, aircraft type, time, and location all in your *Abschuss.*

Then this information went to the *Kommodore,* then to *Oberkommando der Luftwaffe,* and then to the *Reichstluftministerium,* or Reich Air Ministry. It sometimes took months to have a victory confirmed in the official record, even when we painted the victory bars on our rudders in the unit. The unit record was kept, of course, and that was how commanders based promotions and award recommendations, which then also had to go all the way up the chain. I know that Gerd Barkhorn was recommended for the Diamonds, and as far as I know it was approved, but the process took too long. He was never awarded those before the war ended, and he was in the hospital anyway, after his jet accident.

The partnership with Krupinski was a little uneasy at first, but we found that we worked well together. It was

Krupi who believed in my ability, or perhaps psychic ability, to sense when something was wrong with an aircraft. I cannot explain it, but I often knew if there was a problem long before the instruments told me anything. I received a new 109G—well, almost new—but it had not flown in combat. [Heinz] Bimmel Mertens wanted to run his usually thorough mechanical checklist, revving the motor, checking everything. I told him that it would not be necessary, as it had just been flown to the field that morning.

Rall, Krupi, Gerd, and I were the four horsemen, I guess, since Graf had stopped flying on orders. [Graf had been a professional footballer, and he was sent to play as goalkeeper for the *Luftwaffe* team. This was part of the Propaganda Ministry's public relations program.] By that time of our competition, Macky had gone to JG-77. We heard that Macky was getting the Swords, and we sent him a telegram to say congratulations. Then that night and for the rest of the month, we had fresh steaks for every meal. One of the pilots had accidentally killed a cow in a field near the base. Some of us went out hunting. It was not very sporting, hitting a cow, but it was fresh meat.

I started the engine with Bimmel's help and taxied down the grass field. As soon as I lifted off, I set the trim and eased off the rudder and pulled back on the stick. Everything seemed to be good, but I sensed a vibration—something was not in order. I turned around to have Bimmel do his check. I knew he was right. I landed, and as soon as I opened the canopy, Hrabak came out and asked what the problem was. I told him that something was wrong. It was not that he did not believe me; he just thought I was wrong. So, he decided to climb in and test fly it himself. Krupi was standing there also with his camera. He had been taking some photos for his scrapbook.

Hrabak took off quickly, pulled the landing gear up, and climbed. He had not even reached five hundred meters when we all heard this loud bang, and then smoke started pouring from the cowling. Hrabak banked and quickly set the 109 down, and he jumped out as it was still rolling with the ignition and fuel switches off. Later, we learned from Bimmel that a piston had cracked under pressure, destroying the engine. The vibration I had sensed was that one piston that was not working, placing strain on the motor. After that, no one ever doubted my opinions on the mechanical issues with a fighter.

I will tell you one story, and I do not think that Hrabak knows this. He only needed a few kills to receive the Oak Leaves, so the word was passed around that the best pilots would try and be assigned with him, to watch his back, and help him get those kills. During one of these missions, when Krupi collided with a Russian, Hrabak had two Yaks on him. I saw this and I thought he was dead, but Gerd shot down one, and I closed on the other. Hrabak never even knew they were there! We wanted him to have the Oak Leaves.

He was like the father figure to us, although he was only eight or ten years older, but that is old for a fighter pilot. Anyway, everyone wanted to see him get the Oak Leaves, so we all kept the enemy off of him and opened up opportunities for him to score. I learned later that these guys did the same thing for Barkhorn and me when we both were coming close to three hundred kills. It was a way to show appreciation to a great pilot without it looking like charity. I even did this for many others, including [Hans-Joachim] Birkner.

We had a saying that if a leader is good, take him up and watch his back. However, if a leader was bad, let him go up and perhaps he will not come back. That sounds harsh, but I know that [Gordon] Gollob earned his decorations the hard way. No one liked him in JG-3 and JG-54, and when he went to JG-77 he scored his last kills in 1942. Hitler took him off flying status. The rumor was that Diamonds winners were to not fly anymore, but I think it was because there were so many requests for transfers from the units when he was there. It saved face for him. I believe that.

We both had strengths and weaknesses and managed to overcome these problems. It worked out well. Besides, I had to make sure that he came home to his many girlfriends always waiting on him. I won the Iron Cross 2nd Class while flying with Krupi. One of the things I learned from him was that the worst thing to do was to lose a wingman. Kills were less important than survival. I only lost one wingman, Günther Capito, a former bomber pilot, but this was due to his inexperience with fighters, and he survived.

Once I saw Rall almost killed. We were fighting in the Dnieper region, and our base was being attacked nearly every day. We all scrambled and intercepted the enemy fighters. Rall was flying with Birkner as his wingman, and we had all been off the ground maybe five minutes when I saw Rall's plane. A LaGG had hit him from altitude and caused a great explosion and smoke in his cockpit, and he crash-landed. I radioed in, and Birkner said that he was also hit but still in the air. Rall's oxygen bottle had been hit by a cannon shell, and it blew up, cutting his head. There was blood all in the cockpit. He was okay and flew again in a couple of days. I got the LaGG.

I knew that some of my comrades were getting annoyed with me. I would come back from almost every mission with enemy contact or a kill. When I flew in only a *Rotte* or *Schwarm*, we had the most success. The enemy thought "only two or four planes; we can get them." They did not. I had a secret that I learned during a *Rotte* patrol with Junger. We saw a well-camouflaged air base near Nikopol—big but not so easy to see. I knew this because I once followed a Russian fighter to see where he was going. This became my hunting ground.

Obviously, the others wanted to know where I was finding these aircraft. This was where the rumors and questions began as to my victories, I think. I used to take off before the sun came up, so I could be near Nikopol. They would take off at dawn, and I could sometimes catch them from higher altitude. One evening, Rall came to me and asked me when I was leaving in the morning. He wanted to go with me. We took off, and I headed south again. He came over the radio and asked why was I going south. He decided to head north with his wingman and hunt. He had just turned away when I called out this Pe-2 and two LaGGs that had appeared. Junger saw them also, and I told Rall that I was going to have a fight and he could just enjoy the show.

Rall yelled at me to wait—he wanted to join the party—but I had already shot the Pe-2 down and was firing into a LaGG that was on fire. Rall saw both kills, and Junger got the last one. I was laughing about that. Rall said, "So, this is where you have been hunting, you secretive bastard." Rall said he would keep the secret if we flew together and he could get some kills, and I said okay, but his wingman had to keep his mouth shut. We all agreed. That would be our private hunting ground.

Not long after that, I was coming back from a flight and scored three kills but was out of ammunition. I heard Rall on the radio, so I vectored him to the place I had just left. I had shot down three, but there were still about eight Airacobras there, and I knew that they had to be low on fuel. Rall thanked me and took [Joachim] Birkner with him. I learned that he had good kills, and the confirmation was easy. Our Russian speakers were listening to the radio, and they heard the leader of the Red Banner fighters call out the men he had lost to a 109. That was good enough. [The Germans would tune into Soviet radio channels and listen to the air battles from the enemy perspective, hoping to gather intelligence.]

There were so many good friends, most of whom are still alive, but my closest relationship was with Heinz "Bimmel" Mertens, my crew chief. You rely upon your wingmen to cover you in the air, and your teammates in aerial battle, but the man who keeps your machine flying and safe is the most important man you know. Even during the coldest winter, when other mechanics were inside getting warm, Bimmel would be working on my fighter, making sure it was at peak performance. He would let no one else touch my engine. We became best of friends, and none of my success would have been possible if not for Mertens. There is a bond there.

Whenever I received food packages or special things from home, I always made sure that Bimmel shared in these. He took great care of me, and my planes. I can't explain it. It is like having a brother. When I went missing on the mission where I was captured and escaped, Mertens had taken a rifle and went looking for me. He would not give up. That is loyalty you never find outside the military.

Once when I was gone for a few weeks on leave, Gerd Barkhorn decided that, due to his efficiency as a mechanic and his high ratings, that he would take Mertens away from me to be his personal mechanic. Gerd outranked me and could do this, but Bimmel was not happy about it. He did something unlike him, and stupid, that Gerd noticed right away, and he fired him. I came back and Gerd said that Bimmel should be court-martialed for sabotaging his aircraft, and he was upset. I told him I would handle it. I spoke with Bimmel, and he just wanted to come back to me. Many others tried to get Bimmel away from me. He was the best mechanic I ever knew.

The day I went down, the Russians were attacking in our area and Hrabak gave us our orders. Early that morning, the Russians had launched an attack. Our orders were to support the bombers, bomb and strafe all traffic and troops in the open, to stop them from breaking the German line. This was on August 20, 1943, and we took off at first light, barely dawn at 0400. Our mission was to support the Stukas of Hans-Ulrich Rudel in a counterattack. They were flying tank-busting Stukas, with under-wing cannons, not bombs. They were hunting tanks. Rudel is a man I respect, but he was, to be polite, just insane. He was perhaps the bravest man I ever knew, but then again you have to use common sense in combat, at some point. He was probably the luckiest man who ever lived. I just think that he did not care about his own safety.

They went into their attack, hitting tanks, T-34s, and they were burning. The enemy aircraft were at low altitude, perhaps one or two thousand meters staggered, and we were above them, circling. I chased this one Yak down, who was already smoking, and he never pulled out. He crashed into the ground and exploded. We had IL-2s in the air also, and it seemed that we were greeted by the whole Red Air Force. Some enemy planes went down. Then things changed. The Red Air Force was bombing German ground positions in support of their offensive, so my flight of eight fighters located and attacked the enemy—about forty LaGGs and Yaks with another forty or so Shturmovik ground attack aircraft.

I closed in on one IL-2 and fired about ten cannon rounds, and he went down, smoking and on fire to the left. I pulled away and climbed, and then saw others. I went full throttle and lined up another, coming up from six o'clock low, and fired. The IL-2 began smoking and then exploded. I had shot down two of them when a fragment of something hit my plane. I thought that I had flown into the pieces of one of my kills, but it turned out to be flak. It knocked out the cooler, and the engine started to overheat and die. I knew I was in trouble, since I was perhaps twenty or thirty kilometers into enemy territory. I learned later that where I had landed had been no-man's land between the lines. The enemy had advanced far enough to where I was in their territory.

I prepared for a crash-landing—ignition off, fuel off, flaps down just before impact, and then neutral flaps to slide across the ground, just like a glider. After a good forced landing, I was captured by Soviet soldiers. I faked that I was injured, holding my back as they all approached the plane, while I was taking the cockpit clock out of the instrument panel to destroy it. Those were our orders, if we were ever forced down. One man climbed on the wing and tried to lift me out, so I screamed in pain—fake, of course, as I was unhurt. The man let me go and climbed down.

Then a few minutes later, others came, shouting, "Comrade! Comrade!" I was a little stunned at this greeting. I expected to be shot or beaten to death. That had happened before to our pilots. I must have faked being injured well. They placed me on the ground—very gently, I should add—and took a tent canvas and placed me on it, like a litter of sorts, and carried me. They placed me in this truck and we drove away. They believed me completely and took me to their HQ, placed me on a large table, and their doctor examined me, and he even believed me. He tried to speak with me, but he did not know much German and I did not speak Russian. I just reacted to his probing on my spine, as if I were in great pain. The doctor wrote something down and placed a tag around my neck. I guess he was fooled.

The men then brought me some food—apples and other fruits and some bread, I think—but I did not eat anything. I did not trust the food, and I also knew, from my father being a doctor, that people in great pain cannot eat. I wanted to maintain the charade. After a couple of hours, they came and placed me back on this tent, carried me, and placed me in the back of this open truck [which was a German vehicle painted with a red star] on a stretcher. I had been thinking the entire time of how I could get out of this problem. I knew that the longer I waited, the farther east I would be taken, and the chance of escape dropped with every minute.

I was lucky that they thought I had an injured back, which was very plausible in a crash-landing. Ten or so men took me to the village, but I only had one guard and one driver as we were leaving, and their attention wandered. It was as if God said to me, "Now, this is your chance. Take it." The truck rolled along this unpaved cattle road, bouncing and shaking me. I thought that if I did not get out of this truck soon, I would have a real back injury. The soldier sitting with me seemed concerned, as my body bounced a few inches up and then hit the floor again. I played this to the hilt, so he even set his rifle down. Then after only about ten minutes, the guard became nervous, and as Stukas made their attacks nearby, I was certain that our truck would be a target. I was not going to die this way. I thought of Uschi, my family, and friends. I was getting the hell out of there.

Then, as if by divine action, we started driving through an area full of sunflowers, perhaps three meters tall—a forest of them. I thought about my personal things that had been taken. I was pretty sure this guard had my wristwatch, medals, pistol, map, and other things, including a photo of Uschi and me. I thought about looking for them after I hit him, but I decided that every second lost was a chance at failure. I made my move. The guard had his head turned to the front, so I jumped up and I rushed the one guard in the truck. He was not wearing a helmet. He fell and hit the windscreen, and I think he was probably knocked out. The driver acted as if the guard [in the back] had been shot. He must have thought we were hit by the Stukas at first. The good thing was that he had no weapon in the cab with him, as far as I knew.

The guard in the back of the truck fell down and forward, and I went out the back. I heard the truck stop, so I had to keep moving. I do not think I ever ran so fast in my life. I found myself in a great field of very tall sunflowers, where I tried to hide as I ran, and I remember looking at the sun in the east, estimating it was around 0900. I ran for about ten more minutes through this field until I ran into a forest of trees, and nearby was a small village.

The small village was occupied by Russians [civilians], soldiers too—I saw their fur hats and uniforms. I thought that, given the heat, wearing fur was crazy. I figured that they would start looking west, so I decided to return to the area I had just come from and wait for nightfall. As I started, I heard noises, and I looked out and saw all of these people digging trenches, and that meant that I had to be near the front. I remember wishing that I had my map with me, but the Russians had taken that also. It was during this time that Mertens, who spoke Russian, took it upon himself to take off and find me, armed with only a rifle and water, as he was concerned when I did not return. Bimmel had not worn his uniform, and wandered around, even mingling with some partisans and a few enemy soldiers. He asked questions but learned that no one he spoke with had seen a German pilot.

I kept moving, and I was surprised at how quiet it was. No gunfire, no sounds of battle or even aircraft. I reached a secure area in a grove of sunflowers, flanked by tall trees near a stream. I piled stones and dead wood around me, making a small wall, covered by grass among the plants, and took a nap. I was exhausted. The adrenaline is hard to describe, but it tires you quickly after it wears off. I also had not eaten since the afternoon before. Later I awoke in the late afternoon, and when it became dark, I had my bearings and took off again, heading west. I had made a mental note of a hill due west—that was my target.

I walked for over an hour, and then I heard the sound of metal against metal, like a rifle bolt being pulled and a round chambered. At night, when all is quiet and still, sound carries farther. I stopped walking and crouched down low among the sunflowers, listening. I could hear men approaching, low murmurs of their talking, but I could not see them. I passed a patrol of Russians—about ten, I think—about three hundred feet away from me, so I decided to follow them. Even though I could not see them, I could hear them, and I followed the waving of the sunflowers. I knew that they were headed west, and I assumed they were looking for me, or were perhaps a reconnaissance unit. Following them was something they would not expect.

The bright moonlight made this easy, but suddenly they walked out of the sunflowers and into an open meadow, and there was no cover for me. I saw these men walk toward two houses that were on the far side, and I stayed in the sunflowers, concealed, just watching. They passed the houses and I waited, and then I ran fast and hid under one of the houses. The men kept walking, and then walked up and over the hill that was my original target. Then the patrol disappeared over a small hill.

Maybe ten minutes later, I heard a great firefight with rifles and machine guns. The Russians must have walked into a German position. That would have made sense, as high ground would have been used for observation and artillery spotting. Well, as soon as the firing started, I heard these Russians screaming and running back down the hill, coming at me. Luckily, they ran right past me, never stopping or looking under the house.

I knew that this must be the German lines, since the men of the patrol came running back over on my side. I waited for an hour and a half, until all was quiet and the enemy had gone, and then I continued on. I saw spent cartridges and grass that had been pushed down by boots leading both ways. I walked to the other side and saw that it was an empty space. I realized that it was not a fortified German position. The Russians must have encountered a German patrol that fired on them first.

I walked slowly and quietly for about two more hours across this valley, surrounded by small hills. I stepped over a small ditch when about twenty meters in front of me a shadow stood, and in German said, "Halt!" Well, you know that I did, but then the crack of a rifle shot and the whistle of a bullet frightened me, and I felt the bullet pass through my trouser leg. I felt the heat. Then I was angry. Being challenged by a German sentry who then also fired a bullet at me, which ripped open my trouser leg, made me upset, but this man was in complete fear. I screamed at him, "Damn fool. Don't shoot your own people!"

He kept telling me to stop, and I told him that I was a German pilot. Well, I put my hands up as he instructed, but he was the one shaking. The rifle was rattling—he was so afraid. I knew that this guy was not going to help me. He was either an idiot or completely absorbed by fear, so I began shouting louder to anyone behind him. I assumed that he was not alone. I shouted, "I am a German pilot who was shot down. Let me through." A voice said to bring me in, and the guard walked me into their perimeter, but his rifle was sticking into my back. I made it to the top of the hill, and as I walked down, I saw that there was a *Waffen* SS infantry platoon, dug in and well camouflaged.

Well, they threw me into a foxhole, and their platoon leader, a *Leutnant*, started his interrogation. I did not have any identification, as my *Soldbuch* and other things had been taken. I gave him my unit, location, commander's name, when and where I was shot down, all of that. I asked him to call my wing HQ to verify the information so that I could get back. I was then welcomed into their position, given another quick interrogation for intelligence on the village I was in and the numbers of soldiers, vehicles—that sort of thing. The *Leutnant* then explained why all of the questions.

I was told that another group of Russians had entered their perimeter speaking fluent German, claiming to be escaped POWs, and when they came in they pulled out some Tommy guns and killed some men. Their nerves were frayed. They were, of course, suspicious since I did not have any identification. Everything had been taken when I was captured, even my medals.

I stayed with the infantry for the night, had some food, and managed to get some sleep. But at about 0400, I was awakened and taken to an MG-42 position. The *Feldwebel* placed his finger to his lips, told me to follow him, and he pointed. I could not see anything, but I could hear Russians coming closer. They were singing. I finally managed to get a glimpse of them, about two hundred, staggering. It was an unbelievable sight. The *Leutnant* told his men to hold their fire, to let them come closer, to fire only on his order.

Then another group of Russians, obviously drunk, walked toward our trenches as I peeked over the top. Then more came, and soon all of them were very close. The *Leutnant* gave the order to fire when they came within about twenty meters. The bodies were torn apart—the screams and the moans of the wounded rose from the field on the side of that hill. They were all destroyed. The firing lasted about thirty minutes, as many of the Russians began firing back, and the German riflemen picked off those farther away.

I remember thinking, "So this is the infantry. You can have it." A few of the men went down to check the bodies, and I heard a few shots. I guess that they shot the wounded. They went through their clothing for anything of intelligence value. They finished the killing and then sat down and ate. I thought to myself, these SS men are tough, nothing fazed them. Later in the prison camps, the SS men and paratroops were the toughest. They were of a different mindset. I think all the hard ground fighting created a different type of human being.

I asked the officer in command, whose rank was *Obersturmführer*, which was an *Oberleutnant* to us—and who had the Knight's Cross, Close Combat Badge, both Iron Crosses, Wound Badge, three antitank kill stripes, everything—why they shot the wounded, as it was a violation of the Geneva Convention, and that we in the air wing never did that. We treated our prisoners like guests.

He looked right at me and said, "You have that luxury. We would have to feed, guard, and then transport these men back, and that puts my men at risk. The Russians will even kill their own to get to us. We are a reconnaissance platoon. We gather information. We have seen what they do to us when we are captured. You are lucky to be alive. Eat something. We leave before dawn. All that noise will bring more." I understood at that point. I remember thinking how sad it was that we had not evolved as a species enough, to the point where killing was unnecessary, and it is still a part of our existence. I could not pass judgment on these men. They hated the enemy; I did not, but their war was a different one from mine. I would learn to hate later and handle that in my own way.

Finally, after two hours marching, at around 0600, I arrived at the SS Company HQ deeper into the Donets region. The infantry commander, a very serious *Hauptsturmführer* also with the Knight's Cross and Close Combat and Wound Badges, contacted Hrabak on the field telephone, describing me, giving my name. To validate, they asked me to name my mechanic, and I said "Bimmel," and I was okay. They sent me back by car, and after being gone for three days I was met by Krupi, who had just come back from the hospital after being wounded again. I also learned about what Bimmel [Mertens] had done, and I was very upset. The next day, Bimmel came back and we saw each other, and we had a "birthday party." That is a party thrown in honor of a pilot who survived a situation that should have killed him. We had a lot of those.

I had scored 148 kills by October 29, 1943. My award of the Knight's Cross was late, I guess. There were many men who had more than fifty kills who did not receive the Knight's Cross, which I think was unfair. I also thought it unfair that men like Rall, Barkhorn, Otto Kittel, Heinz Bär, Walter Schuck, and Erich Rudorffer and others with over two hundred victories did not receive the higher decoration, the Diamonds. They deserved them because Galland, Werner Mölders, Hans-Joachim Marseille, and others with fewer victories received them. It should be said that the Soviets knew who we were by name, in most cases. We knew a lot of their pilots, too. I knew of [Ivan] Kozhedub, Pokryshkin, Morosov, Litvyak, and the like. I was in the fight, I think, with Barkhorn where Litvyak was killed. The date seems correct, as does the location.

I received the news that I was going to get the Oak Leaves. So did Krupi and Johannes Wiese. That was a strange occasion. First, most of us were drunk. We flew on a Ju-52 into Prussia, and due to the bad weather, we then took a train. Gerd Barkhorn, Walter Krupinski, Johannes Wiese, and I were to report to Berchtesgaden. All of us except Gerd were getting the Oak Leaves; he was getting the Swords. By the time we got there, we were trying to sober up. Walter always stated years later that we had to hold each other up. I cannot remember everything, to be totally honest.

We had been drinking cognac and champagne, a deadly combination when you have not eaten in a couple of days. The first person we met off the train was Hitler's *Luftwaffe Adjutant*, *Major* von Below, who was, I think, in a state of shock at our condition. We were to meet Hitler in a couple of hours, and we could hardly stand. This was in March 1944, and there was a lot of snow at that time, at that altitude. It was warm despite the snow. We had just left the Ukraine. I could not find my hat, and my vision was not the best because of the cognac, so I took a hat on a stand and put it on, and it was too large. I knew it was not mine at the time.

Below became upset and told me it was Hitler's hat, and to put it back. Everyone was laughing about it except Below. I made some joke about Hitler having a big head, and that it "must go with the job," which created even more laughter. I also remember acting like Hitler, as when he gave his emotional speeches, complete with the hand movements. They were all laughing like hell.

Well, we were brought in and lined up in order of the presentation of the awards. I was barely able to stand, and I felt sick. Krupi started humming this silly drumbeat tune as we could hear Hitler coming into the doorway, and Gerd started to laugh. Then Below called us to attention and we locked up, but Gerd was still trying not to laugh, and Krupi seemed oblivious to the fact that we were within seconds of being mere inches from Hitler. Below turned to look at us, as if to see who was making those sounds, just like a schoolteacher looking at a classroom to see which student laughed or said something.

Well, we received our medals and shook hands, such as it was. Hitler had a weak handshake, almost like a woman really—not very manly. Then we were invited to sit at the table while the midday meal was served. We all took off our Knight's Crosses and began putting our Oak Leaves on them, and Gerd removed his Oak Leaves and was replacing them with the Oak Leaves and Swords. Hitler then began talking about his plans for the greatest war heroes. He stated that starting with the men who received the Oak Leaves, then up to the Swords, and so on, that we would all be given estates of our choice in the occupied territories. We would have houses built for us so that we could raise our families. I preferred to stay in Germany, and he said that was fine.

Krupi and I kept joking with each other. Krupi gave me some grief, teasing me about being caught with Hitler's hat. I told him that he should transfer to the Stukas, because when we did not have air combat he would go tank hunting. He used to hit the T-34s; there were always a lot of them, and they carried their fuel on the outside. He destroyed quite a few, but he came back with holes in his plane. I tried that, and I got one, but I was too low. The damned thing exploded, and I had shrapnel in the belly of my 109. Krupi's plane always had damage because of this.

We all sat there and had lunch, and then something strange happened. I knew that Krupi and Gerd smoked occasionally. Krupi actually smoked a lot. Well, he pulls out his cigarette case, and he looked at me and I shook my head, and then Hitler, who seemed to be disinterested in everything up until that time, snapped harshly at him. Hitler was a big nonsmoker and nondrinker. Hitler also hated meat and was a strict vegetarian. He told him [Krupinski] to put away his filthy habit. Gerd was sitting next to me, laughing. He had already been with Hitler, and he knew better, so he did not pull out a cigarette, but no one warned Krupi. Wiese just laughed out loud.

We chatted about the war, mostly light conversation. Hitler discussed digging massive trenches, deep and very wide all along the final line of defense, much like the Soviets had done at Kursk. Then more wine was brought out, but I could not drink any more alcohol. I was done. I drank the coffee. Then Hitler asked Gerd how he was since they had last met, that sort of thing. Hitler then spoke about the new jets and rockets, and all sorts of great wonder weapons that we would soon have. He had this great vision about our ultimate victory. Gerd had warned us about this.

It was interesting that Krupi and Gerd had already heard about the jets, and they expressed an interest in them. Ironically, they would both serve with Steinhoff and Galland in JV-44 at the end of the war, flying the Me-262 jet. Hitler asked about the front and mentioned some of the ground battles, and how we would defeat the enemy. I was certain that he was either severely delusional or badly misinformed.

I found him a little disappointing, although very interested in the war at the front and extremely well informed on events as I knew them. However, he had a tendency to drone on about minor things that I found boring. He rambled about how we were defeating the Soviets, which was news to us, I can say. He then spoke about the Allies threatening Italy, the bombers not being properly dealt with [being shot down], those sorts of things. I found him interesting, yet not that imposing. I also found him lacking in sufficient knowledge about the air war in the east. He was more concerned with the Western Front's air war and the bombing of our cities. Of course, the Eastern Front ground war was his area of greatest interest. This was evident. Hitler listened to the men from the Western Front and assured them that weapons and fighter production were increasing. History proved this to be correct.

The luncheon dragged on and we left to go to the large lounge area, where we sat around. There was a great fire burning in the fireplace, and the room was warm. Several others arrived, high ranks, and then all of us were involved in an interesting conversation. After another couple of hours, we were dismissed. We all had a few days off before we had to report, and I went back home to see my family and Uschi.

Two months later, we had to evacuate the Crimea. This was May 9, 1944, and it was the first time that we had to pack our ground crew into the fighters to get them out, before we were surrounded. We were pushed back west, toward the Ukraine. There were a lot of enemy contacts after that, and even more enemy aircraft. One reason that we had so many pilots score high numbers of victories was because we successful leaders always gave our wingmen the chance to shoot and get kills. That built up their confidence and gave them practice.

I had just landed after a successful mission when I found out that I had been awarded the Swords [the seventy-fifth to be awarded]. This was June 1944. I would fly many more missions before I went back to see Hitler in July for the Swords. I arrived with several other *Luftwaffe* men. *Major* Heinz-Wolfgang Schnaufer, Friedrich Lang, and I were getting the Swords, while Adolf Glunz, Horst Kaubisch, Eduard Skrzipek were to get their Oak Leaves. We all discussed the war—the damage to the cities from the bombings. Some of the men had lost family or friends as a result.

I knew that the Americans were bombing manufacturing places; they were military targets. Uschi was working for the Heinkel Company, as they made aircraft motors. That worried me, but she only did that for about two months, and she stayed with my family when she was not with hers. Right after she left, the factory was bombed; it was very bad. My father's home was safer from the bombings. Uschi would tell me about spending the nights in the cellar because of the bombings, but luckily they were never hit.

I returned to the unit and shot down more aircraft, and was informed that I had to go back to see Hitler again. Then we heard about the bombing that almost killed him on July 20. This sent shockwaves throughout the unit. I was reading a letter from Uschi when the radio made the announcement, and the radio operator burst in and told us. We had also heard about the latest American and British bombing raids, and which cities had been hit the hardest, and I thought of my family and Uschi.

Hitler was going to give me the Diamonds [the eighteenth awarded], and this order came straight from Hermann Graf. I arrived on August 3, 1944, to visit Hitler again for the award ceremony, and there were ten of us *Luftwaffe* guys in all. Then Hitler walked up with *Gruppenführer* Hermann Fegelein, and he was not the same man I had met twice previously, when I received the Oak Leaves.

This was just after the bomb plot to kill him. His right arm was shaking, and he looked exhausted. He walked bent over and had to turn to his left ear to hear anyone speak because he was deaf in the other one from the blast. Hitler discussed the cowardly act to kill him and attacked the quality of his generals, with a few exceptions. He also stated that God had spared his life so that he may deliver Germany from destruction, and that the Western Allies would be thrown back inevitably. Although I was surprised at all of this, I was bored, and I wanted to leave and see my Uschi, which I did later.

Then Hitler talked about the U-boat war, how we were going to destroy Allied maritime commerce, and all of that. I now found him an isolated and disturbed man. He then turned to those of us flying in the east. He seemed very interested in the stories of how much better the Russians were, the pilots and their aircraft. Hitler then stated that if not for all of the American and British military aid to Stalin, we would have already won that war.

I immediately disagreed with him. I told him that "yes, they have a lot of support," but they had moved their industry beyond the range of our bombers. We could not hit their factories. Moreover, I told him simply that the large numbers of available Russian manpower were overwhelming. I did say that, once we could identify a flight leader, if we could shoot him down, then the rest of the flight was easier to knock down. It was as if they could not think independently.

However, this was not true with the Red Banner fighters. They were probably just as good as any American or British pilots, and this was not just my opinion. Even after the war, we pilots spoke about this, and the men who flew on both fronts agreed. The toughest fight I ever had was against one of these Red Banner boys. These men were the best the Soviets had.

I told Hitler about my experiences, that I found that when I used the black tulip [the pattern on his spinner to the cowling], I had more difficulty in finding opponents, who avoided me for the most part. I became known by name. The Russians would mention when I was in the air. Hitler found the tulip-paint-scheme story interesting. I explained that I needed camouflage to gain victories, so I stopped using that aircraft pattern most of the time.

I also explained the difficulties with supply and operations. We seldom had hard shelter, living in tents. The lice were the worst, and there was little you could do but hold your clothes to a fire and listen to them pop. We had DDT and bathed when we could. Illness, particularly pneumonia and trench foot, were bad, especially among the ground crews. I also explained that we moved so often in retreat that we never really had time to establish a long-term airfield, which also made flight operations difficult.

I also explained that we almost always flew from grass strips, and we were often bombed. These strips were easy to repair, although the terrain made every takeoff and landing an adventure. Sometimes fighters would snap their landing gear, or just dig in and topple over. Maintenance was another nightmare, as supplies and parts were difficult to get to, especially when we were moving around all the time. Despite these problems, we were very successful in the Crimea from 1943 to 1944.

I then told Hitler about this one event, a ten- to twelve-minute air fight that I had with three Red Banners. Two of them broke off pretty soon, within a couple of minutes. I do not know why, perhaps fuel. But this one guy stayed with me, and he was tough. I was more of a hit-and-run pilot, not really a dog fighter as such, but I used every trick, every muscle, and I was screaming on the radio for help. I felt a couple of hits in my fighter, but no real damage. This Yak and I were circling each other, each trying to tighten up and get on the other guy's tail. That damned Yak pilot was good, and the airplane was first-rate, I tell you. I had never been so afraid of an outcome, and I was not sure I would win.

I saw streaks fly past, cannon shells. I decided to try something after I saw he was gaining in the hard left turn and I was running low on fuel. I hit the right rudder, pulled back on the stick all the way, pulling a loop to try to end up behind him. As I was inverted and completing the loop, I looked down and saw this guy pulling the same trick, and he was still vertical as I was nosing down. He was just off my right wing and climbing, and I was descending. This meant that he would have altitude on me. Not a good place to be.

I also knew that outrunning him was not an option, so I continued pulling back. My eyes were going gray, and I could not even see the instruments. I was still pulling, going vertical in the second loop, when I felt this explosion rock my 109. I saw a bright flash and debris fluttering everywhere. Pieces of the fighter rattled like stones around my aircraft and the canopy. I was stunned and not sure what had happened.

Then over the radio I heard Gerd Barkhorn say, "He is gone, Erich. You owe me a drink." I was drenched in sweat, and then I heard three others come over the radio. Apparently, they were up high, watching everything, and they were laughing. They were letting me fight this guy, waiting to see what would happen, but they were always there just in case. I was pretty angry with all of them, and when we landed I told them that they were bastards, making me sweat fighting this guy. Gerd said, "You may want to learn dogfighting, my friend," and then the rest of them, including Krupi and [Hans] Ewald, laughed. Then Gerd was walking away when he turned his head and asked me, "You will confirm the victory, right?" I told Hitler all of this, and he laughed at me, too.

I do not recall anyone talking of defeat during our conversation at that time, but I do know that we talked about some of the great pilots killed already, and the news that the American Mustangs were reaching deep into Germany and even farther. Hitler seemed very concerned about this. Few of us from the east had any experience against the Americans, and none of us who were still with my unit at that time, although many old-timers in JG-52 had fought the British. Those few who fought Americans had done so in North Africa, and their insights proved interesting. After that meeting, I had a few days back home with my family and Uschi, and that meant more to me than medals.

I went back to the war, and the battles were becoming even more intense. I shot down something like thirty-five more aircraft in the month after I returned, and on August 24 I scored three hundred, and was the first pilot to do so. I was still in the air, and when I landed the men all came out with warm champagne and a sign that said, "Congratulations on your three hundred victories." The news spread quickly, and there was a telephone call to me from Adolf Galland.

I had finished flying for the day, and had scored eleven victories in three sorties, and I was very tired. I walked away from my fighter and was going to file my third *Abschuss* for the day when I was called into the operations center. This was just a small wooden building that would have collapsed if you kicked it in. I was told that I would be flying the next morning to meet Hitler again. This time I had been awarded the Diamonds. I think that this made me the second pilot from JG-52 at that time to earn this honor. Graf had been the first. Dieter Hrabak and the rest of the guys threw a great party before I left, and I was so drunk I could not stand the next day. It sounds like we were all alcoholics, but this was not the case. We lived and played hard. You never knew what thc ncxt day would bring.

I told Gerd and the others that when I came back, I did not want to see that anyone had tried to steal Bimmel from me again. I reminded them that he had a rifle. I flew my 109 to Insterburg, and JG-52 gave me an escort. I guess they wanted to make certain I arrived after all that drinking. I landed not far from the grass strip and parked next to Hitler's Ju-52. A driver met me and I jumped into the car. When I arrived at the *Wolfschanze*, the world had changed. Hitler had already begun the trials and executions of those involved in [Stauffenberg] the plot, and everyone was under suspicion. You had to enter three areas of security, and no one was allowed to carry a weapon into the last section.

I told Hitler's SS bodyguard commander [SS-*Obersturmbannführer* Otto Günsche] to tell the *Führer* that I would not receive the Diamonds if I were not trusted to carry my Walther pistol. The guy looked like I had just married his mother. He went to speak with von Below, who was an *Oberst* then, and Below came out and said it was all right. Because the others had complied without question, I did not want to be different, so I hung my cap and pistol belt on the stand and Hitler came to me and said, "I wish we had more like you and Rudel," and he gave me the Diamonds, which were encrusted upon another set of silver Oak Leaves and Swords. He then handed me the certificate that went with the award, which was beautifully framed with his signature and very nicely matted in a silver frame. I wondered how I would place this into my fighter without breaking the glass.

We had coffee and lunch, and he confided in me, saying "militarily the war is lost," and that I must already know this, and that if we waited, the Western Allies and Soviets would be at war with each other. He also spoke about the partisan problem, and he asked me of my experience with the partisans at the front. I told him that we in JG-52 had not really had any real partisan problems, which was probably because we had to relocate to different airfields so often—retreating almost weekly—that the partisans probably just could not find us. He did not find that very funny, from the expression on his face.

Hitler asked me my opinion of the tactics used in fighting the American and British bombers. Since I did not have a lot of experience with this, I simply stated what I thought was a fact from my chats with other pilots who had actually flown against the Americans. I told him, in my opinion and only based upon those conversations, that Göring's orders to combat the Americans and the method to be employed was in error. He sighed and nodded his head. He said, "Galland and the others say the same thing to me."

I also informed him of the deficiencies in pilot training; too many minimally trained men were simply throwing their lives away. We had men coming to us with perhaps twenty or so hours in basic flight school, using the He-51 biplanes; or maybe they had five to ten hours on the Arado trainer, and then perhaps twenty hours in the 109. Then they were sent to the front. I told him that the propaganda we kept hearing was ridiculous—claiming that all the new, young pilots needed was greater National Socialist spirit to win.

This was insane. I told Hitler so, and I also told him that even the best veteran pilots were being lost. These new pilots may at most have had sixty hours flying time. Some had less than thirty. I had over two hundred hours before I even saw the front, and another thirty or so before I flew combat. We were just killing young men, and many commanders were refusing to send them to fly and die until they had more airtime. I also told him that if I were a *Kommodore,* I would not let any man engage in combat without at least a hundred hours flying time in a unit with many veterans assisting him.

We were so outnumbered that the new pilots did not have a chance. They were being sent to die, and nothing was coming as a benefit. The 109 was not an easy fighter to fly anyway; just taking off was a trick, because of the propeller torque. Many of these young guys ground looped by not being very familiar with the aircraft. If you gave too much throttle, the fighter would swing ninety degrees on takeoff unless you gave full hard rudder.

Landing caused a lot of problems, as the undercarriage was very narrow. Coming in too fast, not reducing power, or giving full flaps caused many to flip over on their backs. Also, the 109 would stall quickly if you reduced power too quickly. These were just the nature of the beast, so to speak. It was not like the 190, which had a wide undercarriage and was more ruggedly built for field operations. Hrabak held the record for ground loops in the 109, I think, but do not tell him I said that! It was very easy to do on a muddy field or unimproved runway. We hardly ever flew from a hard surface, until much later in the war. Then we began cracking up the fighters. We were used to landing on soft earth, and those habits saw a few pilots bend their gear, so to speak.

Galland and I had spoken about these problems, also, when I was with him in 1944 in Berlin. This was when he was still General of the Fighters. He said that pilot training and quality were the greatest reasons he and the *Kommodoren* were going to speak with Göring. He and Steinhoff had already spoken to *Generalfeldmarschall* Erhard Milch, and that conversation went nowhere. Their meeting with Göring ended badly for everyone.

Göring asked me about the partisan problem, and he was aware that we had lost over two hundred fighters, 109s and 190s from two different groups at our base in the Carpathians. The general in charge of the base was not a pilot, and he ignored our requests to have the fighters dispersed and camouflaged. This was because we had American fighters and bombers going over almost every day. Hitler had also asked me about this. I told him.

Well, one day these Mustangs and Thunderbolts came down and destroyed over half the fighters parked on the air base. The general had apparently written a report to Berlin, saying that partisans were responsible for the sabotage. Hitler also asked me about this, and how bad the partisan problem was. I told him that the report was a lie. I was there; we had no partisan problem there in Romania. Hitler had told me that his generals were complaining of partisan activity all the time, and then he said that he thought that some of his generals were lying to him.

When Hitler and I spoke about the air war, he said that Göring was issuing an order that all fighter units, day fighters and night fighters, would have to go up and fight enemy aircraft whenever they came, even at night or in bad weather. I told Hitler that this was impossible. All the fighter pilots would have to go back to instrument flying school, or blind flying school, which would take about a year for the pilots to qualify. It would be suicide.

I told him that the night fighters, bombers, and reconnaissance pilots had the necessary training and experience. We lost many fighters trying to take off in extremely limited visibility against a bomber raid at Jüterborg; the ceiling was below a thousand feet, miserable. Forty fighters were lost. Hitler also spoke to us about the new weapons and tactics, and afterward we shook hands and then we parted. That was the last time I saw Hitler, August 25, 1944. I flew back to the unit, where an order for ten days' leave waited, and I married Uschi.

We had a really big celebration back home. I was in all the newspapers, and the big party was held in the sports *Palast* in Weil. Everyone was there. There were many gifts, presents and such. The mayor arrived and gave me a document. They were going to build us a nice house, just for us to start a family later. Well, that house never happened, since the war ended, of course, and I would be gone for a few years afterward.

I had my ten days' leave, and after eight days I had to report to [*General der Jagdflieger*, *Generalleutnant* Adolf] Galland, where we discussed the Me-262 situation. He would schedule me for transition training later. I then went back to the front, but was able to return in September to marry my Uschi—that was all that mattered to me. I had my bachelor party, which we in Germany called "Elf Night." The next day I was married, and we stayed at the *Jagdfliegerheim*, and our friend Dr. Rossbach was there. He had been the physician for JG-53 also.

Gerd was there as my best man. Willi Batz, Krupi, Heinz Ewald, Erhard Richter, Ludwig Franzisket, and others attended who could be there. It was wonderful even if we were in the courthouse. But we did not marry in a church, since we were Protestants, and we only had a Catholic church in the village. So, we married in the courthouse the next month, in September. We later remarried in a church after I came back, but that was in 1956. My uncle, my father's brother, was the minister who married us. Interesting was that Franzisket and I knew each other from flight school, and he flew with Marseille. That was where I learned so much about him. It was a shame that he died so early in the war. I would have liked to have known him.

I was still hung over when we started the wedding celebrations, and we had so much champagne it was incredible. Well, the next day I packed my things and so did Uschi, as we were going on our honeymoon. This man walked up to me and handed me the bill. It was four thousand marks. I thought I was going to have a stroke, but then the provost marshal came up and pointed to my Diamonds. He looked at the bill, took it from me, and said that a great hero like me should not have to pay a bill like that! He signed it, so the government paid for my wedding!

Outstanding, I thought, and I thanked him. He just wanted my autograph, and I gave it to him. Well, the place sent the bill again, to my father this time, but all the guests had contributed to help out, so the bill was only 2,500 marks remaining, which everyone [guests and his father] helped pay. The four thousand marks in total were inflated by almost double. They also had a hundred marks billed for cigars, but we had not smoked any.

I did not get to see Uschi or my family as often as I would have liked, of course. After the party, we had another celebration at my parents' home. Then I had to go back, so I borrowed a Fieseler *Storch*, I think, and I flew to Krakow. I received a new 109G and flew back to my unit, which was at Brünn, in Czechoslovakia. I would not see Uschi until December 31, and then again not until March of 1945, when I moved Uschi in with our friends, the Vandekamp family at their castle. I again had ten days' leave, and had come home after I checked out in the Me-262 with Galland and Trautloft there at Lechfeld, during the last week of September and first week of October, I think.

Lechfeld was a nice air base, very modern even then. The runway was asphalt, and the jets were lined up on the sides. One of the chiefs took me to the jet. I climbed in and he stood on the wing and talked me through the start-up procedure, roll out, takeoff, and landing. He was very serious and careful to explain the throttles, and moving them forward slowly was critical, and why that was the case. I was to count to twenty-one before going all the way forward. He said to give the air speed indicator 190 kilometers, and then pull the stick back, and I am on my own. Landing, he explained to "come in, faster than in the 109, half flaps at first, slowly bringing the power down, but faster than starting it up. Do not apply the brakes until you have less than thirty kilometers, or they might lock up." I said, "Okay," and took off.

It was a very smooth and quiet ride, very much like a glider, and I could feel the power. I was in radio contact with the ground control, and the headset was so clear—none of the rattle and static we had in the 109. I took it through a climb and banks. I was not impressed with the turning radius, but the power in the climb was incredible. Landing first with the tail down and then touching the nose gear was a new sensation. I flew a second time later that day. I did two more qualification flights the next day. Before I left, I had ten flights for a total of about seven hours—excellent, really. With four heavy cannons, I could see how these would be great against the bombers.

This was where I met Heinz Bär, one of the best. We really became friends after I came back from Russia, but he was killed in a flying accident at Brunswick in 1957. That was sad, as he would have been a great asset to the new air force, but I think he was done with wearing a uniform also. He was a real fighter and a kind man, and I know that all of the men he commanded and flew with loved him. He told me a story once, about flying against the heavy bombers. He shot down a B-17, and most of the crew parachuted out. He saw the crash site and radioed the position, so all the men were captured quickly. This happened only a mile or so from his airfield. The soldiers had four of the crew marching them towards our base, but there were a lot of angry civilians throwing things at them and wanting to kill them. Their town had just been bombed and there were casualties.

Bär took another pilot with him, and they drove over to the men. There were perhaps a hundred civilians. Some had farm tools and others had guns. He stopped the car and got out, and when they saw his Knight's Cross, Oak Leaves, and Swords they stopped. He spoke to them and told them:

"These are men, soldiers fighting a war that they did not start. They are doing their job. This is a military matter, and they are under my protection. They have rights under the Geneva Convention." Then there were a few of the men who did not care, and they began going for the Americans. Bär pulled out his Walther pistol, chambered a bullet, and pointed it at the ringleader. He told him that he only had a certain number of bullets, but that he knew whom to shoot first if they did not leave those men alone. It was after this conversation that I left Lechfeld.

I then took Uschi to Schöngau along the way. Galland had asked me then to join his JV-44, but I declined. He had been fired by Göring in January, so he was no longer the *General der Jagdflieger*. However, Hitler gave him permission to fly and create his own unit, which he did. I also received a telegram from Joannes "Macky" Steinhoff stating that he was working with Galland along with Krupinski, and that I should join them. Barkhorn also called me; he was joining them. I knew that Macky had been with JG-7 flying the jets. Trautloft also had trained in them even though he was Inspector of Fighters, and he found it favorable.

Galland had selected the best pilots that he could get, even having Macky look into the hospitals and invalid centers, locating men who were not on flying status. Macky said that it was easier to pull a man out of a hospital than have him transferred from an active-duty position. Those transfers took orders, and Galland no longer had his authority, although he did still have his rank. Authority or not, he carried so much respect with the fighter pilots that they basically ignored [Gordon] Gollob, who replaced him.

Galland sat me down, and he simply said that he wanted to end the war with the best men we had, proving that

Göring was wrong about our fighting spirit and that Hitler was wrong about his wishes to use the jet in a different way, as a bomber. They had been arguing about that for almost two years at that time, I believe. There were many other political things going on that I was unaware of and did not know until long after the war. I was too far removed from the center of power, being at the front. Galland and the *Kommodoren* were very much involved, and they rather kept those opinions and details to themselves. And I was not so sure that Galland would be able to create his *Kommando*.

I should also mention that while at Lechfeld we had daily attacks around noon, like clockwork, by the Americans. Mostly P-38s, Mustangs, Thunderbolts, anything, up to thirty or so in waves, would fly in fast, drop bombs, and machine gun everything. They would put holes in the runway and try to hit aircraft also and damage buildings. They did this almost every day, and there were two jets lost. They had a squadron of Fw-190 Doras and a few 109s there. These would take off before the jets and fly ahead, seeing if there were any enemy fighters coming in. They protected the jets in taking off and landing, where the jets were very easy to kill.

He was short on the necessary aircraft, fuel, munitions, support personnel, mechanics—all of these things—although he had no problem getting pilots. These types of requisitions took months for approval, not to mention actual assignments. Also, I knew that even though I would not be a junior officer, or even a junior pilot, I was a lot younger than the old-timers. Besides, I really felt at home with JG-52. With exception of my short time with JG-53, that was the only home I knew, and all my friends were there, except those who were dead, missing, or transferred.

I stayed at Lechfeld for about three weeks, and then I finished flight qualification. My unit had since transferred to Romania, and later one *Gruppe* went to Czechoslovakia, operating from hard landing fields. This placed us between the Soviets and Americans. But, after four days leave I had a telegram, telling me to go to Königsberg, East Prussia. Uschi was, I think, six months pregnant with Peter Erich at the time. That must have happened on our honeymoon.

Our physician was Dr. Rossbach, who was also the attending physician for Gerd and Christi Barkhorn. Christi was also pregnant from their honeymoon, and they had a daughter later. As I told Ray Toliver many years ago, we tended to come home, make babies, and then abandon them. I think about Gerd and Christi, who were in an auto accident. This was on January 6, 1983. Christi died in the crash; Gerd died on January 8 from internal injuries. That really killed me inside; Uschi also. So tragic to survive the war, the bombings, the stupidity of the Nazis, and then die like that. It makes no sense to me.

I returned to my unit on April 1, and I was worried about Uschi and the baby. She was due around the first week of June, I think. I knew that the bombings were a problem for her. Hertha Rall had lost four babies, miscarriages due to bombings. The last was when she was six months pregnant. I did not want that to happen to Uschi. Then there was always the risk of them being killed. I would already be in captivity when our son was born about two weeks early. That was May 21, 1945. I would not learn anything regarding this for ten more years.

I was given a few days off after another crash-landing, where I took some flak. I was stationed near Budapest at that time. I only had enough time to go as far as Vienna, so I sent Uschi a message to meet me. It was not possible because the rail line was bombed out, so I took Bimmel with me. We boarded the train, and they had special cars for officers and others for enlisted men, but I wanted him with me. I had to go to the toilet, and he stayed with the bags. I came back and this railroad official checking tickets was giving him a hard time, being an enlisted man. Once he saw my Diamonds, he brought us cognac and cigars. Nothing more was said.

I feared capture in Russia, and that was an eye-opening prospect. The bombing of our cities also worried us, as our families were dear to us. I suppose I was most worried that Uschi would not wait, so I always tried to see her whenever I was on leave. Medals meant leave, and that was an incentive. If I had the choice of losing her or returning all the decorations, I would send the medals back. She is the love of my life.

It was later learned that the Soviets knew exactly who I was and that Stalin had placed a ten thousand-ruble price on my head. This was later increased to one hundred thousand. Rudel and I had the highest bounties of any Germans during the war, probably with the exception of Hitler and a few of the Nazi elite. Every time I went up, I knew that someone would be looking for me. I had thoughts of the American western films, where the top gunfighter is called out into the street—another person wanting to make his mark. I felt marked, so I had to change my aircraft occasionally. Food was always a concern, especially later in the war, and fuel restrictions made every mission count.

We had a Royal Hungarian unit assigned to us once, as well as a *Staffel* of Croats and another *Staffel* of Slovaks. I knew Ion Dobran pretty well. He seemed like a very likeable and intelligent man and a good pilot. To be honest, we gave them rubbish to fly, not the best planes. If they had been given new fighters and not our old ones, worn out, they would have been a lot better, I think. They were good pilots and fearless in many ways. Good men, but perhaps a little crazy. We had even more contact with our allies, especially with the Romanians when we were stationed there, and this was where we engaged both the Americans and Soviets. This was a very trying time. The Romanians made me nervous. I had reservations about them, about their overall quality in general, although they also had some very good pilots. We were all flying in Russia against twenty-to-one odds. In Romania, it was thirty to one. Later, it was even more.

I would not call leaving Russia an evacuation, but a full retreat. We had to move, and I discovered that when the radio, armor plate, and rear wall were removed, you could stack two men in the tail and another man could be placed behind the pilot. Some would put three in the tail section—they could lay on top of each other—but three was about the most I would try because of safety. The aircraft then became a very heavy animal, and hard to control in combat if you had to engage, but proper trim made everything okay. The engine was strong enough so that I could have put perhaps seven men in the fighter if it would have held that many. Getting off the ground took a little more terrain, and landing—well, you had to be especially delicate with the landing gear. But overall, it was not a great problem.

We managed to save many of our precious ground crew from capture using this method. Hitler had been giving these ridiculous orders, such as stand to the last man, and not a step backward—just throwing lives away. I knew that he had to be insane. I was never a great infantry strategist, but I should think that you pull back, reorganize, and shore up a good defense, and maybe prepare for a counterattack. Hrabak and the other leaders would never follow these stupid orders. I would not. We were not Nazi zealots.

It is interesting, too, that Hrabak also violated his orders to fly west, at first. He stuffed so many people into his fighter, making so many trips, I think he set a world record. When I heard about it, I made a joke that he had actually started his own airline in a war zone. He would only have a quarter of a fuel tank filled, to allow for the weight of the men he carried. He would take off, land, pull them out, and fly back, and do it again a few times. When he made his third or fourth trip and landed, his fighter would not start for some reason, but they had everyone out. *That* is a good leader.

I would say that in our group, there were the majority of us who found all the National Socialist idiocy a little sickening. We used to make jokes about Hitler, Göring, Göbbels, and the rest. They were just too comical in many ways to be taken seriously. Hrabak made it a special point to explain to the new young pilots that if they thought they were fighting for National Socialism and the *Führer*, they needed to transfer to the *Waffen* SS or something. He had no time for political types. He was fighting a war against a superb enemy, not holding a political rally.

I think this approach damaged Hrabak in the eyes of Göring and others, but he was a real man and did not care about anything but his men. Hannes Trautloft, Macky Steinhoff, Rall . . . everyone felt the same as Galland. I would say that Gordon Gollob was the one memorable exception who did not fall into that company, and I will say no more about him.

There is one story I should tell. In 1943, Willi Batz, Gerd Barkhorn, and I had this one guy whom we really wanted to keep. This man was a master shoemaker, leather worker, mechanic, weapons repair specialist, and he even knew how to fix cockpit instruments. He was a mechanic in a Russian fighter unit, a Ukrainian who had defected to us. A watchmaker by profession, he toyed around as a pseudo-inventor and self-educated scientist. He came up with a method of building a still to make vodka, using the potatoes and grains that grew during the warm weather. He could also make alcohol from sunflowers, which had a strange taste but was quite interesting. He could make alcohol out of anything organic, just about. [Johannes] Wiese wanted to buy him from us, and Gerd said that he was not a slave; he could make up his own mind. So, I said let's have an auction, and the bidding began.

Well, this man was about forty years old and was perhaps the happiest fellow I ever met. He was not a soldier, nor a pilot, but a man who had left his unit and walked west until he stumbled across one of our sentries. They brought him in for interrogation. It was easy to see this man was not a wealth of military intelligence, but he had many talents, and I liked him. Well, I won the bidding, and the guy stayed with us for a few weeks. He was later taken and placed in a prisoner of war camp. I never saw him again, but he made me a great pair of sheepskin-lined flight boots.

Those things were very warm, and the soles were made from a tire, about fifteen millimeters thick and lined with felt or something. Wonderful. Rall, Barkhorn, and others also had a pair, and they were very warm. In the summer, I flew in tennis shoes and shorts sometimes. Not regulation, but it was so damned hot in the cockpit. The sun beating down on the canopy turned it into an oven, so we had to open the air vents, but that was not enough. You really wanted to be comfortable and be able to move around in the cockpit, especially with a parachute harness on. I would loosen the straps. I did not like the idea of jumping out anyway.

I was in a duel once with a Red Banner–flown Yak-9, and this guy was good, and absolutely insane. He tried and tried to get in behind me, and every time he went to open fire, I would jerk and roll out of the way of his rounds. Then he pulled up and rolled, and we approached each other head-on, firing, with no hits either way. This happened two times. Finally, I rolled into a hard negative G dive, out of his line of sight, and rolled out to chase him at full throttle. I came in from below in a shallow climb and flamed him. I had bruises on my shoulders from the straps holding me in the cockpit. That was what made me loosen the straps from then on.

The Russian pilot bailed out and was later captured. I met and spoke with this man, a captain, who was a likeable guy. We gave him some food and allowed him to roam the base after having his word that he would not escape. He was happy to be alive, but he was very confused, since his superiors told him that Soviet pilots would be shot immediately upon capture. This guy had just had one of the best meals of the war and had made new friends. I like to think that people like that went back home and told their countrymen the truth about us, not the propaganda that erupted during and after the war, although there were some terrible things that happened, no doubt.

Once I attacked a flight of four IL-2s and shot one up, then another. I had hits on all of them, but only one was a sure kill. Then all four tried to roll out in formation at low altitude, and all four crashed into the ground, unable to recover since their bomb loads reduced their maneuverability. Those were the easiest four kills I ever had. However, I remember the time I saw over twenty thousand dead Germans littering a valley where the Soviet tanks, infantry, and Cossacks had attacked a trapped unit, and that sight—even from the air—was perhaps the most memorable of my life. I can close my eyes and see this even now. I remember that I cried as I flew low over the scene; I could not believe my eyes.

One fight I remember was a duel against this really hot Yak-7 pilot. This man was probably the best guy I ever flew against, and he was not a Red Banner fighter. At least his Yak did not carry their markings. I looked up and Junger was on my wing. I called him out as he started his dive. We pulled up into him, and I saw that he was firing.

Normally, I would think that a pilot firing from so far away was a novice. But this man knew his business, hitting Junger. He was okay, and since we were just ten minutes from the base I told him to fly back. This Yak was alone, and I wanted him. Junger peeled off, and I yanked over into a hard right bank to follow the Yak down. I knew Junger was safe. The Yak was pulling up, and I knew he was trying to get altitude, roll, and hit me with a quick burst and pull away in a dive. That was the normal tactic. I then pushed the left rudder and pulled back on the stick, following his climb.

The Yak could climb well, but not as well as a Gustav, and I hit the booster [nitrous oxide and water injection system]. It could dive like a demon, and turn with my fighter, but I could out-climb him. In the hands of a good pilot, the Gustav was a great and dangerous machine. This Russian was no fool. He must have guessed what I was going to do, and he rolled and then did a split-S. He caught me off guard, and then he ended up behind me. I was in trouble, and instinct took over. He had built up a lot of speed, so I lowered my flaps, reduced throttle, and pulled the nose up.

He had a choice: pass under me or over me, or even ram me. He chose neither. He did the same thing: lowered flaps, reduced speed, staying behind me. We were both near to stalling. I then gave full power, went full flaps, banked left, tightening the turn, then barrel rolled, and as he followed he must have stalled. He began to lose altitude. I took advantage and winged over, fired a quick shot, and saw smoke pour from his engine. The canopy opened and he fell out, then his parachute opened. I waved to him and then went home. I filed the report, but no witness, no victory, but I did not care. I had aged a year in the six-minute fight. By all rights, I should have been the one under a parachute.

There were many times where I could have been killed, and perhaps should have been killed. That could be said of all of us. Look at Krupi, Macky, and others. However, I always felt very bad at the thought of a needless death, not that any death was good in that war for us. However, I always tried to hammer home the point that I learned: Never, ever come home without your wingman if at all possible. During my time in combat, I had two wingmen shot down due to their inexperience, but never killed, and they flew again. I was living proof that an inexperienced wingman is often his own worst enemy. After all, I lost a fighter with nothing to show for it on my first combat sortie.

I did suffer a few heartbreaks when I lost a friend. One was especially hard, when one of my young pilots, whom I had trained and used as a wingman many times and who became very successful, died. He was Hans-Joachim Birkner. He was very successful in JG-52, receiving the Knight's Cross and shooting down 117 aircraft, and he only flew 284 missions—one of the best ratios of the war. He flew many missions as my wingman in 9. *Staffel*, which he took over as

Staffelkapitän. He was killed in a landing accident after he lost his engine at Krakow, Poland. Very sad.

Another time was in May 1944 near Jassy. My wingman, Blessin, and I were jumped by fighters. He broke right and the enemy followed him down. I rolled and followed the enemy fighter down to the deck. I radioed to my wingman to pull up and slip right in a shallow turn so that I could get a good shot. I told him to look back and see what happens when you do not watch your tail, and I fired. The fighter blew apart and fell like confetti.

However, separate from Krupinski's crash the day I met him, one event is clear and comical.

My wingman on many missions was Carl Junger, who had originally questioned my victories. He came in for a landing out of fuel, and a Polish farmer with a horse cart crossed his path, right across our runway. He crashed into it, killing the horse, destroying the wagon, and the fighter was nothing but twisted wreckage. We all saw it and began thinking about the funeral, when suddenly the debris moved and he climbed out without a scratch, still wearing his sunglasses. He was ready to go up again. Amazing!

Then there were the American Mustangs that we both dreaded and anticipated. We knew that they were a much better aircraft than ours—newer and faster and with a great range. We also knew that they were liquid cooled, which sometimes created a problem if you were hit in the radiator. They also had six .50-caliber machine guns, very effective and dangerous. They were roaming all over Europe from their bases in France, England, Belgium, and Italy.

When I arrived in Romania, we protected the oil production at Ploesti, and Willi Batz always made me the flight leader. We had always been in competition with Barkhorn, since we were the top three scorers after Rall left to go to the west, and I always won. That was because Batz was a staff officer and his duties kept him on the ground a lot, and Gerd was wounded a few times and kept out of flying. Then Gerd went to the west to fly 190s and, later, jets, and I had more time to fly. I used to hold up my fingers after a good sortie, showing my victories just to bother him.

Barkhorn would have had many more victories, but if there was ever a question as to who may have scored a kill, he always gave the credit to another pilot. Batz was also the same way. He had great success, and shot down 237 aircraft and has the Swords, but he was transferred to Hungary in February 1945. Batz scored fourteen kills in one day in Russia, so he used to remind me that I had a higher score, but he had more in a single day. That was all right. I then pointed to my Diamonds and asked him, "Where are yours, Willi?" We are still best friends today.

I had been promoted to *Major* on paper, but not wearing the rank at that time, so I was given command at the base in Jassy. JG-52 was split apart, some fighting against the Russians and others against the American heavy bombers. Hrabak had gone to command JG-54 and Graf was the JG-52 commander, the *Kommodore*. It was in Romania where I thought I was going to lose my first wingman. We were flying over Jassy on a patrol, and I was not thinking about much, looking at the photo of my Uschi that I had above my altimeter. That gave me comfort, looking at it occasionally. I then had this bad feeling, the same feeling I would get before a fighter had a problem, this sting in the back of my neck—a sixth sense, I guess you could call it. I looked over at my wingman, a young new guy, and then I saw this enemy fighter closing in fast on him. I ordered him to break right hard and dive. He did so, with a fast reaction, just as the cannon rounds flew past where his fighter had been.

I also knew enough to know that this guy was probably not alone, so I rolled over. This Russian was very aggressive and would not let him go. I was on the enemy's tail and told my wingman to pull up in a shallow right climb, making the Russian think that he had an easy kill. This guy had total target fixation, and I told my wingman to watch, so I shot him down easily. I then told him that was what happened when you did not clear your tail, and ironically this guy was alone. No wingman. We were lucky, but I was very much awake for the rest of that flight. I told myself that I could look at Uschi's photo later; it would still be there.

Once in Romania, we had an interesting experience with both Russians and Americans. We took off on a mission to intercept Soviet bombers attacking Prague, and we counted many American-made aircraft with Red Stars, part of the U.S. Lend Lease. But then, there were American fighters also nearby, and I was above them all by a thousand meters. It seemed that the Americans and Russians were busy examining each other and were unaware that we were around. I gave the order to drop down through the Mustangs, then the Russian fighters, and through the bombers in just one hit-and-run attack, and then we would get the hell out of there, since there were only the four of us [in a *Schwarm*].

I hit two P-51s quickly in my dive—one went down—and I then fired on a Russian Boston bomber; I scored good hits, but it was not a kill. The second element also scored a kill against the Mustangs, and my wingman and I were all right. Suddenly, the most amazing thing happened. The Soviet fighters and Americans began fighting each other, and the confusion worked for us. They must have not realized that it was a *Schwarm* of Germans that started the whole thing! The Russian bombers dropped their bombs in panic and turned away. I saw three Yaks get shot down and a Mustang damaged, trailing white smoke. That was my last fight against the Americans.

This was in the defense of Ploesti and Bucharest, and also over Hungary when the bombers came in and they had heavy fighter escort. B-17s were attacking the railroad junction, and we were formed up. We did not see the Mustangs at first and prepared to attack the bombers. Suddenly, four of them flew across us and below, so I gave the order to attack the fighters. I closed in on one and fired, his fighter came apart and some pieces hit my wings, and I immediately found myself behind another and I fired, and he rolled away, on fire.

My second flight shot down the other two fighters. But then we saw others and again attacked. I shot down another and saw that the leader still had his drop tanks, which limited his ability to turn. I then closed on him and shot him down also. Soon afterward, I was recalled to take over the command of I./JG-52, and this was June 23, 1944. I did have the opportunity to engage the Mustangs again when a flight of 109s was being pursued from the rear, and I tried to warn them on the radio, but they could not hear.

I dived down and closed on a P-51 that was shooting up a 109, and I blew him up. That was my four Mustangs in a single mission. But this success was not to be repeated, because the Americans learned from then on not to be ambushed again. They protected the bombers very well, and we were never able to get close enough to do any damage. I was relieved that this pilot was able to successfully bail out. I was out of ammunition after the fight. As soon as that happened,

I was warned by my men that I had several on my tail so I headed for the deck, with a swarm of eight Americans right behind me.

That is a very uncomfortable feeling, I can tell you! I made jerking turns left and right as they fired, but they fired from too far away to be effective. I was headed for the base so the defensive guns would help me, but I ran out of fuel. The engine stopped and I was losing altitude, and had to bail out, which was my only time in a parachute in combat, although I did have to crash-land sixteen times, sometimes from flak but the rest from my victories. Once I just had a mechanical failure, but we saved the fighter.

I did bail out in flight school at Gatow, as I said. When I bailed out in Romania, I was certain that this one pilot was lining me up for a strafe, but he banked away and looked at me, waving. [This was Capt. Robert Goebel, eleven-victory ace from the 31st Fighter Group.] I landed four miles from the base, where some of our soldiers picked me up at Zarnesti. I had almost made it. They drove me back to the base in their truck. That day, we lost half our aircraft; we were heavily outnumbered, and many of the young pilots were inexperienced.

I knew that if an enemy pilot started firing early, well outside the maximum effective range of his guns, then he was an easy kill. But, if a pilot closed in and held his fire, and seemed to be watching the situation, you knew that an experienced pilot was on you. Also, I developed different tactics for various conditions, such as always turning into the guns of an approaching enemy, or rolling into a negative G dive forcing him to follow or break off, then rolling out and sometimes reducing air speed to allow him to overcommit. That was when you took advantage of his failing.

When I was in Hungary, we still had some big air battles, and the units were scattered. Helmut Lipfert was commanding 6./JG-52 as a *Hauptmann*, and I was there when Graf reassumed command. Lipfert's men tackled the heavy bombers, and they suffered heavy losses. They were very brave, being outnumbered heavily by the American escort fighters.

Since I had qualified in the Me-262, and flew the jet once more in March 1945, Galland asked me to again think about joining his unit, but my heart and friends were in JG-52, and I felt that was where I belonged. I was also told that American fighter pilots had unofficial orders to shoot parachuting jet pilots. I knew Rudi Sinner, and he told me his story. It was horrifying, really. We had standing orders never to shoot a man in a parachute. I would know, as I was a combat leader there in JG-52. The thought of the transfer was exciting, but I did not want to be just another pilot where, in his new unit with all the high ranks already there, I would be like Gerd or Krupi, just another wingman. Unit loyalty to me was very important.

Plus, I had many new pilots at JG-52 who needed guidance and instruction. The new arrivals were getting younger all the time and had fewer and fewer hours of flight instruction before they were thrown into battle. Rall, Krupinski, Steinhoff, and others were transferred to the Reich Defense, where they ended their war. I was torn, but I felt that I made the right decision at the time—I was needed at JG-52, and that was where I stayed. In later years, I realized that my life would have been very different if I had joined with JV-44. I would have never lost a decade of my life, and my health, if I had made that choice.

On May 8, 1945, I took off at around 0800 from my field in Czechoslovakia, headed to Brünn. My wingman and I saw eight Yaks below us. I shot one down, and that was my last victory. I decided not to attack the others once I saw that there were also twelve Mustangs on the scene above me. My wingman and I headed for the deck, where the smoke of the bombing could hide us. We pulled through the smoke and saw once again the two allies fighting each other above us. Incredible!

Well, we landed at the field and were told that the war was over. I must say that during the war I never disobeyed an order. But when *General* [*der Flieger* Hans] Seidemann ordered Graf and me to fly to the British sector with the rest of the wing and surrender to the Americans in order to avoid capture by the Russians, I could not leave my men. That would have been bad leadership. Graf said the same thing.

Graf gave the order to destroy the fighters. I told the men who were not needed to start heading west. Bimmel opened the fuel petcocks, dumping the fuel, so that we could burn the fighters. We did not want them going to the Russians. I decided to fire all of my ammunition, and I did this, but then that started a fire from the fuel vapors. Soon the entire fighter was burning, and I was inside. I felt like an idiot and jumped out, with not too much damage. I only lost the hair on my left arm. We destroyed twenty-five perfectly good fighters. They would be nice to have in museums now.

Some of our men had their families living in these areas, so we brought the women and children with us as we retreated. We had heard stories about what happened to women if the Russians caught them, even children. Many of the families were bombed out of their homes, so they migrated towards the bases. I was afraid for them.

There was still a large bounty on my head. I was well known, and everyone knew that Stalin would like to get me. I was marching with my unit day and night, trying to avoid the Soviets, going west through Czechoslovakia, when we surrendered to an American [armored] unit. We had wounded, both carried and walking. [*Oberleutnant*] Walter Wolfrum was one of those also captured. We carried him, and he would be released soon afterward. It was Wolfrum who managed to get my one letter to Uschi later.

They handed all of us over to the Soviets. Graf had been a prisoner of the Americans, and was then sent to us, where I met him again. I remember Graf telling me that, as Diamonds winners, the Soviets would probably execute us if they got us. I had no doubt he was right at the time. Graf also mentioned that the women, children, and ground personnel would have no one to help them; they would be at the mercy of the Red Army, and we all knew what that meant.

Graf, Wolfrum, Grasser, and I surrendered to the [U.S.] 90th Infantry Division, and we were placed in a barbed-wire camp. Soon there were about fifty thousand people in this camp—soldiers, pilots, civilians, even women and children. Then they separated us all into groups, and our group had over two thousand people—women and children also. The Americans said that we would stay with them. One interesting thing was that they collected our weapons, wristwatches, anything as souvenirs. The conditions were terrible. There were no sanitation facilities, no food or water. We were in American custody for two weeks total. Many men decided to escape, and some were even assisted by the guards, taking their families with them. They must have known something was coming that we already suspected or knew.

We went eight days without any food, and then we were told we were to be moved. This included the civilians. Why they were there I still have no idea to this day. I think it was because they were the families of suspected Nazi Party members or high-ranking officers perhaps. All of us, even women and children, were taken to an open field near a nice lake. We stayed there for two days, and they [Americans] brought food and water.

I and other military men made certain that the children were given the food and water first, then pregnant mothers, the older people, and then other civilians. We were to eat last, after the enlisted men—that was Graf's order, as he was the senior officer in charge, and my commanding officer. It was the right thing to do. Hrabak had been transferred to JG-54 at that time, in the Baltic. I was next in line as a *Major*, and Graf was an *Oberst*. He told all the other men that it was our job to take care of them. For that, I give him great credit.

The officers were separated from the enlisted men, and we officers were kept with the women and children. Then the officers, women, and children were loaded up on American trucks and driven for about an hour going around this lake. The trucks stopped and there were Soviet troops there waiting for us. More of the other civilians had arrived before us, and they were kept away from us. Some were German military women, and some were the family members of a couple of pilots who had lived nearby in the Sudeten region. The Russians then separated the women and girls from the men, and the most horrible things happened, which you know and I cannot say here.

We saw this, the Americans saw this, and we could do nothing to stop it. Men who fought like lions cried like babies at the sight of complete strangers being raped repeatedly by the soldiers. A couple of girls managed to run to a truck and the Americans pulled them in, but the Russians, most were drunk, pointed their guns at their allies and fired a few shots. Then the truck drivers decided to drive away quickly. Some women were shot after the rapes. Some were beaten to death or strangled for resisting.

Graf was a brave man. He said he was going to do something, and Hartmann Grasser was also there with us, along with Wolfrum before they let him go. Graf risked being shot when he ordered a Russian to stop raping a young girl, and he knocked one Russian down, and his Ppsh machine gun went flying away. Graf reached that Russian and started to beat the hell out of him. Graf was a strong and athletic man, and that Russian was bloody. Five others pulled Graf off and began to beat him until one of their sergeants said to stop. The Russian soldiers were under orders to rape, straight from Moscow. Their propaganda specialist, Ilya Ehrenburg, printed the order from Stalin in their papers and broadcast it over the radios. The Russians felt they had a right, and that there was no crime in raping and killing women and girls.

Some of the men, husbands, could take it no more and they attacked the soldiers, and were shot. Little girls and old women also suffered. I watched a few of these young girls, children, being raped by twenty to forty men, and they died. They cried for their mothers and fathers. I could not believe what I was seeing, and I had three Russians pointing rifles at me, Graf, and the others. We could do nothing. Some of the Americans were shouting at the Russians, but I could not understand what they were saying, but I could tell they were horrified at what they were seeing. One little girl was about six or seven years old, holding this dirty rag doll, and they took her too. She died within the hour as they raped her. There were even old women, grandmothers—nothing was sacred to them.

There was this one young American captain, who jumped

from his Sherman, with his pistol in hand and pointed it at a Russian soldier who was hitting this German woman, beating her while another one was tearing her clothes off, and he spoke in Russian to them. The captain told him and the others to stop. They just laughed and pointed their weapons at him and the others. The Russians were about fifty and the Americans were only about half that. One of the tankers rotated his turret, pointing the main gun at the Russians.

The captain was immediately on his radio, trying to see what he could do to stop this nightmare. The news that came back was not what he or any of us wanted to hear. They were told to leave; it was not their problem. I could see in their eyes, those young Americans, that they wanted to help, maybe even kill their allies to save those women. I felt sorry for them also. They knew they were condemning a lot of innocent people to possible death, and worse.

Others were not so lucky. I remember a twelve-year-old girl whose mother had been raped and shot, and then this child being raped herself by several soldiers. The more she screamed and cried, the more they beat her. She also died from these acts soon afterward, because one of the soldiers took her stockings and he strangled her to death. They passed around bottles of vodka and sang songs, as if they were having a party.

Then more Russians came, and it began all over again and lasted through the night. The Russians then pulled their tanks and vehicles in a large circle and put their lights on. They had armed soldiers all around. They were to shoot if anyone tried to escape, although I know that a couple of young boys did. This allowed them to rape and enjoy it all night long.

We stayed in that area [with the Soviets] for almost three

weeks. We buried the dead, trying to keep families together. The children, teenaged girls, were the toughest. I will never forget that. One young girl had been raped by about twenty men, for a full day and night, and she also died during the attack. She was still holding her dead mother's hand, who had been raped and killed beside her. Her father had been stabbed protecting her and her mother, who were raped and beaten to death by several men. They still took turns on her [the mother's] body after she was dead and they knew it. I had never hated before, but I did then. I remembered what that infantry *Leutnant* had told me in 1943 after I was rescued, about how I did not understand these Russians as they did—that I did not understand "his" war. I did then.

During the night entire families committed suicide, men killing their wives and daughters, so that they could not be raped again. Then they killed themselves. I still cannot believe these things as I speak now. I know many will never believe this story, but it is true. We spent two weeks in this makeshift camp. Soon, a Russian general came, took command, and issued orders for all of this to stop. He was shocked at what he saw when he came into the compound. The bodies of the dead and dying women and men had just been piled up, and we were not allowed to bury them yet. The smell was incredible.

The men did not stop [the rapes and beating], and a German woman went to him and told him what had happened. The general asked this woman to point out the men who had raped her. It took several minutes for her to point out the three men who were trying to hide, who had just raped her the night before. This general was serious, and he spoke with them, and they were still drunk. Well, because these Russians did not stay away and came back to rape again, and raped this one woman, those three men were executed on the spot by their own men, on the general's orders, by hanging. Their hands were tied, and he used the large branch of an oak tree.

Well, the Russians who saw their comrades hanged decided that they would not suffer the same fate. They came back that night, and other nights. They simply killed the women after they raped them so that they could not be identified. I have told you these terrible things, and Graf and Wolfrum were also there—they can tell you. I have not told you the worst. There is no need. You understand, I think.

Soon there was an official order for all rapes to stop. I learned much later that American soldiers were reporting these things to their superiors, and Stalin was trying to make the Eastern Europeans he had conquered more comfortable with a Soviet occupation. He did not need uprisings from fear of what may happen to the women in Poland, Bulgaria, Romania, the Baltic States, Czechoslovakia, and Hungary; the Russians in Austria and East Prussia had already made their mark on the women there.

Later, in the camps, I spoke to a man in Shakhty, who had been in Latvia, and he told me the stories of what he saw there, and in Pomerania. Women had been raped and nailed up on barn doors, where passing Russians, hundreds of them, would take turns raping these women, even girls, and in a few cases boys. They even raped them when they were dead. I could not believe what I was hearing, but this man and his fellow soldiers in the *Waffen* SS who were prisoners were forced to watch one of these crucifixion rapes. This tough *Waffen* SS man, almost four years fighting in Russia, broke down and cried as he told me. He felt guilty because they did not stop the murder. I could not say anything to him. I know men who abandoned their faith in God later. They just did not care. Graf is now like that. He decided that God must have chosen His side, or just forgotten about us, or did not care about the innocent victims, so why should he?

I must say something here also. It must be understood that I am not aware of any German soldiers raping any Russian women. It may have happened, and I know that under our laws if a woman could prove she was raped, that soldier he was to be shot. That was a standing order. I never knew of anyone in that situation, or even heard about it, but it was common knowledge. We were under orders not to sleep with these women, as it was the *Rassenfeind* [racial enemy] order. We could be in a lot of trouble if we did, unless a woman who was considered racially Germanic came to an officer, or was working with us. Helmut Lent married a Russian, but she was cleared by Himmler's people, and this I know about.

I always thought that the racial part of our policy was pretty damned stupid, as did the other pilots I flew with. We as young people had been hit hard with this subhuman propaganda, such as Slavs, Jews, that sort of thing. I never really thought much about it. It was the same in America with the blacks. Some believed it while some did not.

We were under strict orders at the front not to even steal, because we wanted to have goodwill with the locals. If we needed something, we bought it or traded for it, and if we took something for military requirements, we had to hand the owner a signed receipt—and only an officer could do this. If we stole anything, we could be shot. Standing orders. It sounds ruthless, but that was our military. These crimes we saw now were beyond our understanding.

Once we were gathered, they finally took the time to take

our names, ranks, personal papers, and looked us all over deciding who would be put to work and who could not work. Some were released, like Walter Wolfrum. He had been badly wounded, and they released him. He carried the first letter from me to Uschi. Once they had their information, we went on a five-day march to Budweis. Then they told us we were going to take a train to Vienna. We boarded the train, and they told us that we could not go to Vienna because of riots or something, so that we would have to go to Budapest. We got there, and then were told that there was an outbreak of some kind, and we were being sent back to Germany. You know that little warning pain I used to get in the back of my neck? It returned. I sensed something was wrong.

The one thing that we were told was that all Germans captured in uniform would be released within a year. That would have been 1946. That did not happen. They did not even have us fill out Geneva Convention prisoner of war cards. The Soviets never signed that convention, so they had no intention of agreeing to it. Later I would learn about the agreement reached by the Americans, British, and Soviets at Yalta. That was what doomed us.

All Germans who had been fighting east of the line they drew were to be given to the Soviets. Those fighting in the west would be in American, British, or French zones. Even worse, the hundreds of thousands of Russians, Ukrainians, Georgians, all these people, who were against Stalin and the Communists and fought with us suffered. Under that agreement, they were also handed over. Most were executed, like General Vlasov. We had some of these men in the camps with us. They were treated worse than we were. We were the enemy. These men were traitors to the Communists.

Well, I was somewhat famous, or infamous, depending

upon your perspective, and the Soviets were very interested in making an example of me. The same with Graf. We were propaganda heroes with the Diamonds. I mean that men like us, who were not from the aristocracy, or not from families with long military traditions, were used by German propaganda. Graf was used even worse, like an exhibit in a circus. He was too simple to see that he was being used by them [German Propaganda Ministry].

Graf's father was a blacksmith, some say illiterate, and Graf was not that well educated either and limited in his intellect, but a good man. He was a brave man, but he was not a deep thinker—more of a reactionary. His peasant background was perfect for the [German] propaganda people. Being famous in Germany during the war did not help us once the war was over. It made us targets, you know? I was harsh in my opinions of Graf for many years, but I have since softened on that. I understand things better. Getting old made me wiser, I think.

We were not treated very well at first, but I was never badly beaten and tortured, just hit a few times, and I was starved and threatened for several years. The interrogations were the worst. Threats against me, against my family back home, coercion. I know that you have interviewed several Germans who experienced the same thing. The stories are pretty much the same, so I won't go into details. The first thing they did was give us physical exams to determine how fit we were for hard labor. Then they put us on a train, which was diverted from Vienna to the Carpathians in Romania. We were placed in another wired prison with Romanian Communist guards for a few days.

This lasted about a week, and then we boarded another train. There was no room in these small train cars. Not all could sit, so we took turns. Finally, we arrived near Kirov and disembarked in a swamp. This was our home for a while. Of the 1,500 POWs who were dropped at this place, about two hundred lived through the first winter. This I know from some others who survived. Those who stayed there were not fed, just worked to death. I was sent to Gryazovets where [Hans] "Assi" Hahn was already. He had been a POW since 1943. It was he who gave Uschi the first full report of what had happened to me. He was released in 1949, I think. He met with Uschi, as did others who were released early. She heard nothing about me for another two years.

Then they said we were going home. Graf and I were with about sixty others in this train car, packed so that you had to stand, and could hardly turn around. He said to me, "Erich, look at the direction we are going in." I then knew that we were going east, not northwest. They lied to us again. That should have been no great surprise. After a couple days, the train stopped. We were in another transit camp. We were given a little food and water, and then after a week put back on another train.

I think that it was a problem of the Soviets not really knowing what to do with us. This train was heavily guarded, a lot of soldiers. We spent two weeks in this hell hole, no sanitation except a single bucket for sixty or so people. When the train stopped, we were in Russia, in the Urals, northeast of Moscow. My heart sank at that moment. I knew that I would probably die in Siberia. This was a slave labor camp, in the middle of a peat swamp. We had to build our own shelters, and we dug the peat out and stacked it up, where they dried it out and the trains would come by and haul it all away. Peat burns as a fuel, and that was also what we used for heating and cooking, if we had food.

There were 3,500 or so of us in this large swamp. There

was no fence, just guards and dogs who walked around, but there was nowhere to go if you did escape. How the hell would you walk out of a swamp, in western Siberia, and get home? I was there for a month, when they came and took everyone with the rank of *Major* or higher. We were then sent to a special camp at Graziwics, I think was the name. One day, about a year later, this *Hauptmann* walked up to me. He had been with us in the peat swamp, and had just been transferred to our camp for some reason that he did not understand, and he told us that only 200 of the 3,500 men we were with were still alive as of a few days ago. They had been worked to death and just buried in the swamp. I was an angry man, and Graf just told me to bury it. Forget about it.

The *Hauptmann* said that within days of our leaving, they had stopped feeding the men, just worked them. Most died within a couple of weeks. They starved them to death. They had to be rid of them, because there was another shipment of prisoners coming in a few weeks and they had to make room. The first thing these new prisoners did was bury hundreds of the rotting corpses of the men they had come to replace. That had to affect morale. The Russians lied to us all the time. I was later sent to Shakhty, where we had the revolt.

Right before I was sent to Shakhty, I had to go before the Soviet court, for the second time. This was when they read the charges and gave me twenty-five years. They said I had the right to appeal the sentence. I told them that there was nothing to appeal because no crime had been committed, unless the rapes and murders by their own soldiers was a crime. Then they said that I was no longer a military prisoner, with certain legal protections. I also told them that under international law, and even in their own manual, which I had read in German during the war, that all military prisoners were to be repatriated back home at the end of a war.

Lenin had even said and written into the Red Army manual that any nation that kept prisoners longer than six months or used them as labor after a war was a capitalist nation and an enemy of the working class. They seemed pretty surprised when I said this; you should have seen their faces. They said that did not matter because I was a common criminal, and they gave the list of my victories, saying that I murdered their pilots and aircrews, and they even had a charge that I had shot something like 780 people. I asked when did this supposedly happen, where, and who made this idiotic claim.

They gave the name of a village, which I had never heard of, and I told them so. I even told them that it was very easy to prove where I was; my log book and the unit record would prove where I was. Their argument was that it did not matter, because when I shot down the aircraft the debris fell on the ground, or stray bullets hit people and killed them on the ground. Then they said that I destroyed a factory making corn meal, or something. That was considered sabotage. I asked where this place was, and they told me and even showed me on a map. I started laughing until I cried, because it was farther east than any German I knew of had ever been, unless they were a prisoner, and I told them that our fighters could have never reached that far and made it back. It was ridiculous, and I had never been in that area and I could prove it. They laughed also and said that it was just a political charge against me.

Well after that, I went back to Shakhty, which was a coal mine. Mines were a death sentence. When we arrived, the other prisoners said that none had ever left the camp alive. They either died of malnutrition, starvation, beatings, or cave-ins. These Russian miners had nothing that resembled a mine safety program. They just found more bodies when they needed them.

When we were told that we had to dig coal, I looked at the other Germans already there working, and some of the officers, and told them to hell with that. I was a German officer, and under the Geneva Convention I was not authorized to work, especially manual labor, and they could go to hell. I think I shocked them, and they looked at the fact that we were several hundred and the guards were only a couple of dozen. Although they had weapons, they could not kill all of us before some of us got to them.

I decided that rather than risk anyone being else killed, and since I was such a high-value prisoner, that I would just go on a hunger strike. It was my first but not my last. The camp commandant threw me into the metal punishment box, and they did not come see me for several days, perhaps a week. You lose time, especially when you can see no sunlight. Then they dragged me out and strapped me to a chair in a concrete room, with large windows that had no glass. They placed a tube down my throat and forced me to swallow that rubbish. The other prisoners saw this. I think that this was the final straw. They saw me as a national hero, an officer, and a man who would support them. They decided then to support me. They had had enough also. I think I was just the spark. Strangely enough, the local villagers were also supportive of us—that was how much they hated their own government and the political thugs who ran their lives.

I was not the senior officer; there were a couple of other *Majors* who outranked me and a really tough paratrooper *Oberst*, a man who had fought at every major battle since Poland. He was not a man to be bothered, and I knew that the guards feared him also. There was a rumor that he had killed a guard in a previous camp in Eastern Siberia, but I did not know if this was true and I was not going to ask. I respected him, and he was no Nazi either. In fact, with exception to some of the SS men and [*Generalfeldmarschall* Ferdinand] Schörner, I never met any in my unit.

Anyway, I heard this great noise, and you must remember I was strapped to this chair. This was late in the afternoon, at the end of the day shift. They also ran a night shift. The men were coming back from working in the coal mine, and word spread about me. Soon the door crashed open, and this guy had an axe that he had used to tear down the door, and more than a dozen prisoners ran in and grabbed the guards. It was quite violent; I mean, a piece of wood the size of my arm flew right past me—a part of the door, such was the force. They then took the camp commander, a Soviet colonel, and the two majors hostage, a woman doctor, and then also rounded up eighteen of the guards, as the men had weapons, and locked them in the cellar. Then the civilians outside began to shout, saying that we should give the GRU [*Glavnoye Razvedyvatel'noye Upravleniye*] men to them, and they would help us escape. That was amazing. They also wanted the weapons.

I told the men that no one was to go outside the camp, even though all of the remaining guards had left. I knew that they would be back, and with a larger force. That would probably get us all killed, and the paratrooper colonel agreed. If we stayed in the camp, then we would be in a better position to negotiate. Then we had the camp commander call his superiors and tell them what had happened. I am pretty sure he thought that either we would kill him, the villagers would kill him, or his own superiors would kill him for losing the camp—or send him to a Siberian camp as well. He even asked us not to turn him over to the people outside, and that told me everything. We told this colonel what to say.

Our demands were simple. We wanted an official from Moscow to come see our conditions, and so on. We wanted representation in an international court. Well, within about four hours or so after that call, a couple hundred soldiers came in trucks with all the weapons you could imagine. A Russian general was in charge, coming from their HQ in Rostock. Then the villagers began shouting at them, telling them to send us home, we had not done anything. Many threw food to us over the fence, and some even came inside with blankets and coats, boots, socks, that kind of thing.

We began yelling in Russian to these soldiers that we were soldiers, not criminals, and one day they may find themselves behind wire. How would they like to be treated? Well, they never shot anyone. I was later sent to the commander, the general, who was angry with me, and there were five of us who were considered the leaders. He asked me what the problem was, as if I were the ringleader. I told him that I was the one rescued, and we were not trying to escape. We wanted better conditions and food. I told him that we officers refused to work. I told him why. Three days later, I was called into the commander's office. There were five others there already from the revolt.

They sent us all to the camp at Novocherkassk, and I stayed there one year. On the fifth month of being there, my name was called. I was accused of creating the riot at Shakhty, creating a revolt among the civilians in the area to overthrow the local government, and that our revolt put us in charge of the occupation of that entire area, an insurrection. I could not believe it because we had never left the camp. They said they had statements from eyewitnesses. I called them liars and demanded that they bring these witnesses to make these statements openly. Four months later, I was sent to Moscow to another special court. There was a general, two colonels, a major, and some political clown. There were many other civilians there also, maybe press people, I do not know.

I was asked some questions, and I answered them. I also told them that I knew there were at least one hundred thousand Germans in camps around the Soviet Union, and the war was over [the number was actually over a million]. Their prisoners that we had in camps had come home. Why keep us? Then the general sent all of the civilians out of the room. This was when they confirmed my sentence of twenty-five years at hard labor. My appeal died. I had no rights under Geneva. Then they sent me back to Novocherkassk. When that sentence was given, it was reported back in Germany as fifty years. Uschi was working in a post office and found out when the papers came. My family was speechless, they told me later when I came home. The first three years of being prisoner were the worst.

One day, a large mob had formed. Hundreds of people from several villages stormed the camp gate, threatening the guards to feed us. They could see our condition. After this, the policy changed. The guards were rotated every few days, moved to other camps in the area. This was to stop us from becoming too familiar with them, and to stop the guards from being influenced by the civilians. That was a major moral victory for us. We had won a small victory. That gave us hope. We also began to get more and better food as a result, mostly supplied from the villages, so we often ate the same food as the guards. Before this, we ate what the dogs ate. That is true. I believe that was mostly mutton scraps, but who knows. I lost twenty kilos in weight. That's a lot—about fifty-five pounds or so, I think. Everyone was ill.

We had these loudspeakers placed high where the towers were, which gave these announcements and told us when we had roll call, giving us Communist propaganda, and the political officers would come around and talk to the guards and the villagers. They would say things to them: "Remember the Germans killed your wives, husbands, sons, and daughters; do not feel anything for them," meaning us, and that kind of thing. The amazing part was that the population did not believe in their own propaganda. I think that even these people had seen enough under Stalin to know they were being . . . I think the word is "screwed."

They would often take us men who were of higher rank into an office. They had these documents in Russian, which I could not read, and they told me that I had to sign my confession. I looked at this man and laughed. I told him that, under the Geneva Convention, I could not be forced to sign anything, and as a senior officer, I could not be forced to work. I also reminded him that under Geneva, officers and soldiers in captivity had to be paid the same wage as the captive military, and that torture was illegal.

Then he laughed at me and said, through an interpreter, that the Soviet Union never signed the Geneva Convention. I then reminded him that, under both Geneva and Hague conventions, that open belligerents did not have to sign them to be held accountable for their actions if they waged war. Then he reminded me that we invaded his nation, not the other way around. Then I told him that he was correct, but I was still not signing his damned paper.

Well, they threw me into this metal box, so small you

could only sit, not stand. They came every three or four days to check on me, but never fed me. No water or toilet facility—just a box, and this was in winter. They took my heavy, wool-lined leather coat and fur boots the old man had made for me during the war. I was there with nothing but my prison shirt and trousers. I was freezing. I started to cough up blood once and thought that I may have tuberculosis. That was frightening.

After two weeks, they finally asked me to sign. They said that I could have hot food, my warm clothes, and a hot bath. I told them to go to hell, and they shut me back in. I did not see them for another week, when they threw a plate of food in on me. I ate it. I would normally have thrown this stuff away, but the cold drained me, I needed the calories. I would have eaten a raw dead dog after three weeks. I kept thinking about Uschi, my family, our son I had never seen. They kept me going.

Many of the men who died had simply given up the fight, and they stopped having the will to live. This was especially true when letters were allowed through, telling them that their wives had divorced them. Graf received one of those letters. That was the time when he made his decision to just accept his fate. He became a psychological wreck. He was a good pilot and a brave man, but he was not an intellectual. I do not mean this in a bad way, but he was not the kind of man who could grasp very difficult things quickly. He did not embrace communism. He just gave up. We rarely had mail from home. I received maybe fifty letters in the ten years I was there, and Uschi had written over four hundred, I think. They held mail as a weapon, or as a tool to get you to sign these ridiculous confessions.

One of these papers stated that I had purposely destroyed

over 350 Soviet aircraft. I agreed, and said that was my job. They said that I had cost the Soviet people over five hundred million rubles and murdered hundreds of patriotic Soviet men and women. They also wanted me to sign admitting that I bombed a school and a hospital. I reminded them that I flew fighters, not bombers, so they should go back to their masters and get the lies straight. They beat me up a little and threw me back in the box, and this lasted for nine months, almost to the day. I think I surprised them. When they finally let me out, they again threw me in a chair and said, "Sign." I told them to go to hell again. But, this time they simply said, "Okay," and put me back with the other prisoners.

Many of the men signed these papers, and I guess that was enough to make them happy. Some went home afterwards. After a while, they seemed to have forgotten about me. At least, that's what I thought. Then a week after the nine months of hell, this guy in civilian clothes, obviously NKVD [*Narodnyy Komissariat Vnutrennikh Del*] or GRU, walked in. He called out my name and I walked over to the office. He began talking to me, saying my wife had left me and my country had abandoned me. I should just be like the rest of my comrades and accept my fate. I told him he was wrong. He again told me this rubbish. He said the German women were marrying the Americans and British soldiers, because they had money, food, and they needed men. I told him that he did not know my wife, and he seemed a little upset I had said that. I told him to produce the divorce document and prove this to me. He seemed very upset that I called him out on this. I then decided that I would fight back.

Right after that meeting, I started another hunger strike. This sounds crazy, because we were not fed much to begin with. I was going to prove to them that they did not have complete control over me. If I was such a high-value prisoner, then to hell with them, you cannot bargain with a corpse. Well, after about a week they grabbed me and tied me to this chair. This doctor came in, and with help from a guard he forced a tube down my throat. They fed me eggs and sugar in a liquid mixture. They did this again and again over several hours, every day for twenty-seven days. Every three for four hours, they would do the same thing. On the twentieth day, this political commissar came in. He was like this good policeman telling me that I was a young man and that I had my whole life ahead of me. I told him that his workers' paradise was not what I called a life that I wanted. He told me that my fate was in the hands of Moscow.

Their orders were that I was to stay alive, but then at any time they could send the order to shoot me. He made it sound simple, such as changing your food order in a restaurant. It was like this American television show, *The Twilight Zone*. I remember this episode I saw once, where there was a police state, and the main man was gathering up his own people, like the Gestapo or NKVD, and charging them with silly crimes. But then he too became a victim of his own political machine, and he too said he was innocent of any charges.

This commissar told me that he had five letters from Uschi, and if I stopped the hunger strike I could have them. This was the end for me. I decided that I would live for Uschi, and I would fight to see her again. These bastards were not going to beat me. He held the letters up, handed them to me, and smiled, like he gave a damn about my happiness. I quickly read the letters, and he seemed pleased that I was smiling. Then he said, "Now sign this paper!" Well, I had already read the letters, so I did not have to sign anything, so I just smiled and very politely said, "No." I found it strange that they did not beat me then.

I was never really ever physically tortured except for some beatings; just mental torture—sort of brainwashing, you would say. They did not break me. I had my faith and I had my wife. They kept me going. I think the reason was because I was one of the only twenty-seven Diamonds holders, and I knew there were at least three of us in the Soviet camps: Graf, me, and Schörner, who also had the *Pour le Mérite* from World War I. As an infantry officer in Italy, he had been with Rommel at the Battle of Caporetto and earned that medal. He was a Nazi, but he was a brave soldier.

Novocherkassk was bad, but in 1948 I was sent to the Pervo labor camp in the Ural Mountains with many others. Word that I was coming had already reached the prisoners. When I climbed out of the truck, a lot of cheers and shouting happened. They had heard about our revolt, for which I was blamed as the leader at Shakhty. Others involved in the riot at Shakhty had been sent to Pervo long before me. I came with a few others by train in a special car for us Germans. Many of the men I was with over the first three years died from disease and starvation. They asked about the remaining men at Shakhty.

I told them. Most died during the brutal winter. There were always more workers, mostly German or political prisoners, replacing the dead. It seemed as if this was their method. They did not care; there were always more living bodies to replace the dead. Despite the brutality of the guards, the Russian civilians actually became angry at how we were treated. Some of them would smuggle food to us.

Others would try to take letters out, with the hope that one day perhaps they would find a loved one missing in the war. None of us ever thought we would see home again.

The guards were less abusive at Pervo, the food was better, and there was less hard labor. Rumors spread that we were to be exchanged for Soviet prisoners, but in hindsight we know that was not true. We were held hostage for financial reasons. Stalin and his empire were starving, but we did not know this at the time. He wanted these trade agreements using his great grain harvests to get money and technology. I guess starving out the Ukrainians did not work out so well for him in the 1930s. Western Europe received the Marshall Plan to rebuild after the war, and the Soviet-occupied nations could barely survive on what they had taken. They were hoping to trade us for money.

We were basically kidnapped. We all spoke of escape, but this was impossible. Even the villagers had to have written permission from the local commissar to travel out of the village. People would report strangers to the police. We stood out also, as there were very few men in this village, mostly children and old people. We learned that most of the men worked as paid laborers in a nearby coal mine or something, and they only came home occasionally.

I have heard stories over the years of men who escaped. I have never met one. I know of one man who was supposed to have escaped from Eastern Siberia through China. I find that hard to believe, but perhaps it was not impossible. If you were in another camp in another country, like the many? in Czechoslovakia, Hungary, Romania, Poland or Bulgaria, I could see the possibility.

We had a fellow prisoner with us who arrived from another camp, another *Major* who was a lawyer, and he had been in criminal defense. This was in the camp at Pervo in 1949. He spoke Russian, and he was an important man in our group. We all began learning some Russian from him, and this worked out well. His name was Ulrich, but I do not know if this was a first or last name. Perhaps it is best anyway, because during the time of brutality he was killed by a guard.

What happened was that he had a relationship with a pretty Russian lady. We used to go out on work details and cut trees, haul hay, other types of work, and the villagers liked us for the help. I knew they understood that we really did not have much choice in the matter. Ulrich managed to get extra food, brought it inside, and helped the German doctor who was with us taking care of the sick men. Meat was rare, but on occasion we did get some. I am not really sure what kind it was. I was a little disturbed to have never seen any household pets running around, but I did not think too much about that. The guards had dogs that ate better than we did sometimes. This was definitely true at previous camps.

Sometimes we would be visited by these clowns who wanted information, mostly technical information, and with me it was always about the Me-262. I kept telling this guy that I could start it, fly it, land it, and look at it, but I was not an engineer or a mechanic. I did not know anything about the technology. He became very angry and told me I was lying. He told me that all German prisoners were given a minimum of twenty-five years hard camp labor. I looked at him; he had a Makarov pistol in his holster. I also told him that I was like a farmer with a couple of horses, pulling a harvesting combine. I know how to run it, but I could not build it.

I asked him, since he carried one, if he knew the exact

muzzle velocity of the bullet, or if he knew the exact barrel-to-breech tolerance measurements, or the amount or pressure created upon firing to force the bullet out, the speed of the bullet, the maximum effective range of the bullet, and the pressure required to eject the spent cartridge. He looked at me, knowing that I had him, and he flew into a rage and hit me with his cane. That was a mistake, because I took the chair and used all my strength to hit him with it. He was knocked out and he landed on the floor very heavy, so I opened the door and called the guard. I felt pretty sure that this one thing would get me shot for certain.

The guard came and took me to the commandant's office, and they sat me down. This older guy poured some vodka, gave me some and some bread. That was like a shot of adrenaline, and he said that I would go back to the camp, and he shook his head. He was trying not to laugh, I could see. I gathered that he did not think very much of this idiot commissar, either. I went back to the camp and shared my story, and it gave the other men hope. They had heard the fight in the room, and they knew I was in there. They did not know that I was beating the interrogator. They all had a great laugh and it lifted their spirits. This was the kind of information that raised morale, and high morale; likewise, our military bearing and discipline kept us together. We all knew men who had been released, and we also knew that any man leaving would get the truth out to our families.

I then received the letter from Uschi, who told me our son had died from pneumonia. This was in, I think, 1950. Times were hard for the people in Germany then, with little food. They did not yet have penicillin, which was a big reason that we lost so many soldiers. Antibiotics may have saved Peter's life. Infections killed more people than bullets. The

Americans and British had it during the war, but they kept it a secret.

In 1952, things had been going well for us, for the most part. Then again, I was brought in for interrogation and placed in this chair. My interrogator was there with a girl interpreter. She asked me about being a "beater," and I was confused. She said my file claimed that I had beat up a commissar; I said that was true, but that he hit me first. I met with these people and this girl for about two months on a regular schedule, every few days. What they hoped to get from me I still do not understand. Maybe I was a curiosity. I had met Hitler, more than once. I was a Diamonds holder, akin to a three-time hero of the Soviet Union. I was like a rare, exotic zoo animal to them.

If I remember correctly, they asked me for the first time where my Knight's Cross with Diamonds were. I told them that I threw them away rather than have them placed into their hands. In fact, I had thrown them into the river before we surrendered. I also told them, honestly, that the decoration I wore was a replica, that my wife had the real thing. This was a common practice, since they were very valuable. They did not believe me, but what else was new? I learned how to play this game with these people. I pretended to be nervous during the questioning. If they scream the words *fascist*, *criminal*, *Nazi* and those things, then they think they have you.

But if they changed tactics, and were kind, telling me that I was a good man, intelligent, and asked personal questions about my wife and family, if I had enough to eat, was I being treated well, then that was a warning for me. Again, they tried to get me to sign some new documents that I had not seen, and these were again in Russian. I was read these stupid charges, saw that my twenty-five years at hard labor was upheld by the court again, and they said that I had to sign this paper to go home. I told them that no one in their right mind would put their name on those lies. I told them that I wanted to see the actual charges in my language. They said they would translate them after I signed. I told them that they would grow very old waiting for that to happen.

You have to understand their crazy system. If you were to steal something, they really did not punish you. It was expected, not a problem. If you said something bad about Stalin or even Khrushchev later, then you might get shot. It was an insane system. People in the West, our world, would not understand this mindset. Their system is so corrupt. I tell you that they keep their people under fear and bribing. The people could not revolt, or have another revolution and be rid of the Communists, because informers were well paid, given better houses, jobs. No one trusted anyone. Students reported on their parents to teachers, that kind of thing.

We also had many Russians in the camps with us, and these were political prisoners. I met this one man I can never forget. His own son turned him in to a teacher, because he had said that farming more land would do no good, since he would not see any additional profit or grain; the state would just take it all. That was enough to get him placed in the labor camp. That was the time when Graf told the Russians that he would just accept his fate and fly with their air force. They did not take him seriously and moved him out and to another camp and let him write about the war, that sort of thing. He had been a professional goalkeeper on a football team, and he played for the *Luftwaffe* team also. He was apparently quite good, and he had also played as a defensive fullback. If I remember, they wanted him to work as a sports coach or something.

The strange thing about that was the Russians did not want Graf, or even ask him to fly or work for them. In my situation, it was different. They wanted to send me to Moscow for school, and work with them. I was not sure if they wanted a pilot or a spy, but I said no anyway. They told me that I was too young to have been indoctrinated into National Socialism, and they knew that I was not a Nazi Party member, so I had potential. When they again asked me to work for them, I said that they had to let me go home to see my family and then offer me a legitimate work contract, an offer to be negotiated. I would never work under coercion or threats. They could just kill me and save us all a lot of time. They said, "Okay, we will send you home. Just sign this paper. You are no criminal. Sign and go home."

I have to tell you that it was very tempting. Graf and many others signed, and when they did they were allowed to go home. I asked them [Russians] if this meant that I had to be a spy, and they said no. I asked them then what did the paper say, since I could not read it. They said it was an agreement to work for them later, if I should want to, and that I had been fairly treated. I said, "Well, if that is the case, then type it out in German and I will read it. But I am not signing anything that would place me in a prison back home." They became angry again.

They [Russians] also asked me what I honestly thought of Hitler, Göring, Himmler, and the rest, how I knew them, how often did we meet, that sort of thing. I told them what I thought about Hitler and Göring, as I had a lot of contact with them, but that I had never spoken to Himmler. I did meet him briefly once in Berlin, but I did not know him, so

I had no opinion. Then they told me of the camps, the Jews, their prisoners. They mentioned some places and said that I had to know what had happened. I told them that I had absolutely no damned idea what they were talking about.

My father had also died later in 1952. I did not know of this until I came home. The best way for prisoners to get information out was to write everything down. We sewed notes into the coats of those being released. When they arrived at home, the leaders in Germany, and our families, learned firsthand about how we were being treated. The Russians kept us as hostages for future bargaining. Why they thought this would work I have no idea. They very seldom released any staff officers. Captains and below maybe, but most of the men released early were either unfit for work or enlisted men. Graf and a few others were the rare exceptions.

Once, we had a typhoid epidemic. We also lost many of our men in the Soviet Union to such illnesses. The Russians did not care. There was always an endless supply of free labor. I was in several camps—Shakhty, Novocherkassk—where they kept me in solitary confinement, and then Diaterka. I had become famous when I did the hunger strike to protest the slave labor conditions and the fact that the Soviets were simply working men to death out of spite. It would be a long time before we received any Red Cross packages, and when we did, things were missing and food was rotted, so it was really a waste of time.

I was ironically placed in a camp at Kuteynikovo, where my squadron had been based in 1943, and I once again crossed paths with Hartmann Grasser, from JG-52. When we arrived, we saw a sign that read "Our Work Makes the Soviet Union Strong." Well, if that was so, then we may never go home, so I said to hell with that. This was when others and

I refused to work, again invoking the Geneva Convention. They [Russians] placed me back in solitary. This was a work camp for mining, and many men were tired of it; many had died, and I think my being gone started the problem.

In comparing the camps, Shakhty had been somewhat isolated, about fifty miles from the nearest town, but there were a few houses and small villages along the way. We had barracks and a large building where the meals were prepared. It was strange that often the civilians would come and look at and speak with us. Many had been transplanted from farther west, and had been in the German-occupied areas. Many fled east; others were deported. I never met a single Russian civilian who hated us, believe it or not. They seemed to hate their own government and the commissars, though. This was especially true at Shakhty.

I knew why they [Russians] placed us in the Soviet Union. The Russians were so terrible to the people of the occupied countries, with the starvation and poverty they had to live with, that the occupied peoples would have been very good to us. I know that some German prisoners were held by the Czech, Bulgarian, and Romanian Communists in those countries. I spoke to a few men from those camps, and they said that the local people were very friendly, even the guards in many cases, as they had been our allies in the war. They hated the Russians for the most part. Even today, if you go to these countries as a tourist, you are welcomed as a guest, not as a former enemy.

Some of these people [Russian civilians] were also workers in the coal mines. A few were paid and others were political prisoners, not paid, and kept in a different camp. The mines were a short walk away, about two miles perhaps. At this time, I was the only fighter pilot. The others were ground soldiers. I created my first problems here when I refused to work, under the rules of Geneva and the Red Cross. They [guards] were less than happy with me. I told the camp commander this. He said he would review my case, and the charges against me, and I could possibly be released. I was not holding my breath.

They [Russians] placed me in a barracks alone. Two weeks later, the commandant asked me again if I would work, and I again told him no. I think I said something like it would rain rubles before I worked in a mine as a field grade officer. After my hunger strikes and the fact that we learned that news of our condition was well known by Moscow at that time, the order came that field officers did not have to do manual labor. Sometimes they [guards] violated that order. This was the beginning of what led to the later revolt after my next hunger strike.

Diaterka had a high fence, then a dead zone with a walkway for guards and dogs, then another fence with watchtowers with more guards and machine guns. There were long rows of barracks, which were not insulated, and the winters were quite cold, I can tell you. Each barrack held between two and four hundred prisoners depending on its size, and there were rows of wooden bunks in tiers of three to four.

The camp was divided into maximum and minimum security sections, with us being in the most secure section. The ultra-maximum security section housed elite members of the Third Reich and special Soviet political prisoners, which was another section even within our part within its own wired enclosure. This was where Hitler's SS *Adjutant*, [*Obersturmbannführer*] Otto Günsche, and others from the bunker—including [SS-*Brigadeführer*] Wilhelm Mohnke, Rochus Misch, and Hans Baur, among others—were held. I spoke with Mohnke years later. He was held in solitary confinement until 1949. He was released with me in 1955. Baur was released a little later, minus his leg. I stayed there at that camp until 1954, when I was sent back to Novocherkassk. This was my last camp.

I still see Günsche on occasion, and he lives here near me. He has a medical company, and they make pharmacy medications. You know, he was the man who burned Hitler's and Eva Braun's bodies. That was one of the reasons the Soviets treated him so harshly. They interrogated him constantly, as they did Baur. Misch was also kept in solitary confinement. They [Russians] kept asking him details of Hitler's telephone conversations. Misch said that he had no idea; he placed and received calls, but never listened in. They thought he was lying, that he had to have eavesdropped. I think that the only reason they kept him alive was the hope that he would say something, proving that maybe Hitler was not really dead. They did the same things to Baur. Then they began recruiting agents.

Yes, they offered me the opportunity to return home if I worked as an agent for them, which was out of the question. [They] did not like this, either. I was assigned kitchen duties as an inducement to become a converted Communist. I think that they believed that if they could get us high-ranking and highly decorated officers to convert to communism, their job would be made much easier. They converted Graf—well, broke him down, which was a shame—but he did not embrace communism. He looked at it as a pragmatist; it was either the Western way or Soviet way, and he was already there. They did release him in 1950 [after signing the confessions], but I would not be so lucky. I know that they really tortured him, I mean brutally.

Well, he signed and came home. This was the reason that he was thrown out of the *Gemeinschaft der Jagdflieger*. He was seen as a traitor. I think that is very harsh, but that is the way it was, and still is. He was the only holder of the Diamonds to fall from grace, you could say. He was released on Christmas Day in 1949, because they had no use for him. I think those who turned their backs on him, and did not live through our years of torture and starvation, beatings, had no right to pass judgment on him.

Those of us who resisted the Soviets were punished much longer. They wanted me as an informer, and even gave me a list of names of officers they wanted information on. They promised me early release if I did this. They wanted me to work as a spy in the camp. I refused. Actually, I think I told them to go to hell. They placed me in solitary a few times, sometimes for a long time. After Stalin died [March 5, 1953], things became better for us—better food, better treatment. We were even given German doctors, also prisoners, who could handle our medical needs. I did get one postcard from Uschi at that time, I think, but it was two years old.

I still thought of my Uschi. She kept me going, and the thought of my family waiting for me. They once threatened to kill my wife and son, or forcibly bring them to Russia, and they spoke about doing terrible things. All of this was intended to break me down. We were allowed only twenty-five words on a postcard to send out, sometimes a lot less, and this was not often. The letters I smuggled out with returning POWs provided the information the family needed. There was also information on men still alive and those who died or disappeared. Many men just disappeared, and we never learned what happened to them. I received about fifty short letters from Uschi in the ten and a half years, but she wrote over four hundred. Getting a letter was the greatest morale boost you could imagine.

Again, I was called in and asked about my Knight's Cross, Oak Leaves, Swords, and Diamonds. Well, I told them again that we had agreed never to surrender our Diamonds to the Soviets. My originals were with Uschi, and a copy was taken by an American, and another copy I had thrown away. This NKVD officer leaned towards me and told me that Graf had given his, and they were on the table of the NKVD officer when I was called in. I was shocked; they looked like the originals, not a copy. He wanted mine also. He was angry that he did not get them. I remember thinking that it had been a few years since I became a prisoner. What made him think I would still have them? I did not even have my coat and boots! They again also wanted detailed information on the Me-262, [because] they had several captured machines they wanted to evaluate. I did not help them; what could I say?

I would have to say again that our discipline kept us alive. We never lost our military bearing, and our rigid system and mutual respect for our own authority maintained us. We had the rank structure and presence of mind to form our own leadership committees. Even though we wore no rank, everyone understood his place and all worked within the system. That was our strength, as well as many of us having our faith in God. I thought of my faith and my Uschi, and that got me through. Many men found it difficult when word would come that their wives had divorced them, or that a relative—such as a parent, spouse, or a child—had died.

The greatest heartbreak was when my son, Peter, died while I was a POW, but I only learned of this much later, a year or more, as I also learned of my father's death when I came home. I learned more when I was repatriated in

1955 along with Hans Baur, Ferdinand Schörner, [*Oberst*] Hajo Herrmann, Johannes Wiese, Wilhelm Mohnke, Otto Günsche, [*Standartenführer*] Gustav Lombard, and several others. Assi Hahn was released earlier than the rest of us, like Graf, as was Walter Wolfrum, who had been badly wounded before our capture and taken by the Americans. I was relieved to know that Wolfrum had smuggled the letter to Uschi for me, which let her know I was still alive in 1945. The letters sent by our families could not contain any questions or names of other missing Germans—that was a rule—and we could not mention any of them in our letters home. Many of us used code words that only our families would understand.

It was good to learn that our country had not forgotten us. The wives were crucial to this process, as was Chancellor Konrad Adenauer. My mother had written Stalin and Molotov on my behalf without any response. She wrote to Adenauer, and he replied personally that he was working on the problem. The Soviets wanted a trade agreement with the West, especially West Germany, and part of this deal was the release of all the POWs. I knew something was going on when we were allowed to go to the cinema to see a lousy film and were issued new clothes—suits of a kind, and not prison issue. I was in Novocherkassk when I heard that we were going home. Of course, no one believed it. There were over a dozen or so men in one jail cell at a time when we received the news.

We even had hot showers, with soap. That was a first. They gave us a good meal, the best I had ever had in Russia. That meant something was going on, because they did not ask us to sign any papers or interrogate us before we ate. We met the commandant. He shook our hands, and he seemed honest when he said that our countries should have never had a war, and he wished us all the best in the future. He said something interesting to me alone, very quietly. He said, "You are going to freedom. Never forget this place." I think he was trying to get me to explain how bad things were. This man had replaced the previous commandant, and he was a good fellow. He saw to it that we had better food, rest, and did not allow any guards to harm anyone. He also said that there would be no stealing from prisoners. The guards used to do that all the time.

We boarded a bus to Rostock, where we spent some time. Every town or village I saw in those ten years was a very gloomy place. No one smiled; everyone walked and looked the same. Then we went to Stalingrad, which they called Volgograd by then, I think, then Moscow, Bryansk, and Poland. Everywhere there was poverty—poor, unhappy people. This was true even in Moscow. I saw long lines of people waiting to get food. I had not even seen such things this bad in Germany in the last months of the war. The people were all poor, and I thought that if this is the success of communism, then they can have it. It was almost unreal. I felt very sorry for these people.

In Poland, we had a strange situation. We stopped in a small town and left the train because we had to wait to get another train. One of our men who had left the train was attacked by an East German, a young man, and was hit in the head. He thought we were trying to escape. And he was a German also! But he was too young to have been a soldier in the war. There were a lot of these young men on the train platform, waiting to go to Moscow. Then later that day we took another train to Warsaw and then to Poznan, and stopped in Slubice. This is on the East German border.

When the train stopped in Germany and we got out, hundreds of women and men were holding photographs of sons, brothers, husbands, and fathers, all asking everyone they saw if they knew of their loved one. We knew almost all the names of the men on our train, and none of their missing men were with us. Some of us said that more trains were coming, perhaps later. I knew in my heart that most of these people would never see their men again. It took many years for the names of those who died in Siberia and in Eastern European camps to come out. Many thousands had died, and there was rarely any communication back home to anyone as to what had happened, unless men were released with that information, so many never returned and the families knew nothing. They were simply ghosts who vanished.

Once the train stopped, a policeman came on board and called out two names. These were prisoners who had parents living in East Germany, and they wanted the men off the train. The men said no way, and they did not want to stay in the Communist sector. We all grabbed the East German policeman and threw him from the train. Then our Russian guards surrounded us and protected us from the other policemen who came to get us. They disconnected all of the train cars except those carrying us and told the driver to get going.

Then, after about six hours, we changed trains at Frankfurt at the Oder. Then we arrived in West Germany. It was October 1955. Other trains would follow, with the last coming in December. As soon as the train stopped at Herleshausen, I was able to send a telegram to my Uschi. She would know I was free. Other prisoners arrived in December, like Baur and I think also Hajo Herrmann. The tragic part was that more than seventy percent of the Germans held died in the camps.

I learned that many things had changed upon coming home. The country was divided. The west was occupied. My son, Peter Erich, and father had died while I was in prison; that was a hard thing for me, and I will say no more. Yet my mother and lovely Uschi were there waiting for me. She looked at me and cried, as I only weighed about a hundred pounds. My normal weight was about 140 to 150 pounds. I was weak, and walking took a lot of energy. I have a photo of that too—here it is.

They never gave up hope, and I think that my belief in their strength was what got me through the most terrible mental torture or starvation. Whatever the NKVD or GRU did to me, I thought about my family and focused on them. I was alive and I was home, but I still thought like a prisoner. I always felt as if I was being watched, and I know that this was simply paranoia, but that stays with you.

I have always been amused by the stories of how we Germans were so terrible and just killing everything in our path, especially in the east. I know that some bad, very terrible things happened, but I just did not see these things. I also learned after the war that these killings in the camps and such were also very top-secret, and I can understand why that was the case. It was still evil, and I feel bad about that and how our nation still pays the price for that time. There are some things that I may never understand. I saw little from the Soviet side that was much better, to be honest. I was just glad to be home.

I thought that when I came home it was all over, but this was not so. I had to be interrogated by my government intelligence office, *Amt Blank*, where Krupinski had been working with Organization Gehlen. They worked with the CIA. Well, I was three days in Berlin being asked about everything, like names of anyone still missing, conditions, interrogation methods, locations of camps, all of this. I know that they were trying to account for all the men still missing. Most of those captured were not on any list. They just disappeared.

Remember that over 90,000 men surrendered at Stalingrad [out of 250,000 in the 6th Army]. Less than six thousand came home, and I was with a few of these men on the train. These men had been prisoners since February of 1943. They were zombies, broken men. They spent over twelve years, most in eastern or northern Siberia in the mines, or working on the railroad, cutting trees, and work such as that. This explains the great numbers of the dead and still missing. I was told that only one man in fifteen survived those far eastern gulags.

Well, the first things I wanted were a good meal and a hot bath! But to see my Uschi was the greatest dream. I also read everything I could find—newspapers, books, and magazines. I wanted information. I had been in an intellectual vacuum for so long; I wanted knowledge. Of course, Uschi and I had our church wedding, long overdue. Yes, a big party was planned, but I declined it. I did not feel that it was appropriate until everyone was home who was still alive. I also could not believe the rebuilt areas and numbers of new cars, cars without clutches, the airplanes in the peaceful sky. Stores full of food, clothes, even car dealerships.

I saw Mercedes and BMW cars being sold, nice cars—new styles of automobiles that I found interesting. Later, I met with Ferry [Ferdinand A.] Porsche, who inherited his father's business—Professor Ferdinand Porsche [senior] built the Volkswagen and the Tiger tanks during the war—and he said he was building sports cars soon. He showed me some design drawings. He said I could be one of the first to drive one, and he kept his promise. In 1963 or so, I drove his new car, called the 901, and I liked it very much, but it was not a good family car. I took it on the Nürburgring, and it was excellent—like a 109 with a steering wheel!

There were a lot of Americans and British around too, and they were very friendly, but I was afraid to speak with strangers. I seemed to have lost all of my social skills. Some people, even Americans, knew who I was, and they knew that I had been in Russia for a long time. They were interested, because now the Russians were their enemy.

The streets were not full of broken building and bricks, which was also amazing to me. The clothes style was new—all of it was new. One of the first people to meet me was Assi Hahn, who had been home five years before, who was the second man to bring news to Uschi about me. I then met again with Walter Wolfrum, who had recovered and he was a very good friend, and always has been. Soon it was a major meeting with all of my JG-52 comrades from the war. Everyone came, except Graf. He is something of a hermit now, and always has been.

There is always the thought that you may once again be in the same situation. I know that many of the men who lived to come home still are not right in the head. Many of them lost their families, wives, and children, and they came home to nothing. Some committed suicide, even after living through the gulags. I know that Graf still has some problems, but he will not discuss this with most people. They call it postwar or prisoner shock.

I still have the dreams sometimes. I understand. I was lucky. I came back and had my Uschi. Seeing her was wonderful, and the first time we touched and we hugged, I did not want to let her go. I knew I was all right when she kissed me. My life would be okay after that. I had my love back. Uschi said that she never lost faith, that she knew I was a survivor, and she waited. She prayed at the church every week, and every time another prisoner came back with news, it made her stronger. She knew about the revolt and my treatment. She was afraid they would just shoot me. She always said I had a thick head—stubborn, you know?

I was thirty-three when I came home, and that is late in life to start a career. I had lost touch with much of the world, but the one thing I knew was flying and the military. The thought of fighting another war also frightened me. I also thought about the needs of my country, and my old comrades had rejoined the military and were pressuring me to do the same. Krupi called the house, and we spoke, and he wanted me to join him and Gerd Barkhorn on a flying trip to England. Dieter Hrabak even came and talked to me at the house with Marianne. He and Macky had joined. So I gave in and I joined in 1956. The old boys were back, but Uschi was less than enthusiastic. I had also thought that after my experience I would never wear another uniform again, but then she came around, too.

I was the only Diamonds holder to join the new air force. Galland said no and Rudel said no. Graf was never invited, I do not think, and Gollob was the same, but for different reasons. Schnaufer died after the war [July 15, 1950], before I came home, and he was a good guy. Maybe he would be alive if we had started the air force earlier. Who knows? I think that the political problems with the men who took the high positions were the big issue.

There was a lot of resistance to former *Luftwaffe* officers, especially decorated veterans, being in command. Werner

Panitzki, who was in charge as inspector in the 1960s, was a *Major*—the same rank, same as me, when the war ended. He never flew or fought in battle. He was on staff duty in Munich and Berlin, and in seven years he became a *Generalleutnant*, three stars, and had resigned with Heinz Trettner. They disagreed with the conflict between the civilian government and the military. I tried to stay out of it.

Steinhoff and Hrabak gave me the best help and advice. They were good friends, and still are. Rall would say to me, "You are still an idiot, but a great idiot." Steinhoff would call me a clown. Hrabak called me "Wonder Boy." Krupi called me "the bank" because whenever we went drinking, he was always broke and borrowed money from me. I think he still owed me money, and I asked him about that when I was back home in 1955. But he had given Uschi and my mother money to help them while I was gone, as had others to help her out, and I said that I owed him. He said "rubbish," that I owed him nothing. They loved me; they just worried about me, I think. Trautloft and his wife, Marga, have always been the same way, like the Ralls, and the same with Galland. I sometimes spoke my mind without thinking, and it got me into trouble. Galland understood that problem all too well.

Steinhoff was then asked to take over when Panitzki retired, and he said that he had to think it over, that he would not rush into anything. He had personal and professional reasons for waiting, but they never forgot that hesitation. Steinhoff managed to survive the politics, only because he is a powerful character and supremely intelligent. He was always right in an argument. He never debated unless he knew he was right. That was his greatest asset. I think that, like Galland, any man who could stand up to Göring would have no problem with these [political] types. Steinhoff also addressed many other issues, such as better pay for pilots and mechanics.

These [new air force] men, especially pilots, would join, complete their military service, get their training at great expense, and then leave for Lufthansa or go overseas and fly for better pay. We did not have a professional full-time air force, and the constant rotation and training of new pilots was very expensive. These men knew that there was no career in the military with the bureaucrats running things. It took a long time before we had separate rules and laws from the civilian side. A military organization cannot function like a civilian organization. The requirements and discipline are too great. The military must exist in its own world; otherwise, it will not survive.

I got back into flying again, and it was great. I had a friend who let me fly his light plane, and I certified again as a private pilot. Heinz Bär was also a great help, as were others. I took refresher and conversion training in Germany, England, and the United States on the newer models. I had decided that if I were to be a senior officer and command fighter pilots, I needed to be trained and qualified in the newer aircraft that we were flying. I finished all of this training in America, and I liked Arizona, but Florida and California are better. I went to school to learn English, or at least learn it better.

I was asked to give lectures on my escape in 1943, how to avoid and evade the enemy. I was also asked to give lectures on Soviet interrogation methods. These were very important, to let the young know what to expect in the very best and worst of cases. I met some of the Americans who were shot down and escaped, or held in Hanoi during Vietnam, and others from Korea. Dieter Dengler was born in Germany and went to America. He became a navy pilot and was shot down. He escaped from Laos, and he learned the hard way. He was lucky. There were many examples, like Rudel, who was shot down about thirty times and once had a great escape in Russia.

Now, the United States has the SERE [Survive Escape Resist and Evade] school, which is a good thing, and many NATO pilots go through this, and we have one similar. During the war, Franz von Werra escaped from Canada to the United States, through South America and back to Germany. That was only possible because he spoke the language [including Dutch] and did not look much different from the locals. Canada and America are open societies, with no papers required to travel and no informers. We now get training in resisting interrogation, with a better understanding of what to expect.

I was made the first *Kommodore* of the new JG-71 "*Richthofen*," and I was very proud. However, there were some problems in the air force. The reconnaissance types had taken over, which would not have been so bad but for the fact that they created infighting with the fighter boys. Rall made the comment that, after the fighter leaders took control, now that the fighters control the air force, and all the senior officers who are in charge were old JG-52 men, we should stage another Fighters' Revolt. I knew he was joking, but we had a lot of serious issues to discuss. One was the [Lockhead F-104] Starfighter Program.

The Starfighter was a great plane but it had problems, and I did not feel that Germany needed it, or that our pilots could even handle this machine without a lot more experience. The old pilots compared the transition from the F-86 or F-100 to the Starfighter like from going from a glider into the Me-262. The leap in technical difficulty and the great differences between the two fighters meant that a lot of additional training had to be done for our pilots. The F-104 was an interceptor, like the *Komet*, not a true fighter.

Steinhoff totally agreed with me, since he qualified in the F-104, and he argued hard to allow the pilots more training time, especially in America. I not only supported him, I told even the higher-ups that if they did not authorize this, then they should either retire or be charged with murder. Every dead pilot was their fault. One thing that the war and captivity taught me was to never, ever take any rubbish from anyone ever again. Even Josef was on my side. He had no problem telling people to go to hell and pointing the way to get there. It is not so much pride but a feeling of being. I had never and will never bow to any man. I answer only to God and Uschi.

Many of those higher up felt that I was out of line, but I stated what I thought was accurate, and I was proven correct, but this made me enemies. Rall did not completely agree with Macky and me, but Krupi did, for the most part. In fact, he led the charge in the United States in expanded training in the F-104. This was in 1959, and I was at Nellis Air Force Base near Las Vegas. Later we had the F-4, but I did not fly the F-104 or F-4, and we had already spent many hours in the F-86 Sabre. I always had a philosophy: Never ask politicians or senior officers their opinions about an aircraft. Talk to the young, fresh pilots and also to the maintenance crews. That is where you get the real information.

The pilots who flew it loved the F-104 in the air, as it was the fastest and best-climbing fighter of that day. However, when away from their superiors, they complained about the high maintenance after very few flying hours, the dangers of landing, the long turnaround time. Plus, there were many problems with the hydraulics, engines, and landing gear. I would compare the 104 to the 109, as both had a narrow undercarriage.

The mechanics explained that there were a lot of difficulties in getting spare parts. Many were substandard, and the airframes did not last long at supersonic speeds. They also mentioned the fact that the flight controls had a tendency to freeze, until the pilots dropped below fifty thousand feet. I immediately thought that this one factor, along with any hydraulics issues, may have explained the high number of crashes. I spoke with Macky about this, and he had gathered the same information.

I then met the safety officer for the training squadron, a nice young captain who allowed me to read all of the reports. It was a damaging set of documents. I then knew that I had to stop Germany from buying this aircraft, and Steinhoff carried the banner since he was my superior, and a firm believer. Josef, while understanding, told us to shut up and say nothing. The decision to buy the F-104 was a political decision, made by non-fliers, who just wanted the newest thing. It would have been better to just accept the F-100 and F-102, as they had been thoroughly tested and proven. But no, the idiots in Bonn had the final word.

I was asked my opinion along with Steinhoff at this *Kommodoren* meeting, regarding the records on the F-104. But I also ran into trouble there. I explained my position in great detail. I could not understand this mindset they now had. There was none of the old teamwork that we were so used to during the war. It was all about the individual. Rall also complained about this, as did Macky, Hrabak, Trautloft, Barkhorn, and all the old tigers. Politicians making tactical military decisions had lost us the last war. When Steinhoff became commander in chief, that mindset changed—he saw to it. The bomber boys always had the teamwork mind because they had to. Each man on a bomber had a job; he was not alone in a vacuum.

I also did other things that were considered criminal, such as having the unit's F-86s painted with my old tulip pattern, and then I created the squadron bars, like in the old days, and this raised eyebrows. We were told to take them off, but it is funny how now they are used again. I felt that morale was important, and building camaraderie through a unique and distinguishing emblem was needed. The bars were killed under superior directives, although today all squadrons have them. I did have supporters, such as *General* Josef Kammhuber, but he was a rare breed from the old days.

Kammhuber stood by his pilots, and this was clearly demonstrated in 1961. One of the F-84 pilots took his flight into East German airspace, to West Berlin, just to prove they could beat their defenses. It was embarrassing for the East Germans, who raised all hell. The leader of that group [*Oberstleutnant* Siegfried Barth] was relieved of his command and threatened with a court-martial. Kammhuber argued that he had provided a valuable service. We now had good intelligence on their defensive weaknesses and response time. He won, and the pilots were reinstated.

Kammhuber is a great intellect, a great thinker. Kammhuber was the single most important person in rebuilding the *Luftwaffe* after the war. He and [Wolfgang "Wolf"] Falck saw the future of night fighting, and the Kammhuber Line, as it became known, was a very effective defense. If Falck and Kammhuber had received everything they needed, I know beyond all doubt that RAF night bombing would have been stopped in 1943. Kammhuber's strategy and Falck's tactics were a lethal combination.

I still flew after I retired. They really forced me out.

Kammhuber told me that my promotion to *Brigadegeneral* was killed for political reasons. It just would not seem politically appropriate to have a Diamonds holder in such a position. I said to hell with them. I retired, instructed, and flew at a few air clubs as well as in an aerobatics team with Dolfo Galland. Later, I just decided to relax and enjoy life. I have my family and friends and am always meeting new ones, like you, Colin. We have spoken often for many years, but I feel that now is the time to say some of the things I have never really spoken about. There is always a time for everything.

I had many chances to get together with my comrades from the war—all the men I mentioned, plus many I have not. I always felt that Graf received a very unwelcome response after he came home. He is a good man. He was a good pilot, a good leader, and he took care of his men. I flew with him in JG-52 after he received the Diamonds, and unlike Gollob, who was a Nazi, Graf continued to fly whenever possible, violating Hitler's personal order, so that he could be an example to his men. That is a real leader. You must share the danger and lead by example, and Graf was one of the best, like Steinhoff, Hrabak, Rall, and the others.

Many in our small society felt that Graf had been turned by the Soviets. That was not true. I was there. He was simply a pragmatist, as I think you would say. We were in the Communist world, with no guarantee that we would ever get home. He just wanted to get out of prison and fly, if possible. He was never a Nazi, never political. But the heavy propaganda that was done in the radio and newspapers that told the world about us heroes, especially fighter pilots and Diamonds holders, did us no good in captivity. It just made us more visible targets. The one good thing was that such notoriety meant that to the Soviets, we were high-valued prisoners, so we were much less expendable than the hundreds of thousands of others. I call them the *Geistesoldaten*—Ghost Soldiers, the dead who would be forgotten, never to return home. Our own nation ignores us; they do not care about us, either.

Graf decided to try to make the best of a bad situation. He lives in Düsseldorf still, I think, near Hajo Herrmann. He does not come to the *treffen* or anything. He lives like a hermit, really, very sad. I see him sometimes, and many of the others will sometimes visit him. His health is not good these days. His spirit was broken when he received the letter and papers that his wife had divorced him while we were in Russia. She was an actress, a famous one too. That happened a lot. That was my greatest fear with Uschi. If she had left, I would not have cared if I came home. They could have just killed me then. She is my life, along with our daughter, Little Uschi.

During the war, I flew around 1,456 total sorties, about 1,404 combat missions, I think, but I am not sure of the exact number. Coming out of the sun and getting close was my game; dogfighting was a waste of time. The hit and run with the element of surprise served me well, as with most of the high-scoring pilots. Once a Russian was shot down, especially the leader, they became disorganized and easy to attack. This was not always the case, especially later in the war, and there were special units of highly skilled and disciplined pilots, such as the Red Banner units who would make life difficult.

I was very lucky, unlike Rall, Barkhorn, and Krupinski and especially Steinhoff, who was almost burned alive. All of them were badly wounded on several occasions. I was almost killed by a German sentry once while I was trying to get back to our lines from a brief period of captivity. That was too close for me. I still have that image of Punski walking out of that fireball when he crashed, the day I met him.

I was never shot down by an enemy plane, but I had to crash-land fourteen times due to damage from my victories or mechanical failure, but I never took to the parachute but one time. I never became another pilot's victory. I did go through a few fighters, though, and I made about fourteen crash-landings. I think that being a captain and a Diamonds winner at that age, and later a *Major*, forced a lot of responsibility upon me. I think that I was able to handle all of that responsibility because of the strength and friendship of my comrades.

I would say that I was ambitious and eager; I cannot think of any fighter pilot who would not have those qualities and be successful. Becoming a hero is not always easy, as you find yourself living up to the expectations of others. I would have preferred to just do my job and finish the war anonymously. It would have made life as a Soviet POW much easier [not being so famous].

I would also say, given the many years that have passed, that Hitler's decision to attack the Soviet Union was a very bad idea. Even though we had the technological, tactical, and perhaps on occasion the strategic capabilities to win there, it was the country, more than their military, that destroyed us. The country was so vast, it just swallowed us up. We were spread too thin, and with our resources dispersed all over Europe, North Africa, it just did not make any sense to me.

And also, the stupidity of the invasion without preparing for a winter campaign in 1941 was inconceivable to me, and not just me. Sure, you can think you will destroy an enemy in short order, just like we did the rest of Europe, but you still plan for the worst case, not rely upon hopes and dreams.

Seventy percent of our casualties in 1941–1942 were from the winter then. I experienced temperatures that took us from perhaps ten or fifteen degrees [centigrade] down to minus-forty degrees overnight, and we had winter clothing. I could not imagine not having those clothing items. Motors and weapons could not function; it was terrible.

I knew that once America entered the war, and especially after we lost Africa and Stalingrad, that the war could not be won. That is a very bad feeling to have. To know that you are fighting, losing good men, wasting lives and money, and risking the destruction of your nation and the lives of your people, civilians, your family, only delaying the final outcome. I wish the bomb plot would have worked and Hitler had been killed.

I will always think of Count Stauffenberg and the others as the true heroes. They knew more than we did, and they tried to do something about it. I thought a lot about that when I was in captivity. I wondered how our people and our families were doing. What was Germany like now? What would our future be like after Hitler? I assumed that it had to be a better place even with an Allied occupation, but I was uncertain.

I served under Graf, von Bonin, and Rall when Hrabak was *Kommodore*, and both were excellent commanders. Rall was also my commander in the 1960s, and we all answered to Steinhoff—again JG-52, who ran the air force. I served under Gerd Barkhorn for a while, when he was my *Staffelkapitän*, until I became a *Hauptmann*. Gerd and I were always in heavy competition with each other in scoring, but we were always the best of friends until he died. They were good, honest men who are still well thought of by the men they commanded.

Many of our men decided not to join the new military in Germany. Grasser was asked by Henri von Maltzahn, another good man, to join, but he refused, and he went to train the Indian and Syrian air forces after he was released from Russia in 1949. This was because he was not considered a National Socialist and he was not as high-profile, although he did have the Oak Leaves from Hitler. We are still great friends, and he is a very good man, very steady. Helmut Lipfert became a schoolteacher, and he is also a hermit. He was lucky and did not join us in Russia.

One thing I learned is this: Never allow yourself to hate a people because of the actions of a few. Hatred and bigotry destroyed my nation, and millions died. I would hope that most people did not hate Germans because of the Nazis, or Americans because of slaves. Never hate—it only eats you alive. Keep an open mind and always look for the good in people. You may be surprised at what you find.

The Luckiest Man Alive

Generaloberst Johannes Steinhoff
September 15, 1913–February 21, 1994
976 missions, 543 combats, 176 kills
Knight's Cross, Oak Leaves (Nr 115),
Swords (Nr 82)
German Federal Cross of Merit with Star
Legion of Merit (US) and
Légion d'Honneur (France)

JOHANNES STEINHOFF WAS TRULY one of the most charmed fighter pilots in the *Luftwaffe*. His exploits became legendary, though his wartime career ended tragically. Steinhoff served in combat from the first days of the war through April 1945. He flew more than nine hundred missions and engaged in aerial combat in more than two hundred sorties, operating from the Western and Eastern fronts, as well as in the Mediterranean theater. Victor over 176 opponents, Steinhoff was himself shot down a dozen times and wounded once in combat, another time in a crash. Yet he always emerged from his crippled and destroyed aircraft in high spirits. He opted to ride his aircraft down on nearly every occasion, never trusting parachutes.

Steinhoff, a self-assured and quiet intellectual, lived through lengthy exposure to combat, loss of friends and comrades, the reversal of fortune as the tide of war turned against Germany, and political dramas that would have broken the strongest of men. He openly defied his corrupt national leadership and was never intimidated, even when the Gestapo came calling. His defense of his pilots at any cost almost proved suicidal, yet he never backed down.

Pilots such as Steinhoff, Hannes Trautloft, Adolf Galland, and many others fought not only Allied aviators but also their superiors, who were willing to sacrifice Germany's best and bravest to further personal and political agendas. In both arenas, they fought a war of survival.

Aces like Steinhoff risked death every day to defend their nation. Moreover, by voicing their opposition to the incomprehensible decisions of the Third Reich high command, they risked their careers and even their lives. Steinhoff was at the forefront of the Fighter Pilots' revolt of January 1945, after Galland was replaced as General of the Fighters. A group of the most decorated and valiant *Luftwaffe* leaders confronted the *Luftwaffe* commander and deputy *Führer*, *Reichsmarschall* Hermann Göring, with a list of demands for the survival of their service, and their nation. Their main concern was the *Reichsmarschall*'s lack of understanding and unwillingness to support his pilots against accusations of cowardice and treason. The officers of the Third Reich were blaming the pilots for Germany's misfortunes. Steinhoff's frankness got him threatened with court-martial and banished to Italy, with similar penalties imposed upon others in the mutiny. Adolf Galland was almost shot.

Steinhoff was one of the few men to have lived and flown from the age of fabric biplanes to the jet age during wartime. He flew the world's first operational jet, the Messerschmitt Me-262, in combat. Steinhoff's recovery from injuries suffered during a near-fatal crash in a Me-262 jet near the end of the war on April 16, 1945, again illustrated his strength of will and character and his amazing ability to overcome even the most difficult obstacles. His former comrades always praised his abilities and leadership. His former enemies were proud to call him a good friend after the war, including three prominent Americans: President Ronald Reagan, Senator Barry Goldwater, and World War II hero General Matthew B. Ridgeway. Steinhoff retired a four-star general.

His story is an inspiring tale of moral and personal courage. It also illustrates the power of the human spirit. Steinhoff died in February 1994, shortly after this interview. He had one brother, Bernd, who lived in Ohio, and he is survived by two children. His son, Dr. Wolf Steinhoff, is a retired ophthalmologist living in Germany, a profession for which he trained partly because of his interest in the eye problems his father suffered as a result of the Me-262 crash. He is also survived by his daughter, Ursula Steinhoff Bird [wife of retired Colorado State Senator Michael Bird], who lives in Arizona. Steinhoff has four grandchildren and seven great-grandchildren. During the interview, Steinhoff spoke candidly about many topics, including the war, his superiors both during and after the war, and his philosophy about his country's role in the postwar period following the collapse of the Third Reich.

I was born in Bottendorf, Thuringia, on September 15, 1913. This is a region in the middle of Germany. My father was a mill worker, mostly agricultural work, while my mother was a traditional housewife. She was truly a wonderful lady. My youngest brother, Bernd, is an engineer and lives in Columbus, Ohio, in the United States. My son, Wolf, is a doctor, and he lives here in Germany.

With regard to my education, I attended gymnasium, which is a little more involved than your traditional high school, where I studied the classics and languages such as French, English, Latin, and Greek. It was truly a classical education that later served me well. I picked up most of my English in the countryside and during the war, speaking to captured aviators and such. After the war, I went to school to become more fluent. [Steinhoff perfected his English by reading Western novels and watching American television Westerns while assigned to Luke Air Force Base.]

I studied how to become a teacher, in order to educate people, but with the economic conditions in Germany when I was a young man, I could not find a job. I joined the armed forces and enlisted in the navy, where I served for one year. I was in the navy with another friend of ours, Dietrich Hrabak, and we both became naval aviation cadets. Later, we were both transferred to the *Luftwaffe* after Göring became the commander in chief.

That was in 1935, and I was in school along with Hrabak, Trautloft, Galland, Günther Lützow, Werner Mölders, Herbert Ihlefeld, and many others. We trained at the same school and became friends with many other flight students, most of whom became very successful and highly decorated aces. Unfortunately, not all of them survived the war, and now every year we lose someone else.

Flight school was easy for me; I took to it quickly, as did the others except Mölders. He suffered from motion sickness, and he often threw up and carried a special bag in his cockpit, as he was tired of cleaning out the cockpit. Despite this problem, he was an outstanding pilot—I would say of the same quality as Hans-Joachim Marseille. Mölders was a natural in the 109. I met him again in advanced school. He would land and come out looking as white as a sheet, barely able to stand, and I did not think he would survive flight school, but he was at the top of the class in basic flying, and then in advanced fighter training and gunnery.

Mölders somehow managed to fight through this problem with airsickness, and he became a very important person in the fighter forces later. I think that his ability to conquer his medical condition, which also included vertigo, made him less sympathetic to others who were unable to do their job when he became a commander. He was tough, but also a fair man. Mölders, Galland, Lützow, Gustav Rödel, Erwin Sawallisch, Eduard Neumann, Hajo Herrmann [bombers], Rolf Pingel, and Ihlefeld would join the Condor Legion and fight in Spain. I was not allowed to go, even though I was not married at that time. I was a new pilot and did not have enough time and experience. That always ate away at me.

My first combat mission was late 1939, well after the Polish campaign, while I was assigned in Holland. We were flying against the Royal Air Force [RAF] bombers that were attacking coastal industry. My unit, IV./JG-2 "*Richthofen*," had the Bf-109E, while Wolf Falck's unit flew the Bf-110. That was long before the Battle of Britain, but I could see that things were going to get more difficult for us. This was when I was *Staffelkapitän* IV./JG-2 until the end of 1939.

Falck also scored a kill and claimed another that I do not think was confirmed due to a lack of an air witness. We destroyed half of the bomber formation, shooting down twelve bombers. It was rather uneventful, but later on December 18, we were told that there were forty or so aircraft headed to us—bombers, apparently. I was vectored to one sector and attacked a flight of Vickers Wellington bombers near Wilhelmshaven. I shot one down, and then another I hit also started to plunge down to the sea. There were about twenty-two that I counted, but as you may expect I was rather busy.

Falck's guys did well in the 110s, and assisted us in shooting down half the formation. This mission ironically made us famous. This was the first time large numbers of British and German aircraft had engaged, and we won. Falck, [*Oberst* Carl-August] Schumacher, and I were ordered to Berlin. The Propaganda Ministry went mad over this, over the top really, and we became nationally known in the press. Even the foreign press was there, and this was when I first met William Shirer, who was the American war reporter living in Berlin at that time. He was a very nice and interesting man.

This was the first time I had met the big guys, such as Josef Göbbels, Hermann Göring, Joachim von Ribbentrop, and others, and I must admit I was not very impressed with any of them. They seemed more interested in getting their names and faces in the newspapers than in anything else. I looked at these men, and I wondered how such weak-looking creatures could be running such a great country. Hitler was not there during this meeting, and I would not meet him for another couple of years. I did have many occasions to meet and speak with Göring, which was always an unpleasant experience. In these early days, he was energetic, enthusiastic, pompous—well, he was always that, but he was just a very inquisitive person. He would ask all sorts of questions, about every small detail of the action, or any action. His interest was evident, but his breath was disgusting—sickening, really.

Göring seemed to be living through his fighter pilots, almost as if he felt like he were part of a unit just by discussing the combat. He seemed to miss the old days, I guess, when he was a fighter pilot and hero. I found him annoying, exhausting, and intrusive. He loved to grab you, almost hug a man and slap your back. I found this uncomfortable. I have never been a man who liked being grabbed and touched all the time. Also, his voice irritated me.

However, if Göring were intrusive and annoying, Göbbels was calculating, opportunistic, and, after a few drinks, he became extremely vulgar. I disliked him immediately, and I just as much told him so. I think he thought I was joking, but I said to him, "*Herr* Minister, please keep your distance, if you do not mind." He was always coming into immediate contact with the others and me; I hated that. Many of us made jokes about these men. We called Göbbels the "Limping Elf" and the "Garden Gnome." Of course, we called Göring the "Fat One." The reasons were obvious.

I learned early to detest these men. I measure a man on his merits and character. I did not see very much of either in these clowns. Well, we did our interviews, shook some hands, had the photographs taken also with Wolf Falck, and then I left as soon as possible, after receiving a few days of home leave.

Later I took over as the temporary *Staffelkapitän* of 10./JG-26 "*Schlageter*" [10th *Staffel* (Squadron) of *Jagdgeschwader* (Fighter Wing) JG-26 for a short time until I was transferred to 4./JG-52 in February 1940, where I remained until the start of the French campaign and then the Battle of Britain. We had a lot of time on our hands, mostly flying patrols along the borders, but no enemy contacts. After the December 18, 1939, raid, the British all but abandoned their daylight bombing missions, and then began to bomb at night. This would last throughout the war.

During the Battle of France, combat was not very grueling for me, personally. We had all of the advantages in aircraft, superior numbers, training, and experience. Very few of our pilots had any contact or any success until the summer after France surrendered. By that time, we had more fighters from the factories and more trained pilots. The Battle of Britain was a different experience for many reasons. First, we had to fly over water, the English Channel, to England and back. This meant less than twenty minutes of flying time, once you reached your target area, if you did not get into high-speed combat. If we did engage the enemy, then we had perhaps five to seven minutes at full throttle. This did not leave a lot of loitering time. If we were on escort duty, then that was another headache, and I will explain why later.

The British were born fighters, very tough, well trained, and very enthusiastic. They were brave, and I never fought against better pilots at any time during the war, including the Americans. We were almost evenly matched with the RAF in fighters against fighters, so true dogfights—even in the *Schwarm*—were possible. They would take off and engage us, and with their radar, they knew where we were. They had a lot more fuel for the fight. The Battle of Britain, in my opinion, was the truest test of men and machines, and only the best survived. You learned quickly, or you did not come back.

Our 109 could out-dive, outrun, and out-climb the Spitfire. We were a little faster, and almost as maneuverable.

They could out-turn us, though. The early Spitfires had a serious problem; they would stall out in a steep dive due to their carbureted engines, whereas we had fuel injection. Often we used the tactic of diving away to avoid being chased by Spitfires, and then we would pull up and bank around. While the RAF pilot tried to restart his motor, he was vulnerable. Soon they stopped trying to dive on us, and they would just climb and wait for us to pull up, and then enter into a shallow dive, hit us, and then climb away.

We developed a tactic to deal with that problem. The decoy and sweep was Galland's idea. This was when the *Schwarm* would split into two *Rotte*. One *Rotte* would dive, luring the Spitfires, unless they climbed. If they chased the Germans down, we would chase them. If they climbed, the top *Rotte* would follow them, keeping them busy until the second *Rotte* regained altitude. It worked every time.

We did not need to use this tactic against Hurricanes. They could never catch us unless we were in a turning fight. They were very maneuverable, and could out-turn us easily. The later Hurricane carried up to four cannons in each wing, and it was a dangerous animal, but slow, and not as maneuverable as the earlier Hurricane I, but still more maneuverable than our 109Es. Later, the 109F model canceled that advantage out. The Hurricanes usually went for our bombers, and the Spitfires would come get us.

Well, Galland had a meeting with all of the squadron leaders in JG-26, and since I was with JG-52 at the time, I decided to go over with a few of the others from JG-52, and I again met my friend Dieter Hrabak. Galland had a plan, and this was a good one. There were about thirty or more of us from different units, and I again saw and actually sat next to my old friend Herbert Ihlefeld. Galland began his briefing on the new tactic that he had started using, and he was doing well with it.

He admitted that it was not his idea. His friend from the Spanish Civil War, Wilhelm Balthasar, had actually thought it up, and Galland thought it was worth trying. It worked perfectly, especially for us on limited fuel over England. He introduced Balthasar, his best friend at the time and a fellow squadron mate from the Condor Legion in Spain, who was leading the *Staffel* from 1./JG-1 at that time. Balthasar stood and began speaking. He had a chalkboard, and he pulled a cloth away from it. The diagrams were already drawn, and I could see right away what they were going to say.

The plan was this: In flying in the *Schwarm*, if only using four fighters on the mission, two fighters should engage the Spitfires, which had also started using the *Schwarm*, which they called the "finger four" formation. The two 109s would attack and then dive away, hoping to draw the Spitfires into the pursuing dive. If they did, then the top cover *Rotte* [two fighters] would then drop and close on them in a dive.

The first two German fighters would then pull up. If the Spits had stalled, the trailing German could hit them. If they did not stall, then when they followed the first two 109s and likewise pulled up, they would be shot down from behind. The first two 109s would climb and bank around, using the speed in the dive as increased climbing speed and then cover the tails of the second *Rotte*. This allowed them to get a kill when they turned onto the enemy fighter. Even if they kept diving, the 109s could catch them. Either way, they were an easy kill from behind or from above.

This plan was so simple, and the JG-26 guys had scored several victories using this method. Galland had over twenty kills like this, and Balthasar also. The tactical meeting lasted for about an hour, and then we had lunch. Then, after about ten minutes, the door opened and [Ernst] Udet walked in followed by Theo Osterkamp. We called him "Uncle Theo," and he was a very respected fighter pilot from the First World War, and he not only had the *Pour le Mérite* from that war for thirty-two victories, he also had the Knight's Cross for scoring five victories in the new war, and he was almost fifty years old.

Hitler personally ordered him to stop flying, and he was promoted to *Generalleutnant*. He was a great guy, and one of the few the Fat One would listen to without interrupting. The same was true with other old knights from the Great War, such as Robert *Ritter* von Greim and Eduard *Ritter* von Schleich. For some reason, Göring did not show Ernst Udet the same respect. I think it was because Udet was the highest scoring ace from that war to survive, with sixty-four victories. Göring's ego could not take that, as Udet became a very famous name after the Great War all over the world. Göring was remembered as an incompetent leader after von Richthofen was killed, when he took over command.

Udet and Osterkamp, both men wearing their Blue Max medals and Osterkamp also with his Knight's Cross, sat down and just spoke with us as if they were also junior officers—just bullshitting, you know? They were not the typical rank-conscious officers that expected you to snap to attention and click your heels. They were pilot's generals, like Galland later, just real men who had been there and understood what the fighting was about. This was especially true of Osterkamp, and we all knew that the recommendation for his Knight's Cross had been made some time ago. He would get that a couple of months later after he scored five victories in this new war. His leadership was outstanding.

We learned a lot about our enemy. Later models of the Spit, like the Mark V and IX, also used fuel injection, like us. The Spit XIV and later models were a real problem for us after 1943. We had some incredible fights over the Channel, and over England it was even worse. If we went down, we were prisoners—no escape—and many men drowned or froze to death in the Channel. The RAF had radar, so they could save time and fuel by vectoring right into us, and if we were on a bomber escort, that was even worse. But, what made the situation crazy for me, and for all of us, was this stupid policy of having to stay with the bombers and not engage the fighters. Galland said "to hell with this" and created his own method, which I rapidly adopted.

After the bombers had been hit badly a few times, especially the Stukas, which were always destroyed in large numbers, Göring ordered the fighters to fly close escort. He did not want us engaging the enemy Hurricanes and Spitfires; just shoo them away. Well, it really did not work like that. Galland would send a few fighters ahead early, flying at high altitude, leaving perhaps twenty minutes [as scouts to engage any enemy fighters] before the rest of the fighters [second echelon] took off to rendezvous with the bombers. Galland's plan was perfect.

The four to eight fighters sent ahead would draw the RAF up. Once that happened, his men [the first group sent ahead] would engage, allowing the bombers a better chance of getting through. The fighters escorting the bombers would take over from the early fighters, who would be low on fuel, and then take over the combat. By this time, the British would have to start thinking about returning to base. That was when we in the second wave had the advantage with a reserve of fuel. That was how many of us scored kills.

Then we were ordered to escort the Messerschmitt 110 Destroyers. Now this was Göring's pet aircraft. He claimed all the great benefits that the 110 would have in the air war a few years earlier. These lumbering machines were worthless, unless in ground attack or as night fighters. Even with the rear gunner protecting the rear of the bomber, the 110s fell in large numbers. They could not maneuver, but they did have powerful forward-firing guns.

After the Battle of Britain, things pretty much became quiet again for us. I really did not do much operation flying for the rest of 1940. The next great campaign was the Balkans in the spring of 1941. We learned a lot from the air battles against Britain. First, there was the range limitation of our fighters. After arriving on station, we had about twenty minutes of combat time before we had to return home, and the British knew it. Second, we were sent on many bomber escort missions, which eliminated our advantage of speed and altitude, both of which are essential to a fighter pilot's success, and we therefore lost the element of surprise.

Another factor was the British use of radar, which was a shock to us pilots, although our leadership knew about it. This early warning system allowed the British to concentrate their smaller force with greater flight time over the operational area, engaging us at our most vulnerable moments. Another problem that truly hindered our success was Göring, who would not allow the war to be prosecuted according to logic. One example was when he altered the *Luftwaffe*'s targets from military and RAF targets, such as airfields, to cities and docks, which proved disastrous in many ways.

We knew that we would have to change our method of flying in the future. We learned a lot from fighting the British, and we became even better fighter pilots. After this period on the Channel and before we invaded Russia, Wolf Falck had been trying to get me to join his night fighters. He had offered me a staff job, but the only way I would consider this was if I could still fly when I wanted, and I was not talking about flying a desk. The new job meant a promotion, and that was always attractive to me.

I was in Fürstenwald when Falck arrived, and we caught up on the events since our Berlin gathering. He informed me of the night fighter program that he was starting, and that [*Generaloberst* Ernst] Udet had recommended his plan to Göring, who then had approval from Hitler. At that time, Wolf Falck was probably the most powerful *Hauptmann* in the *Luftwaffe*. First, he was the very first *Kommodore* of our generation along with Galland; the others were old eagles from the First World War.

Second, he was a *Kommodore* and still only a *Hauptmann*, and this was unheard of, when at that time the title of *Kommodore* required the rank of at least a *Major*, or *Oberstleutnant*, if not an *Oberst*. That requirement of rank would drop as the war continued, of course, with men ranked *Major* and *Oberstleutnant* appointed to *Kommodore* quite often. In some cases, even a *Hauptmann* would be given a full command, like Falck, in the case of a special unit. We in the *Luftwaffe* learned that rank meant little compared to experience. Many very young found themselves promoted and appointed to important commands because of their abilities. Men such as Walter Nowotny and Erich Hartmann became *Majors* at age twenty-two or twenty-three. That was the way it had to be.

Not long after this meeting and after Falck left, I received a phone call. Göring had given Falck written authorization to fire, hire, and staff his new unit any way he wanted. I found out one day that he was my new commanding officer, and I had orders to fly down and report to him. This was at the end of June 1940. I jumped into my 109 and took off; the flight should have lasted no more than an hour.

Well, I saw this small group of bombers, Bristol Blenheims, and I thought, "Why not?" and I attacked one. I hit him solid in the right engine, and he started going down, burning brightly. There were no parachutes that I saw, and this was almost near the airfield where I had to land anyway, and I was low on fuel. As I reduced my speed, lowered my flaps, and lowered the landing gear, I watched the smoke trail as the bomber impacted into a nearby village. I felt bad, thinking that my victory had probably killed some Germans on the ground.

I shut off the motor and climbed out, collected my bag and flight log, and walked across the airstrip to Wolf's headquarters office. He looked angry, since I was almost an hour late, and I apologized for arriving late and reporting in flight gear. I should have been in my dress tunic. He asked me why I was late, and I told him that I had encountered some British bombers and shot one down. He smiled and said all was forgiven and that he wanted to go to the crash site.

We drove over to the crash in his car, and when we arrived, the wreckage was still burning and smoke was everywhere. The cockpit crew were still strapped in, and another man was crushed in the wreckage. There was another dead airman who had been thrown clear from the impact. I then saw something that made me lose my mind. Some of the villagers were poking at the dead man with sticks, and a couple started kicking the body. I ran toward them, my hand on my pistol. I had opened the holster, yelling at them. Wolf grabbed my hand, and I realized what I was doing. I still screamed at them and told them they were no better than animals. I told them these were men who died for their country. They were airmen and they deserved the same respect as our own men. I told them that I would shoot the next person who went toward them.

Then a policeman walked up, an older man who was a veteran from the last war, infantry type. He agreed with me, and he said he would arrest anyone who harmed the bodies. The crowd then fell silent, and it seemed as if they felt ashamed at themselves. None of them would look me in the eye. Falck said, "Let's see to it they have a proper burial, and get their identification. Their families should know what happened. I will take care of it."

I apologized to him for my outburst. I am sometimes an emotional creature but not often, and that sort of thing I could never tolerate. I would later learn that my sense of morality and honor was not unique in the *Luftwaffe*, but it would cause me great harm years later. Against the British and later even the Americans, it was not difficult to keep that mindset. They were like us—educated, Western, and professional men. We could relate to them. Later, in Russia, we would be in an entirely different war and attitude altogether.

The only problem that we really had was strafing later in the war. Those of us who were later jet pilots in the Me-262 were not safe once we bailed out. The problem was that they [American fighter pilots] had a tendency to shoot jet pilots in the parachute or even strafe us on the ground. Later I learned that this was not a direct order, but it was quietly ignored when it happened. They believed in error that we were high-value targets. I know for a fact that Rudi Sinner was strafed badly flying in JG-7. I also spoke with Georg-Peter Eder, who was strafed twice, once in the parachute and again when he was on the ground. Luckily, they [Americans] missed both times.

From that point forward, I flew from the airfield near Bonn as a night fighter pilot in the 109E, and this was just insane. We never shot down anything. Then Falck got permission to use his 110s for night fighting, and then we began having success. In September 1940, I would meet Göring again. He had called a meeting to discuss the failure of the night fighters to score victories. He was smoking this large cigar and listening to the people around the table. Falck had finished speaking, as he gave the requirements for his night fighting unit.

Then Falck looked at me, so I raised my hand. Göring nodded his head, and I then stood and told him what the problems were. We needed better aircraft, longer range, better directional equipment, and a way to find the enemy, other than just by following the searchlights. I also said that given the altitude at which enemy bombers fly, it took us a long time to reach them, and by that time we were already low on fuel. The men around the table nodded. However, Göring just told me to sit down and shut up. He said that once I grew up I would be able to speak like the adults at the table. I was humiliated, but I knew then and afterward that the old generals and colonels at that meeting were on my side. Well, I had had enough of this nonsense. This was when I was sent to the Channel Coast to JG-52. I would stay with that wonderful unit for another three years.

I did meet many of the more colorful characters in the *Luftwaffe*. Some stand out more than others for obvious reasons. You ask about [Hans-Joachim] Marseille; this guy was a real clown. Marseille was transferred into my wing from LG-2, where Herbert Ihlefeld was his squadron leader. He joined my 4./JG-52 just before the Battle of Britain ended. I was his squadron leader, and I watched him. I knew he was a brilliant guy who was very intelligent, very quick and aggressive, but he spent too much time looking for the girls, and his mind was not always on operations. He actually had to be taken off flight status on more than one occasion because he was so exhausted from his nights on the town.

I was commanding 4./JG-52, and we were waiting on replacement pilots, which usually came from Schwechat, with a couple of hundred hours behind them. When I was told that I was getting this guy with seven victories and a lot of flight time, I was excited. I normally never received experienced pilots. But, as I always said, if you looked a gift horse in the mouth, it was very often missing teeth, and so I learned with Marseille. I had requested his service record book, and I was very surprised to see that with his time in the service, and his experience, that he had not yet been promoted.

Then I received his disciplinary record, and I could not believe it. I thought we probably had a real, unassuming hero. But no, these were not commendations and awards; these were reprimands, punishments, proficiency reports. You name it and it was all in there: confinement, disobeying orders, public drunkenness, disrespect, violations of flight regulations, low buzzing airfields and control towers, auto theft, being out of uniform, late to report for duty, drunk on duty, breaking formation without orders or authorization . . . I could go on.

His list of crimes was long. There was even a letter signed by Eduard [*Ritter*] von Schleich, the school commandant whom we all knew, attesting to his "great flying and shooting skill," but he was completely apathetic regarding command authority or having any understanding of military discipline or personal conduct. Von Schleich was also a holder of the *Pour le Mérite* for his thirty-two victories as a fighter pilot in the Great War, where he was known and respected on both sides as the "Black Knight."

I also saw that he only needed to lose one more German fighter to be an Allied ace. I called him in, and this was the first time I met him. He looked like he was fifteen years old, and I looked again at his birth date. I saw this child standing in front of me, and I asked him, "What the hell is this? It is almost as thick as a telephone directory! Let's take a look!" As I held up the thick file, I leafed through the many pages and mentioned the dozens of problems. I asked him, "What do you have to say to this?" and so on. In typical Marseille fashion, he replied: "I never wrecked an airplane, *Herr Oberleutnant*!" I think he meant that he never wrecked one without being shot down. I did read where he ran out of fuel and landed on the beach. He did that with me once also.

I called my old friend [Ihlefeld] and asked him about Marseille. He told me: "Sorry, Macky, but I had to send him somewhere; I did not mean to do that to you. Good luck, you will need it." When I asked him what the hell he had done to me, he hung up. Herbert showed up at my base later that week, landed on the airfield, and we had a good chat, or perhaps not so good. That was when I discovered how badly I had been screwed over. At least he brought some good French brandy with him.

I had summoned Marseille, and he just walked in as casually as entering a *pilstube* [a bar]. He did not report properly and was not even in complete uniform. He did not even salute me! However, once I snapped at him, he was locked up at rigid attention. Well, at least his version of attention anyway. He almost poked his own eye out with the salute he gave. His hat fell off his head, and I suspected he was drunk.

I made him stand there, not because his folder was thick with enough violations for an entire *Geschwader*, but because he was a day late reporting for duty. You know why he was late? He was with a girl in a hotel, after being home for a few days just before Christmas, and he lost track of time. He admitted this. Marseille was many things—a drunkard, playboy, rebel, occasional idiot, car thief—but he was never a liar. He always admitted to his mistakes. I could never tell him this, but even when I was at my angriest with him, I had to wait until he left before I often laughed silently to myself. It was just very hard to hate the guy.

But the moment I met him, I knew he was trouble. He had many gifts, and I saw this. His greatest gift was luck. Herbert had sent him to me because he was overstaffed on pilots and that he did not have enough fighters. I told him that was because the man he had sent me had crashed all of them. Then he said, "Macky, you are a great father figure, you know how to work these men, you are a very good leader. I know my shortcomings, and I hope that you can help this guy. He does have promise."

Well, I had that telephone in my ear and looked at the thick folder on Marseille, and just said, "All right, I will do what I can." I had a feeling that I was making a huge mistake. I soon enough came to regret my decision. Most of us by this time who were squadron leaders or higher had had a couple of years of flying combat. We knew our business, but the best of us knew that we did not know everything. Every mission, every encounter with the enemy, provided another valuable lesson, all of which a good pilot learned—and quickly. Failure to do this would mean death, and there were many ways for a pilot to die: outnumbered, engine failure, bad weather, and bad luck. But dying due to being an idiot was unacceptable.

Marseille had a natural flying talent. I guess you could call it a gift. He would pull stunts over the airfield, doing amazing things. His problem was that he knew he was good, and his ego always got the better of him. Once, I flew with him as the *Staffelkapitän*, and I think this was the first mission I flew with him, and we encountered Hurricanes over the English coast, and of course we flew the *Schwarm* formation, or "finger four" as it was called by the British. Each pilot had a wingman, and that wingman had only one job: keep his *Rottenflieger* alive, clearing his tail if necessary.

Once the enemy had been called out, Marseille disappeared. He left his flight leader all alone. No one knew where he was. Suddenly over the radio, we heard, "Got him," and it was Marseille. [Marseille claimed a "damaged" but did not confirm this or any victory while with JG-52.] Then we heard, "Oh shit, he got me," and it was again Marseille. He had flown into a simple trap, lured in by a lone fighter and jumped by three others. Only his awareness and reflexes prevented him from being killed, or having to bail out over England or in the Channel.

We shot down three fighters on that sortie and escorted Marseille back, as his fighter was leaking glycol and smoking slightly. He finally called out his fuel warning. He had to slide the fighter down on the beach at Calais, which was not his first crash-landing. He was fine, and the fighter was later cannibalized for spare parts, but he was on my shit list. He broke the most cardinal rule of combat. He left the formation without orders and, even worse, without telling anyone. I grounded him for a week to teach him a lesson.

For that week, he worked with the ground crews, pulled sentry duty, those kinds of things. It never occurred to me to restrict him to quarters, and that was my fault. He stole my car, went into town, and came back drunk, with two girls in varying degrees of undress. They were also drunk, and one was driving my car! I was beyond angry. Well, I had him call a taxi for the girls and made him pay for it. I then restricted him to the base for a month, restricted to his quarters, and after a week of this he was finally allowed to fly again. The only way out of his quarters for the rest of that month was to fly a mission. Once we returned from the mission, he was back under guard. Even his meals were brought to him, and I fined him a month's pay as well.

But, I did not nail the back window shut. Now, this was a very small window, like a porthole, but he managed to climb out. As the guard was posted at the front door, and there was not a back door, I did not know anything was amiss. In fact, early one morning I shaved and walked outside, and I thought I saw that my car had been moved. I asked the officer of the watch if anyone had driven my car. He said: "Yes, sir. Marseille left late last night. He just came back about an hour ago." I was livid and could not understand how he managed it.

I asked the *Feldwebel* on guard duty out front if Marseille had left, as he was not allowed to go anywhere. He told me that he never left the building. I walked in and Marseille was sound asleep. I could smell the beer on him. I kicked his bed and he tumbled out of it. I told him to get up, and just as I did, the order to form up was given. He jumped up, did not go to attention, and did not salute. He just fell over drunk and landed half on the bed, and then on the floor. I just looked at him and told him to pack his bags. I said that

I would tell him what I had decided to do with him after we flew our reconnaissance mission.

I had him for over a month when I finally decided that I had to get rid of him in late January, early February. This guy had no concept of military bearing. Either he respected you as a man or not; your rank really meant nothing. He was a womanizer. The day he reported for duty, his only question was which town had the prettiest girls. Many of the men quietly requested that he not be assigned to their *Schwarm*. They did not trust him in the air. That is very bad for unit morale.

Once after a reconnaissance mission, a Gestapo *Sturmbannführer* [*Major*]—an old Party type, Blood Order, Great War Iron Cross First Class, the works—paid me a visit. This guy was looking for a pilot, name unknown, but he described Marseille perfectly. I thought quickly and asked him what had this pilot done? He told me it was a personal matter, and he was visiting all the local air bases trying to find this guy. He simply said he would keep looking, and I offered him a drink. We spoke, and he said that the man he was looking for had taken advantage of his daughter, who was visiting him from university. Everything clicked in my head. She must have been one of the two undressed girls I saw in the car.

When Marseille returned, again with a partially dressed woman, I had to reprimand him. Then I had to cover for him, since she was apparently the daughter of the same local Gestapo officer. I felt as if I were more of a truant officer or a probation officer as opposed to his commanding officer. It was at about this time I had to get him the hell out of the unit without making clear the real reason. He could have gone to prison.

Once, Marseille was late for a pre-flight briefing. As I was finishing the meeting, I heard a car pull up outside. I opened the door and saw him climb out of a car and kiss the girl driving it. Then another girl climbed from the back-seat and sat in the front. He was still getting dressed into his uniform as he walked in the doorway. I asked him if he had a good explanation for being late before I grounded him. You would not believe his answer: "Yes, sir, I was too drunk to get out of bed, and when I did, I realized I was too late for the briefing. Sorry, sir, I will try to not let that happen again." Well, it did happen again, so I dismissed him and sent him packing to Edward "Edu" Neumann in Libya.

It was quite ironic. He left France in disgrace and then became a living legend. If there had been girls in Africa, I do not think he would have had such success. Although he was a chronic problem, I actually liked the guy very much, but I think that in sending him away I actually saved him. I cut his orders the next day, and within a week he was gone.

He was the perfect playboy, but a real fighter. Yet he was an individual, not a team player. He had seven victories when I fired him, not because he was not good, but because he was shot down four times while getting those victories. That was with Ihlefeld. He had three claims that I remember, and he probably did score the victories, but there were no witnesses because he broke off and went crazy, without any wingman support. When they crashed into the Channel, you could not just fly over and confirm the wreckage an hour later. Unless there was a witness, a crash site, or the pilot was recovered, it was not confirmed as a victory.

He had no concept of *Rottenflieger* [i.e., a wingman's responsibility], and many men did not want to fly with him as their wingman; several asked to be transferred from our *Staffel* if Marseille was to continue flying. They did not feel safe with him. It can destroy a unit, so I thought the best thing for him and the unit was to transfer him away from the women, and he became a legend in North Africa, of course, winning the Diamonds to the Knight's Cross and scoring 158 victories.

He was a true character and the epitome of the First World War fighter pilot, but we were not fighting the First World War. He was the ultimate individual. I can still hear that damned record player and his music, which was all right and we liked it, but then again his musical tastes were not exactly what the national leaders would have considered as appropriate. He was one of those young people we called swing kids, the jazz lovers. I liked some of the music also, and I did not go out of my way to irritate the higher powers, but this clown did not care. He also had a wireless radio set, and he used to tune in to the BBC and other forbidden channels. I did not lecture him about it, as we all did it. I just told him not to get caught, and if he was caught, that I knew nothing about it.

One day while he was still with me, we had a visit from some high ranks from Berlin. They were doing an inspection tour of the coastal fighter units. *Generaloberst* Hans Jeschonnek, who was the chief of staff for the *Luftwaffe*, was the senior officer. All the men were lined up for inspection. Jeschonnek went down the line, looked the men over, and then he stopped at Marseille. What happened next was strange. Jeschonnek looked at him and asked him what he was doing here. He thought that Marseille was over with Ihlefeld. Marseille, always thinking quickly, said: "I was, sir, but they said the hunting was better over here." Jeschonnek did not even smile and he said, "Yes, perhaps, but then again most of these girls are off limits to you." Every man in the unit started laughing, and I did also. Even Jeschonnek laughed, and he hit Marseille on the head, knocking his cap off, then continued walking down the line.

Another time I was walking through the barracks just doing my usual inspections. Some of the men had posters of film stars and other women on their walls. I had no problem with that. However, when I walked into Marseille's quarters, I stepped on an empty bottle. My foot rolled out from under me and I fell on my backside. The bottle rolled away under his bunk. I then reached under the bunk to get it as evidence and saw over a dozen empty bottles—different kinds of alcohol; some of them were quite expensive. This was even worse than I thought. Marseille had a drinking problem, and I would have to find some way to address it.

I called him in and sat him down. I thought perhaps I could reach him better with a more fatherly approach, as opposed to the superior-officer method. I was right, but I also knew that I could not run a unit acting as a father to every problem child. I had to get rid of him, but I did not want his career ruined. I wanted to get him help. I had already learned about his father, mother, and the family situation [divorce issues]. That seemed to really be the center of his problems. He had an inferiority complex, and he always felt persecuted. I told him that he brought most of that upon himself, and he agreed. I told him that I was getting him out of here for his own good. I mentioned the Gestapo officer, and he was almost packed before he left my office.

I really wish that he had survived the war. I think that it would have been good, in later years, to have sat down and spoken with him, had a drink. He would have been older, more mature, and with Neumann and the others sitting around having a drink, we could have laughed at his stupidity with the clarity of hindsight. Well, in 1941, he was gone, and the war had started in Africa. Then we soon had our own new war in the east.

The Russian Front was a totally different kind of war. Most of the battles were below three thousand meters, since the Russians flew their aircraft almost always as ground support, or as flying artillery. They were very effective at ground attack missions. Early from June 1941 through the next year, we did not have much competition in the air. We in JG-52 simply destroyed everything that they sent at us.

When we shot down a British, French, or other Allied pilot, there was no animosity, nothing but real admiration for the RAF. They were well trained, educated, good fighters, and natural hunters. We knew that when we flew against them, there was still a code of chivalry. We did not shoot men in parachutes, and they did not either. Both sides went out of their way to save each other's downed airmen in the English Channel or North Sea. Often we would radio on their frequency if a downed enemy was close to their shore, so that he would not drown or freeze. When captured, they were treated as honored guests.

However, in the Soviet Union, it was a totally different war. There was no sense of mutual respect. We had a similar culture and society to the British, and other Western Europeans, but we were not like these people. The Soviets had no concept of chivalry as a whole. Often pilots and aircrews were murdered when they were shot down. This happened a lot, and the few men who were captured and kept alive spent many years in Soviet camps. I made up my mind that I would not endure such a thing if I were shot down in enemy territory. I kept my pistol loaded at all times, and I knew that they would have to kill me before I allowed them to take me as a prisoner.

There is often a misunderstanding as to why most of us rode down our damaged fighters rather than bail out. It was not so much that we did not trust the parachutes. If a fighter was on fire, I would certainly go over the side. The reason was because it was easier to glide closer to our lines, and be covered by our fellow pilots, than if we were in a parachute. The other reason was that Soviet pilots, in almost every battle if possible, would shoot us in the parachutes. Remember that they did not sign the Geneva Convention. They did not care about chivalry or human life.

The combat that lasted throughout 1941 until January 1942 was almost over by the end of the year. In August, I received the Knight's Cross in the field. We flew on until October, but there were just a few engagements. We were in the southeast of Russia, flying a lot of aerial reconnaissance missions. But it was during one of these missions that I actually had my first real dogfight since flying against the RAF.

I was in a flight with Günther Rall, Alfred Grislawski, Walter Krupinski, Hermann Graf, and a few others in October 1941. We were involved in a big fight, and Krupinski was shot down and wounded pretty badly. I saw him go down. Then I was hit, and Grislawski claimed a kill, an I-16, as did I, and then he radioed that he was also hit, heading back with Punski, which was a name we often called Krupinski. Rall scored two kills and Graf had two or three—I do not remember. We were not all assigned to the same *Gruppe*, but we were thrown together a few times for missions if machines were not working, or some other reason. We lost two fighters, no one was killed, and we had around seven victories. I was cut by a piece of metal that struck my face, but it was not a bad wound.

We were headed back after we followed Krupinski and Grislawski, and saw that they had crash-landed safely, when we were attacked again. This time we were hit by Yaks—about five of them—and they came in fast from above us at three o'clock. I called them out, and we all banked left and climbed to meet them. Rall and Graf then continued their climb. I could see them. We engaged, fired, and I saw no hits. I did feel a few hits in my 109. We had the F model then. I pushed the left rudder and threw the stick left to roll over and chase these guys. They were fast, and three of these guys rolled and then pulled up.

That was when the Russians made their mistake. They tried to climb away and ran right into Rall and Graf, waiting upstairs. Just like against the British a year before, the enemy flew into the top trap. All five went down in just a few minutes, and I had another claim. Rall called out that his engine was losing compression, and we saw glycol coming out of his cooling system. In five minutes or less, he would seize up and become a very heavy glider. My fighter had a few holes but no other problems, and Graf was fine. Grislawski radioed that he had landed, and was okay. Punski also called, and he was safe, but wounded.

The winter hit us quickly and very hard also. Oh, it was very difficult. In many cases, we had no operations. We often had heavy snow and low cloud cover limiting visibility. The cold would freeze all machinery and moving parts. Sometimes we could not fly because the snow was piled so high that we had no way to remove it. It was very poor weather, and navigation without instruments was absolutely impossible. So much of the country was flat ground. There were no great landmarks to refer to, unless we were near rivers. There was just so much area to cover. This and the cold were the greatest handicaps. That was absolutely the worst time. The winter from 1941 to 1942 was the coldest I had ever experienced. We were grounded much of the time, and the enemy would still attack our airfields.

Early in the war, the Soviets were not well disciplined. Later, that changed. They became very disciplined, if not principled and somewhat intelligent, but still not well trained in tactics. They were very brave for the most part, but unlike the British and Americans, they would break off combat after only a few minutes and a couple of rotations. The Soviet pilot was for the most part not a born fighter in the air. But, there were a few of them who were different.

In fighting the Soviets, we fought an apparatus, not a human being. There was no flexibility in their tactical orientation, no individual freedom of action, and in that way they were a little stupid. If we shot down the leader in a Soviet fighter group, the rest were simply sitting ducks, waiting to be taken out. This was in the early days, and for the most part this was true until 1944. The only exceptions were the Red Banner, or Guards units, as they called them. They flew the best planes, had the best pilots, and they began using our tactics. This was about late 1943 when we began running into these guys on a regular basis, especially in the Caucasus and Ukraine.

Our success was easy to explain. We fought as a team from the beginning. We had excellent training schools and great combat leaders from the Spanish Civil War, as well as the early campaigns in Poland and the West, who led by example. We learned our trade during the Battle of Britain, and that knowledge saved many German lives. We were very successful from the beginning of the invasion from June 22, 1941. We did not have a lot of competition until the next year, as our greatest enemy was the weather.

During that first winter after November, when the snow really came down and the temperature fell even lower, we did not have many spectacular missions. Once the summer and autumn were over, the fighting in the air slowed down. We just did not have as much activity as we thought we would when November ended, although we did have occasional battles.

Since we were stationed more to the south, we were not that involved in the great air battles around Moscow. We had some fierce battles in November while in the Caucasus, and we were all in the air the day Rall was shot down, and we never thought that he would come back to us. He had broken his back. We were with Army Group South in the Ukraine, and the army was still driving into the Caucasus. Hitler had wanted the Baku oil fields, and we got them. This mission was to help Germany with our oil supply problem, as we were almost completely relying upon the Romanian oil.

It was so damned cold, and I really mean cold, even for a German. Minus-fifty and -sixty centigrade temperatures were normal at night, and from November until February it never reached above zero as far as I was aware. Our engines would freeze; nothing mechanical would work. We had a guy that was a prisoner, and he was very happy to be out of the Red Air Force, as he was a Ukrainian. There is a long history between Russians and Ukrainians that explains this hatred they had for each other. Well, this guy showed us how to keep our engines running and stopping the oil from freezing solid, so we were able to keep the fighters running. Once we learned this technique, Hubertus von Bonin sent out a memorandum explaining this process, and that really saved a lot of our fighters and other motor vehicles.

When not flying, we pilots all sat around, talking about our families, home, the war, comparing notes on the last few missions. [This is what we were doing] when we were informed that the Japanese had attacked America at the naval base in Hawaii. I then knew that it was over for us, and when we heard Hitler declare war against the United States a couple of days later, we all looked at each other. "Is he crazy?" You have to understand. Our treaty with the Italians and Japanese did not require us to declare war. That was Hitler acting on his own.

When this happened, we were in the middle of the first Russian winter, and we were too busy to think about it. I was just south of Moscow when I heard the news. However, it later penetrated my mind that this was a decisive step. The Americans had tremendous willpower and an unmatched industrial capacity for building big bombers, fighters, ships, and so on. It was only time that determined how long we would survive.

In all the combats I was in up to that time, even when we were outnumbered, I never really felt in danger. I did not like the idea of flying over enemy territory, especially in winter, but that was just part of the job. The enemy pilots were amateurish and not well trained at first. They almost never used anything that resembled a coherent tactical formation. They would fly in loose groups and then attack individually, almost as if they did not have an assigned wingman.

I was once flying a mission with Johannes Wiese, Krupinski, and others in the Caucasus when the ten of us encountered about twenty enemy fighters—Yaks, Ratas, and others. This was the first time I saw the Russians try to ram our fighters. They really wanted to do this. We shot down several of them and had no losses, but that was eye-opening. Later, I would see this a few times. Incredible. I was never sure if it was bravery or desperation.

The Soviet pilots did get better over time. In fact, the famous Red Banner units had some of the best pilots in the world. I fought against them in the Crimea and Caucasus later. But the hardest thing about the Russian Front was the weather—that damned cold. The second thing, and probably the most important, was the knowledge that if you were shot down or wounded and became a prisoner of war—that is, if they did not kill you first—you would have it very bad. You were safe only on your side of the lines.

I first met Hitler around September 2 or 3, 1942, when he awarded me the Oak Leaves. I had only recently been the full-time *Gruppenkommandeur* of II./JG-52 since March after my promotion to *Hauptmann*, leading the second *Gruppe*, and I had been told by a few of the others who had already paid Hitler a visit that he was a rather odd fellow, to just be patient with him if he started one of his philosophical lectures. I flew my fighter to an airfield and then took a transport. I opened up the newspaper that was sitting inside and saw that Marseille had been awarded the Oak Leaves and Swords earlier. I thought, "That bastard, he finally did something right." Then we heard the news that he had shot down seventeen British fighters over Egypt in three missions. To me, that was incredible. I wrote him a letter while on the plane and posted it when I landed, before I met Hitler and the Fat One. I do not know if he ever received it.

I was standing there with the other guys, including Nowotny and Rall, when we received our medals, and then we had a short chat before the lunch was served. Hitler seemed to be in good spirits, smiling and even happy. I can tell you that would change as the war went on. He was never an impressive figure, and became less so each time I saw him.

He asked us about the war, which we were supposed to be winning, and what we thought about the new territory being incorporated into the Reich in the east. I mentioned something to the effect that "I hope the *Führer* will not become too attached to it, because I don't think we will be taking up long-term residence." He looked at me as if he was going to suffer a stroke. When he asked me to clarify my statement, I simply told him that since the United States had entered the war and they, along with Britain, were supplying Russia, and we had no method of attacking their industry beyond the Urals, I did not think we would keep making great gains.

He sat silent for a moment, then said something like, "We will finish Russia soon, and turn our attentions to the west once again. They will see that supporting Bolshevism is not to their benefit." Well, I looked at Rall and he just shrugged his shoulders, and he answered some questions Hitler asked him in his turn. After the lunch, we were dismissed. I met with Hitler again outside Stalingrad a few weeks later when he toured the front, meeting the various units, and JG-52 and JG-51 were not that far apart.

Galland came in later and spoke with Göring and then with *Generalfeldmarschall* Erhard Milch, who asked us if there was anything he could do for us at the front. Rall and I looked at each other, and I decided to take the lead. I mentioned the ammunition and fuel shortages, which was nothing new to Milch, I was certain. But there was another problem we all shared. Two of our pilots had been visited by the Gestapo, and interrogated. They were accused of being Jewish. Now, at this time I had just learned that Milch was also half-Jewish and had received protection from Hitler and Göring, who also awarded him the Knight's Cross.

The two pilots were Heinz ["Johnny," aka "Rudolf"] Schmidt, whose grandparents had been apparently deported some time ago. I think his mother was still around Bad Homburg, but I do not remember all of the details. I told Milch, "You of all people should know how difficult it is to fly missions against Russia, all day fearing the Gestapo might be waiting to interrogate you when you land." I told him that Schmidt had the Knight's Cross and would later receive the Oak Leaves. I had flown with him during the Battle of Britain, as he was a longtime member of JG-52, and he was leading 6. *Staffel* at this time. He was a good pilot, and he did not deserve these actions. I knew there was some kind of mistake. He asked me about the details, and I told him.

We had just landed after a mission back at our airfield. It was a very hard fight against greater numbers of Yaks, and we had lost two of our men. This was the beginning of the Stalingrad campaign, actually just before we were relocated again. Schmidt would be recovered after his crash-landing and would come back in a few days, but the other, whose name I cannot remember, died when his fighter blew up. I had over a dozen holes in my fighter. We had shot down around eleven aircraft, I think. We saw that there was a black staff car there, and we were told immediately that the Gestapo wanted to speak to us.

Well, I can tell you that Krupinski, Rall, Graf, Ihlefeld, Hrabak, von Bonin, Barkhorn, Grislawski, and all of the others were pretty angry about this. The more we spoke about it, the angrier we became. I should mention that Ihlefeld was the acting *Kommodore* at this time, as Hrabak later came back [from leading JG-54 on temporary duty] to take over command from him.

By the time we actually met these Gestapo clowns, we had been drinking, celebrating some of the pilots receiving medals from von Bonin. The pilots had been talking to other guys in several *Gruppen*. Several of us were called in and questioned about two men, Rudolf Schmidt and the man who had just died on the mission.

I do not know why we did it, or remember whose idea it was, but we all took turns urinating in the back of the automobile. It was a warm time, early autumn, and with the doors closed and the windows rolled up, I am certain that after a couple of days that car must have smelled terrible. Well, we all swore ourselves to secrecy. No one was to speak of it. A couple of days later, I was in my tent and I heard the greatest string of curse words in such a rapid delivery in my life. The two Gestapo men were getting into their car, and I assumed that our prank had apparently resulted in the desired effect. They looked around at all of us gathering, most knowing what had happened, a few being the culprits, but everyone laughing at them. They filed a complaint at the headquarters tent and had a chat with Ihlefeld and Hrabak.

I was told about that conversation with the Gestapo guys an hour later. In fact, I was asked, along with the others, by both Ihlefeld and Hrabak about this. I told him that it was a real shame that this had happened, and I also told him that I hoped that they could catch the culprits who treated our Gestapo friends so badly. It was unfriendly. Hrabak then smiled and said, "Do not bullshit me, and I do not care about a bunch of juveniles pissing in their car. But, I am curious as to who took a shit in it and placed that dead dog in the back?" At that point, I must admit that I was stunned, because I was unaware of anything beyond the group urination. We had a pet dog in the camp that just died a few days earlier, and no one had buried it yet. That was apparently the dog he was talking about.

He saw the shock on my face, and he knew that I was unaware of it. Then Ihlefeld said, "Macky, to be honest, I do not even care about that; I am just glad they are gone," and we laughed out loud and he offered me a brandy! This was the kind of unit we were, very close like brothers, and we stayed that way all of our lives. I do not know whatever became of that visit from the Gestapo, since later Schmidt went missing after he never returned from a mission. We do not know what happened to his family. I would like to know more, to be honest.

I know that they spoke to Rall about not only this but also about his wife, Hertha. She was his doctor after he broke his back in the Caucasus the year before. He told me after the war, and I was shocked at what he and Hertha both told me about Hertha getting Jews out of Germany. She was under suspicion, and by association so was Rall, but they never had enough proof to do anything about it. Ask him about that; he will tell you. Rall had it rough, to be sure.

Göring and Himmler investigated these pilots because they believed that they were both Jewish to some degree. Göring and Himmler were annoying and very arrogant, and I told the one Gestapo guy that they [he and his friend] would probably be lucky to get out of Russia alive. He asked, and he was very nervous, if the air situation was really that dangerous. I told him no, that he had just made enemies of forty pilots who were yet to add a Ju-52 to their victory count, and theirs was sitting on my runway. I think he received the message. Later, when I was in Berlin, Galland and I had a meeting about this with Milch. That was the first time I knew that I hated the Fat One, but that is another story.

We did a lot of escort missions and even ground support. We had a good relationship with the army and even the *Waffen* SS troops around our bases, and this was especially true when we were at Gonschtakowka. However, this was around the time when we had the visit from the two Gestapo types asking about our pilots. I really hated those guys, as did almost all of the other pilots. Von Bonin told us to be courteous to them, and then we could shoot them later. I knew he was joking. However, this would not be my last meeting with these types of men.

Hitler was on a tour of the Eastern Front, and he was paying all the frontline air units a visit. We were at the airfield, and it was cold as hell in the morning, though it was supposed to warm up later, and we waited for his Ju-52 to land. We heard his plane coming, with an escort of Fw-190s, and they flew away after the transport started to land. We had sent two fighters up to cover the approach as well, just to make certain that there were no nasty surprises for Hitler as he arrived.

The aircraft rolled to a stop and the ground crew opened the door. Two people came out whom I did not know, and then Hitler, followed by [*Reichsführer*-SS] Heinrich Himmler, *Generalleutnant* Hans Baur, and [*Obergruppenführer*] Karl Wolff. I had never met either of them before, but everyone knew who Himmler was. I would later meet Himmler and Wolff again—Himmler a couple of times—and I would see Wolff later in Italy, and again many years later after the war, along with Hans Baur, whom I also met for the first time on this occasion.

Baur was a likeable man who flew combat in the First War. He looked at our fighters while Hitler went to relieve himself. Then Hitler walked back to us and asked us all basic questions, making small talk, really. I was speaking with him directly when he told me: "Now I have Russia, now I have the Caucasus. I am going to penetrate the River Volga; then after that the rest of Russia will be mine." I remember looking at the others around us and thinking that this guy was nuts! His great plan was news to us, and the topic of many discussions among us pilots long after he left.

I met Hitler the next time on July 28, 1944, when I received the Swords to the Knight's Cross. That was a week after the bomb plot to kill him, and he was not the same man—perhaps more withdrawn and living in a fantasy, as far as the war was concerned. You know, after the July 20 plot to kill him, we were never allowed in his presence with our side arms, which were part of our service uniform. He trusted no one. I simply turned to walk away when I was told this, and von Below came up to me and said, "Steinhoff, where are you going?" I told him that I was not leaving my pistol or anything else to meet with him. "Bring your weapon then," and I did. I was bowing to no one.

All I wanted was to get my medals and get the hell out of there. I could not stand Hitler. He rambled, and his right arm was shaking. He looked like a gray ghost, bent over. He looked pathetic to me, a broken man. He spoke to us about the great massive push against the Russians he had planned, the new tanks and bombers coming. I asked him "what about fighters" since we were on the defensive, and we were under-strength to combat the American bombers and fighters in the west.

"I am taking that situation in hand, Steinhoff. The new jet bombers will destroy their airfields and aircraft and destroy their troops." Well, I looked around at the others in the room, and [*Major*] Werner Baumbach was there, and he just nodded his head like an idiot. He was a brave man and a great hero, of course, but he was a narrow-minded man. [*Generalmajor*] Dieter Peltz was a more pragmatic man from the bomber arm, and he was also there, and he said nothing, but I did.

I told Hitler that anything less than a thousand fighters per month, and better fighters than what we had now, would be a waste of time. Even the Russians were coming out with better fighters, and well trained and experienced pilots, while we received teenagers who would not survive five sorties. The jets would be better in the hands of the fighters to eliminate the bomber threat, although I told him that it still may be too late.

"Steinhoff, you are too pessimistic," he told me. Then Galland walked in and he overheard the conversation, and he could not resist joining in. "Steinhoff is correct, *Mein Führer*. I would say that three thousand fighters per month would be required, along with the proper training and recruitment of suitable pilots, not the children *Herr* Göring keeps sending us." I was a little shocked at that, because Galland addressed Göring as "*Herr*" instead of his title. This did not go unnoticed by anyone else, especially Hitler.

"The *Reichsmarschall* has his own problems right now, Galland, but I do understand your concerns. But the fighters have failed me too many times. I have the reports from Göring to this fact, and . . ." Well, Galland cut him off sharply, another eye-opening moment, and he said, "I would take anything coming from the *Reichsmarschall* submitted with a bag of salt." I was stunned, but more things would happen in a few months to explain everything to me. I was aware that Göring and Galland had a love-hate kind of relationship.

Well, the next time I was summoned to Hitler, we *Kommodoren* were with Galland in Berlin to meet with him and Göring, just prior to the revolt. He was pacing back and forth, mumbling about the weapons we had, how we would show the Allies a thing or two, and so on. It was depressing to know that our country was in the hands of this madman and the lunatics around him. Then the Fat One pointed to Galland and said that everything was his fault. He did not inspire his fighters with the proper attitude, that a trained chimpanzee could do a better job. Then he said, "Do you not agree, Steinhoff?"

I looked at Galland, Trautloft, Neumann, Lützow, Hajo Herrmann, Rödel, *Ritter* von Greim, Peltz, Ihlefeld, and the others, and I knew that my character and loyalty was being put to the test. I said, "*Herr Reichsmarschall*, I believe the problem is that you do not understand this war, or the men who are fighting it, being so far removed from the real world. And no, I do not think that a trained chimpanzee could do better, as I have seen this exact method of leadership in Berlin for quite some time. It has not worked well yet."

There was an immediate hushed silence until I heard someone explode in laughter behind me. Of all people I knew, the most serious man I ever knew, Günther Lützow was laughing so hard his Knight's Cross, Oak Leaves, and Swords were bouncing up and down hitting him under the chin. Göring turned purple with rage, and he pointed his finger at me. He screamed, "You have a great sense of self-importance, little man! I could have you shot for saying that."

But he was not finished, "And you, Lützow, what in the hell do you find so goddamned funny?" Lützow did not hesitate. "I am laughing not because it is funny, but because it is very true, and even the silent cowards in this room know it. Only they will not be as honest as Macky." Galland was the next target.

"Galland, so this is your leadership? Insubordinates and cowards? No wonder we are in the state we are in! Your pilots do not deserve the medals they wear, including you." Galland was not taking that sitting down. He stood up, took off his Knight's Cross with Diamonds, Iron Cross, Spanish and Gold Crosses, and all the other medals and dropped them on the heavy table.

"Then I will not desecrate the uniform by wearing these undeserved medals anymore, *Herr Reichsmarschall*," and he turned to leave. Göring then screamed again that Galland was not dismissed, and Galland responded that any further discussion would be taken up with Hitler. Then all of us fighter leaders took off our Knight's Crosses and threw them into the pile with his. The bomber boys just sat there—awe-struck, I think. We just turned our backs and walked out, and the Fat One was still screaming. In a couple of hours, I was in the staff office with some of the others when an orderly came and brought our medals to us. Galland refused to wear his for a while.

Then there was a meeting with Hitler, and Göring was not invited. In fact, I do not even think he was told about it. The next day, we arrived and Hitler was already there. He asked us some basic questions, and then Galland said that he had chosen Walter Nowotny to command the first jet fighters at Achmer. Hitler agreed, and said that he would give him the chance to prove his ideas. Then Hitler said something interesting: "Do not worry about Göring; I will take care of that." I was not sure what he meant, but I think I smiled to myself.

Hitler knew where Germany was going and the situation we were in. Yes, he created the situation for himself. He could not have cared less about anyone else. But, it was our fate to pay for his crimes, and Germany will never live that down. Historians only now, I think, are telling the full story. We fighters were just overwhelmed, and the ridiculous people who controlled the country had delusions. We had combat reports showing the growing American and Soviet strengths. Our men were fighting and dying for a lost cause. I think our people saw us, the fighters, as their last hope.

However, we were receiving the blame officially, and most of it came from Göring—hence, the revolt. He made all of the grand promises, and he boasted to Hitler that his men could accomplish anything at any time. The first failure was at Stalingrad. I watched an entire army die from the air. Unfortunately, he did not consult us before he made these grand overtures. That is a question you historians will continue to ask long after we are all dead. I think that the mentality in Berlin was one of pride and ego. But at that time, it was too late anyway. Our problem was the American bomber and fighter forces.

It was in April 1943 that I first came in contact with the B-17 four-engine heavy bombers, but I only saw them. After the death of Joachim Müncheberg, I was appointed as the *Kommodore* of JG-77, where I stayed until December. At that time, we knew that North Africa was lost, and we were just defending, and covering the ground units from the beachhead of Cape Bon, northeast of Tunis. This was the last piece of Africa, where the last of the *Afrika Korps* and the Italian army were pushed into. Later, they surrendered.

After a dogfight with a few Spitfires, we were prepared for landing when we looked up and saw this great armada of bombers that we had never seen before. We could clearly see them in the sky, as it was sunny with no clouds. There was not enough time for us to take off and reach them; it was too late for making an attack. We were aware of these aircraft, of course, the American heavy bombers, but they usually did not fly in Russia and in the Mediterranean and Africa, in our areas.

After the exhausting battles in the Caucasus and Crimea, I had some home leave. I had just arrived in Munich and spent some time with Ursula when I had a call from Adolf Galland. I had a choice: a command in France or North Africa. Well, as my wife will tell you, I have not always made the wisest choices, so I took the job in Africa. I had never been there, and I think the adventure appealed to me. Soon I was in Rome to get my orders, and then on to Sicily and then Tunisia to join JG-77—this, I think, in late March 1943.

Well, I arrived at the unit and looked into the eyes of these men who had in many cases been fighting in the desert for a year or more, always outnumbered, although the great majority of the pilots were new replacements. Finding a pilot over the age of twenty-one was difficult, and so many of their faces reminded me of Marseille, who was now long dead. Most of the old-timers were already dead, captured, or crippled.

These men of JG-77 had worshipped Joachim Müncheberg. I knew him, and he was a great pilot, good man, great sense of humor, and a fine gentleman. His men loved him, and they were sizing me up as much as I was them. I was the new stepfather to the family, eyed with great suspicion. I had been in their shoes, so I knew. Most of these men had not fought on any other front, so this was the only war they knew. I learned rather quickly just how good the British were at that time when a Spitfire shot out my engine and radiator, forcing me to crash-land in the desert.

Well, we were already on our heels at that time. Then, I received my orders to take over command of JG-77 during the evacuation in Trapani, Sicily. JG-2 had a *Geschwader* there, JG-53 also, as did almost all of JG-27. All of the fighter units forced out of Africa went there. We knew that the Allies were coming to Sicily. It was a very lovely place, with Mount Erice in the background, great white-sand beaches, like a tourist place. The sea was as warm as a bath. You really had to see how these men were. Veterans of Libya, Tunisia, and some even in Russia, we did not look anything like a disciplined military unit. Half the men wore sandals and shorts, and we went shirtless until the order came down to stop that practice. No sunburn was allowed.

The first combat I saw there was against B-25s [Mitchell twin-engine medium bombers], but I was not involved. We had an alert that they were coming. There were about sixty of them, and that meant that they might have fighters with them. They usually did; P-40s or Spitfires from North Africa would join them. We could hear the battle over the speakers. We had one pilot missing, one shot down who was safe after parachuting, and one enemy bomber had been shot down, with several damaged. Usually, the first we knew of an air attack was when the flak started firing. We did not have radar or even a good early-ground warning or relay system.

We were still consolidating our forces and preparing for the invasion that everyone outside of Berlin knew was coming. Not long after we had relocated to Sicily, which was May, we had several important people finally come visit us. Field Marshal [Albert] Kesselring arrived within minutes of an enemy attack against our airfield. His aircraft landed and the tires were torn apart from shrapnel on the field. He was doing his inspection tour, meeting with pilots and speaking with leaders. We called him "Smiling Albert" because of his seemingly always happy attitude.

Let me just say that we had developed the beach mentality. We were hardly ever in proper uniform, as it was just too damned hot. We had our cotton tropical shirts and shorts. Many of us wore sandals, headscarves, and hats, carried umbrellas, and sat around in deck chairs getting suntans. Except for the fighters nearby, we could have been mistaken for a group of tourists at the beach. This was what Kesselring saw when he landed. I jumped up and ordered the men to form up at attention, and they tried. Some were drunk, or had just awakened from a deep sleep after days and nights of little sleep due to nuisance raids. Kesselring was not amused.

"Steinhoff, do your men know that there is a war on?" he asked. I was always sort of a smart-ass, and I said, "Yes, *Herr Feldmarschall*, we have been fighting it for about four years now." Well, "Smiling Albert" was not smiling at that time. "Tell your men to at least pretend that they are German soldiers. This is a disgrace. What if the *Reichsmarshall* had come here and seen this?"

My response was not planned. I just said what came to mind. "I do not think we have a chair that would support his weight, *Herr Feldmarschall*." Everyone started to laugh so hard they fell to ground, abandoning the position of attention. Some were throwing up the meager meal they had just had. I did not even smile. I was serious. Kesselring screamed for attention, yelling, "*Achtung*," and even then it took a minute for the men to regain their composure.

Well, he asked me specific questions, and I gave him direct answers: "No, we were not combat ready," and "No, we did not have enough aircraft and ammunition." "Yes, my men were exhausted and needed a rest." "No, I did not have much confidence in Berlin, or think that anyone in Berlin knew shit about what was going on, since they had their heads up their asses."

Well, Kesselring had more than his fill of me, and he turned to some of the others. I will never forget one of my junior officer's comments to Kesselring. He said, "Well, if the great *Führer* is so concerned about keeping Sicily away from the Allies, then why did he not give us what we needed in Tunisia, to prevent us from being here at all?" I laughed when he said that, and Kesselring, while not a Nazi by any means, was still visibly upset at the comment. "Just follow your damned orders," was his response. He also denied my request to give my men leave after many months of hard fighting.

As Kesselring left to get into the staff car waiting for him, he called me over. "Steinhoff," he started to say and then began laughing like hell. "I had to hold back, but that joke you said about Göring almost made me piss myself. That was pretty damned funny, but I would not say that around too many people. Good luck to you." Then he left. I returned to the men, and they were still laughing. I remember thinking that I had at least given them some comic relief.

Galland, the General of the Fighters, came to see us with Lützow in late June, as did Neumann and Rödel from JG-27. We also had a squadron from JG-53 assigned nearby. Hitler was serious about making Sicily stronger. I spent some time with the JG-27 men, as I knew most from the early days. I also knew Franz Stigler, who was there, and Werner Schroer. All of the leaders came together for the meetings, where Galland and Lützow gave us lectures on what had been learned in Western Europe about fighting the heavy bombers. Every one of us knew that we were never going to hold Sicily; we were not stupid. The threat of the heavy bombers and the growing enemy escort fighters was why he was there.

When Galland was there, he also inspected our airfield defenses, revetments, runways, and all of the things that our airfields needed for operations. We were still in the process of completing these fields all over Sicily at that time. We were also still receiving some light antiaircraft guns for our own airfield defense, including some heavy machine guns. The heavier 88mm guns were controlled by the flak division, separate from us. These guys were getting radar sets, and that would help us with detecting incoming enemy aircraft. This was also how we had confirmation of a new incoming air raid. Learning how to attack these heavy bombers was of great interest to me, and I read Egon Mayer's reports.

I knew Egon Mayer from the early days in flight school, and had met but did not know Georg-Peter Eder at that time. I came to know him better later at JG-7. They had worked on head-on tactics to engage the four-engine bombers. I knew that they had been working on that project. Eder had been running a fighter school in France after being wounded badly again. One of his students was my friend Ihlefeld, who became successful at hitting the "giants," as we called them.

Well, the rules were pretty simple. Our problem had been that our gun sights would fill with the wingspan of the bombers, but firing was a waste of time. This was because the bomber was still too far away to hit. You had to be three times closer to a bomber than a fighter to even begin getting good hits. We learned "never fire too early," "wait for the wing roots to fill the reticle instead of the wing tips," and "know that you will have a fifty percent chance of being shot down on a rear attack." I also learned that we had a fifty percent chance of being hit during a side or flank attack, but being shot down was only twenty-five percent due to the speed of the attack perpendicular to the formation. It also offered a wider target.

I began the discussion with questions on the head-on attack, which I wanted to try. The head-on attack greatly reduced the risk of being hit, let alone being shot down. However, apparently the head-on method also greatly reduced accuracy and the time on the target. You had maybe two seconds to fire and pull away. Those two seconds had to count. I later tried and found that it was a technique that I could not master.

You had to have nerves of steel, and be able to aim and shoot while in the approach, usually a dive from above, so that you had the altitude converted into air speed to get through all of the defensive fire. Galland enjoyed the conversations. He loved being with his pilots and away from Berlin. He told me that he felt quite young and lighthearted to be with his men, as he called us. He dreaded going back to Berlin, and told me that he wished he could be demoted so he could lead a squadron again. Strange that he should have said that, since less than two years later he would be leading a squadron of jets. I would be with him.

There were so many Knight's Crosses around during Galland's visit, it looked like a convention. During this time, I was able to speak with these men who had also flown with Marseille, and who had come to know him much better than I did. They told me the stories, and we sat around, drank, and laughed ourselves sick as we all compared notes on him. I still wonder what it may have been like if he had lived.

Galland had created these manuals, training aids with drawn pictures and instructions on how to attack the four motor bombers. He had a wood-carved model of a B-17, with wires twisted into circles and with spokes. These showed us the defensive fire radius of the bomber and allowed us to seek the weak or blind spots. At this time, the B-17 and B-24 bombers did not have front guns, or what you call nose guns. This was why the head-on attack was effective. Later that changed, which meant that instead of attacking head-on level, we would have to attack from above and dive into the front, at a higher closing speed. This way we were only exposed to the top turret guns.

I remember something funny that Rödel said, when he asked Galland, "Where is the lavatory in this diagram? You know that we are all going to piss ourselves doing this." Everyone laughed except Galland. He just smiled and said the best way according to Eder is to have a *Schwarm* attack, single file, one behind the other. At least one if not two fighters will do enough damage to bring the bomber down. Then he went into explaining how to use the best escape methods. I was actually eager to try it. Not that I was suicidal, but it was almost like having a new math problem and being challenged to solve it.

The finer points of the doctrine for attacking these bombers had not yet been worked out in the air, but a few principles had nevertheless already been established. These were:

1. Attempt to break up the formation; single planes are easy to shoot down.

2. If you succeed in leading your concentrated fighter force, in frontal attack on collision

course, right into the bomber formation, you will be sure to break it up.

3. Maintain your fighter force in the closest formation possible and do not open fire except at shortest range, but then fire from all buttonholes, as we used to say.

Some of the pilots had previously engaged the heavy bombers, and they admitted that they had made the mistake of firing too soon, because in their rear attacks, the gun sight filled up and they hit the triggers. But as I said, a bomber's wingspan was much greater than a fighter, so the rounds did not reach the target. It did alert the bombers that they were going to have an interesting day. By the time that the first or second fighters wasted their attack, the rest of the group knew that the Americans were on the alert. That was when our losses rose.

The secret, as we were told, was that if attacking from the rear, we were to wait until the wingspan was well outside the reticle. However, if attacking from the front when the wingspan started to fill the sight, and you had the estimated distance from the target, and if you knew your air speed, then count. Starting the attack from level flight straight at the bomber, and beginning from at least a thousand meters, was preferred, and then you started counting one, two, three, four, fire, pull up, and then climb or dive. This, of course, changed when the front guns, or chin turrets, were added.

Some pilots liked climbing so that they were already in a position to bank around and attack from altitude. Some preferred to dive and pull up, and only expose themselves to the ball turret gunners underneath and a few waist gunners. They could in most cases completely avoid the tail gunners, unlike those who climbed. The disadvantage was you had to regain altitude and convert that into air speed. The positive was that if you had escort fighters chasing you, your fighter was already in a dive building up air speed for an escape. Bad news if the enemy had a top flight waiting upstairs for you.

The purpose was, of course, to shoot down or at least damage the bombers. The least we should be able to do was scatter them to break up their large and very effective formations. This would make stragglers that we could then attack. Lone bombers were easier to kill than many in a formation due to the heavy defensive fire. We called it "attacking battleships" or the "flying wall" due to the massive amount of machine gun fire.

Then, of course, attacking the bombers only worked out if they had no fighter cover, or if we could break through the fighters. Once we did break through, then we had to worry about them after we hit the bombers. If we were damaged after passing through the bomber formation, that meant we were at a great disadvantage against enemy fighters. This was where most of our pilots were lost—not due to the bombers, but from the fighters who got to them afterward.

Attacking these bomber formations would certainly awaken you. They flew in these close defensive boxes, a heavy defensive formation, and with all of their heavy .50-caliber machine guns that could overlap and interlock their fire; they were not easy targets. I had some friends in France who had been fighting these bombers, and I had the chance to speak with a few of them. We finally adopted the head-on attack pioneered by Mayer and Eder, but only a few experts could do this successfully, and it really took nerves of steel.

You had a great closing speed of sometimes over nine hundred kilometers or more per hour. That is a very fast approach. That became interesting when you were flying through your own flak. Baling out at that speed was also a good way to get killed. Later in the war, we jet pilots used different methods to attack, given our greater speed, and we all mostly preferred riding a damaged jet down if possible. Being shot in your parachute was not a nice thought, and it happened often to us jet pilots.

Well, I can tell you, as soon as I took over command of JG-77, I was shot down on my first mission while attacking B-24 Liberators, and I knew right then that it was a totally different war from 1940. I was flying with a few of my men, and we were headed straight into a large formation, perhaps a hundred bombers, and no fighters. I thought, "This will be easy." I was wrong. I remembered the class we were given on the head-on attack, and I was in a perfect firing position: twelve o'clock high with almost two thousand meters altitude advantage.

I put the nose down and attacked from a forty-five degree angle. I remember that my heart was pounding as I closed in. The bomber I focused upon grew bigger very fast, and then I fired. I could not even see where my rounds landed until I pulled back on the stick, rolled over, and pushed the stick forward to continue the climb. I looked back and saw no smoke or fire. My wingman called out that he was hit and breaking off. I then rolled back level and banked around for another attack, when a minute later I heard thumps and bumps in my fighter. The engine went dead, smoke began coming in, and I smelled fuel. I knew right then that I was not riding this bomb to the ground. Then as the fighter rolled and became a brick, the canopy shattered as more bullets ripped the glass out.

Their defensive fire tore my fighter apart, and I managed to open the shattered canopy and tighten my parachute harness, which I always kept loose in flying because I wanted to be able to maneuver. The 109 was going into a nosedive, so I pulled back on the stick. I still had my control surfaces, so I managed to level out, and as I unfastened my seat belt the fighter started a flat spin, pinning me. I tightened the parachute harness again and tried to stand up, and I pushed with my legs. I popped out like a cork from a champagne bottle. I started to tumble, and I looked down to see my fighter still spinning in.

I then straightened out my body and prepared to pull the rip cord, and when I did nothing happened right away. I thought, "Great, all of this and now no parachute." I realized that I had not pulled the wire all the way out, so I pulled again. This time I thought my back was broken. The force of the opening shock cracked every vertebrae I had. I saw stars, as well as tracers. My neck felt as if it were in a fire—whiplash, I guess. I would not be able to turn my head properly for weeks after that, and I had dislocated my left shoulder upon the parachute opening, and when I hit the ground it popped back into place. I then realized that I had a few cuts along my upper right arm and a grazing wound across my left thigh.

I also realized in hindsight, as my plane tumbled out of control and I took to my parachute for the first and last time, just how much I had forgotten. I assumed either I had a lot to learn or I was simply a lucky idiot so far. It was different fighting the Soviets as opposed to the combined British and American forces, even though the Soviets outnumbered us even more. The Western Allies had improved their already first-rate equipment. They fought their battles at higher altitudes, since the Soviets did not have the heavy bomber forces.

I had also forgotten how flexible the Western Allies were and how they could alter their tactics to fit the situation and orchestrate brilliant attacks. The Soviets were not very flexible, and for the most part they were slow to learn from their mistakes. I did learn that the head-on attacks seemed to break up the formations better than anything else. Even captured aircrews told us that the frontal attack was what they feared most. A tail gunner told me that the front attacks did not bother him so much. He liked the change.

We also learned that some of our units in France and Germany were mounting under-wing rockets, or mortars, on their fighters to hit the bomber formations. Others were dropping proximity-fused bombs from above, to blast them. That seemed crazy to me. I heard that these added weapons only reduced their speed and maneuverability against Allied fighters, and resulted in few successes. Due to the limited range of the enemy fighters, these heavy fighters were placed deeper inside the Reich, beyond the fighter escorts range. Once they turned back, our heavy fighters went to work against the bombers. Later, the escort fighters would fly all the way to Berlin and back, especially when the Mustang came into the war, and also after the Allies landed in France and had their air bases there, as well as in Belgium, but they still kept trying that method against the bombers. I thought that it was insane, personally.

We had about 120 fighters and were well prepared for the coming air battles. JG-77 and JG-27 were the most visible units, while a few JG-53 aircraft were also there. During this time, the 12th U.S. Air Force was flying out of North Africa, and Sicily had been bombed steadily, being softened up for the invasion. On June 25, 1943, during Galland's visit, our radar stations in Italy reported an enemy bomber formation approaching, coming halfway between Sardinia and Sicily—heading for Naples, we thought.

Well, it seemed that we were the target this time. We had been bombed before, but this time the American bombers were really targeting our airfields. We heard the engines high overhead, coming from the east over Mount Erice, but it was too late for us to get airborne. Soon, the bombs began to fall. I ran with many of the others and jumped headfirst into a slit trench, about two meters deep, that had been prepared for these attacks.

Then bombs began falling, so many and so hard I was bounced upward a few times—so high I was above the trench and could see the explosions, the sky, and even the B-26 bombers overhead—before gravity pulled me back on top of another man. I fell right on top of Franzl Larsen. I could hear all the breath blown out of him as I landed on top of him. Once we were blown upward together. It was almost comical. We just looked at each other as we went up and down. We were both badly bruised from the impact of our bodies hitting each other. The dust then settled over us. We could not even see each other except for the outlines of our bodies when it was all over.

We could hear the screams of the wounded, even through our deafened ears. The orderlies had been running, even through the bombing, to gather men who were torn apart. The damaged and burning fighters were exploding as the fuel and ammunition were ignited. I thought that my eardrums were shattered. To this day, I sometimes have a ringing in my ears, and sometimes it is so bad it blinds me with the pain—tinnitus, I believe. My ears were also full of dust, and my eyes. We were coated with the stuff. Then it was over.

Larsen climbed out, coughing from the dust, as were all the others and myself. We sat on the edge of the trench, not sure if we would have to jump back in again. The damage was extensive. Larsen said, "I guess we know how the infantry feels now." I agreed with him, only nodding my head. I could not speak, as my throat was full of dust. Breathing was hard. I ordered all engines, guns, everything that could be salvaged collected. We had to cannibalize damaged fighters to make others flyable, until we received replacements. I told Galland about these experiences when he arrived. We needed better early-warning methods.

I had no sooner walked to the medical collection point to check on my wounded and dead men when my orderly called out to me. Since the phones were down, a Kübelwagen had arrived. It was Galland's aide, and I was to call him as soon as possible as they were repairing the phone lines. He wanted a damage report. I told him I still did not know the extent, and I would contact him later when I had a full report. He also apologized for not getting the warning to us sooner. The bombers had come in under the radar, on radio silence, so the attack was a complete surprise to everyone. That did not make me feel any better. I was disgusted and went back to look at my men. I will admit that I cried when I saw the shape they were in. Young men, simple guys, they did not deserve this. The phone rang and again it was the general, who told me that there was another raid, heavy bombers this time. They thought the target was Naples.

I had my doubts as to Naples being the target, since there was nothing of any real military value there, unless they wanted to strike the port. Then he told me that there was no way we could intercept them inbound, but that we could catch them on their return. Well, I asked him if he knew the route they would take, and he said no, but we would be vectored to their formation while in the air. We no sooner had the canopies closed when we were told that the target was actually the ferry traffic in the Straits of Messina. I was vindicated.

This was our maritime supply line, with fuel, men, munitions, everything we needed. It was a logical target, of course, and I knew that the bombers only had one route to return to Libya from there. I had it marked on my map. By the time we were airborne, the bomber formation was already returning to North Africa. We knew that they flew either from Algiers or from Benghazi. To get off our radar they had dropped to the deck, wave-hopping inbound to attack the shipping. They stayed low during their return. They were less than ten meters above the ocean; it was incredible flying. We had the reports from our boats and coast watchers.

My headset was ringing with reports. The Allies were attacking the port of Messina, then the general's orders came over the radio. I acknowledged, and switched the radio channel to my men. I gave the order to scramble. I looked around at the smoking, burning, and broken fighters, the tents covering the makeshift hospitals, and I thought about the letters I would have to write to their wives, mothers, and children. I sat there lost in my own mind until I saw the green Very flare go up, then I opened the throttle.

I released the brakes and gathered speed and then lifted off and saw my wingmen, Straden and Bachmann, also off the ground, and then I looked behind and saw all the others taking off. I had checked my magnetos, manifold pressure—all seemed well. Then I wondered how many of us would die. I cleared my head and focused upon the mission. My body still hurt like all hell, as I was bruised from the bombing. Larsen had a cracked rib. Bachmann had a concussion. My formation of about twenty fighters was able to take off with about a hundred aircraft in total, stationed all over Sicily poised to attack. We were then sent to the area between Sardinia and Sicily. Other groups also scrambled to intercept, so we probably had eighty fighters in the air in total. We rallied over Mount Erice.

I had previously briefed the men that we would attack as a wall, a phalanx, by *Schwarm*, overlapping the attacks. This would maximize our force and allow the rear guard to locate any damaged stragglers. That was the plan anyway. Then the general came on the radio with me, by my call sign "Odysseus," which seemed fitting given the dire circumstances, and he gave us the vector grid coordinate. I relayed the vector to my men and told them to follow me in.

After ten minutes or so of flying, we found them—over a hundred as I looked down after banking—as we were at about three thousand meters altitude. I was then informed that I was overall commander for the one hundred German fighters on the attack, and the enemy was at five thousand meters. Well, I then ordered radio silence until further notice. It was about that time my drop tank went empty and I had to switch to the internal tanks.

Soon after an hour of flying, we had seen nothing. I almost hoped that we would miss the bombers, because we had no air-sea rescue and we were single-engine fighters over the open sea. Visibility was somewhat limited due to strong haze on the water, and I could not see all of my men. I could see *Oberleutnant* Freiburg's *Schwarm*, but no one else. I dropped to three thousand meters again to try to see something, but I could not risk a radio check. They were all somewhere in the fog.

But, just at the very moment when I hit the microphone, telling the men to return to base because of our fuel shortage, I saw the bombers. They were big bastards, too. Then, rather than aborting, I told my men to form up in the overlapping attack formation as planned. We would hit them in waves. Suddenly the radio erupted; everyone was calling out bombers. One great problem with us German fighter pilots, we were notorious for chattering mindlessly on the radio. That was our only real lack of discipline. Otherwise, we felt that we were invincible, as young men will. Armin Zöhler was screaming so loud I thought he had been shot. I told him to shut up.

The B-17s were flying in a wide formation, very spread out, only a few yards above the sea, in a formation so huge you could hardly see where the formation started and ended. They were painted in a desert-sand color, like our fighters on top, so we could see them clearly against the turquoise blue of the water, and the sun was reflecting off the water. It was beautiful.

I rolled over into a dive, focusing upon a small box of bombers as they were coming at us head-on, and then focused on one near the end of the formation. I was at maximum speed when I leveled out and saw a dozen of my men following me. I had no idea when to fire, and I was just over the waves myself. I thought my propeller would clip the water—that was how close I was.

I called out that I was attacking. I saw the nose of the bomber, the sun shining off the glass nose as I closed, and fired. I closed so quickly, I did not see the immediate result, but I screamed overhead and inverted as I climbed. Looking back, I saw the huge geyser of water where my bomber had gone down. The column of water was at least ten meters high, and then I rolled back level and continued to climb. I was hoping not to be hit by those damned .50-caliber bullets.

At that time, we had no experience attacking bombers near the ocean surface, so making a proper attack was impossible. No sooner had I flashed over the bombers then the radio was active again, every pilot calling in zero fuel, asking for coordinates from Trapani. I told them all to shut up, listen to me, and set a course for one-three-zero degrees. We were landing empty; some fighters would have to dead stick without power.

I had just stopped rolling when Straden jumped on my wing, confirming my kill, and he told me that he almost flew right into the waterspout I created when my bomber went in. I was unaware that he was right behind me at the time I fired. His fighter had been lightly damaged from pieces of the bomber that exploded on impact with the sea. When he pulled up, he ran into some of the debris, and his prop was slightly damaged and thrown off balance. He limped home on empty tanks and a wobbly propeller.

Overall, the mission was a disaster with only that single kill, and after the first launch with the fuel-warning lights on, our entire formation went into a panic because of being over water, and because the majority of the pilots had to be directed back to our bases by radar. We lost six aircraft due to defensive fire and most ran out of fuel, landing wherever they could. I told Straden to have all the flight leaders meet me in operations immediately. I had just walked in when I found out that the general was on the phone.

I answered the phone and he wanted a situation report. I told him that I had to debrief the men but that we only had one victory, due to sighting the enemy when we were already almost out of fuel. We had gone past our emergency reserves. Almost as if God had intervened, saving me from that call, another air raid hit us just at that time. I dropped the phone and ran to the trenches, jumping over Larsen in the process. Once again, I took a headfirst dive into a deep trench, and instead of landing on someone else I hit the sand. Then someone fell on top of me. I could not even breathe.

After the raid, I went to meet with the men for the mission debriefing. We sat around and discussed what went wrong, and we all had the same opinion. Being low on fuel over the sea was not the best position to be in. If that had not been the case, given the fact that the bombers did not have a fighter escort, we could have done a lot more damage. I resigned myself to this fact. Later, I was able to meet with Galland at his request. He already knew what had happened. We had a chat, and I could see that he was very disappointed in me. He simply said that we would discuss the matter later, and he left.

Well, the phone rang very early next day, probably three in the morning. Galland had just received a teletype directive from Göring personally, and we were stunned. He read it to me over the phone. Göring's direct order was that one pilot from each of the fighter units at the *Gruppe* level involved against the bombers was to be chosen at random for court-martial for cowardice and desertion in the face of the enemy. Under German Military Law, that was a death sentence. Galland ended the call by telling me not to worry, he would intervene. However, not worrying was an impossible task.

I waited all day, thinking how I was going to bring this to their attention. I waited until after dinner and made sure all the men had their meal before I called the meeting. They had to be told, and this was not something I wanted to do. I still had to finish writing the letters to the dead men's families, but I could not focus on that. I assembled the men, and then I just told them plainly what Göring had sent to Galland. There was a deafening silence. The men looked at each other, and then at me. They knew that Göring was asking men to be sent to die as a punishment for failure, just so that he could save face. I heard a voice in the back grumbling. It was Freiburg, who said, "What the hell, I will volunteer. I need a vacation anyway." The men were grumbling. I could hear their muttered conversations, gallows humor. Suddenly a light went off, and then I had an idea.

I told them what Galland told me, that he would intervene, and that tended to tone down the dissent somewhat. Then we had another air raid, almost on cue. Wellingtons were hitting us again, so once again we headed for the trenches as the windows started to shatter. Luckily no one was injured, and I began looking around. I had to stop myself from laughing when I saw Freiberg emerge still holding his bottle of wine. He had fled the building with it and had been passing it around in the trench.

We gathered back in the ready room, which was still intact, and Freiberg came up to me and handed me the bottle. He said that all of the leaders were going to volunteer for the court-martial. They decided that they would rather take their chances in a court, where they could tell their story to people who knew nothing about flying fighter combat. And as a result of our solidarity, every single *Staffelkapitän* and above to the *Geschwaderkommodoren*, including myself, submitted our names. We were either going to be vindicated or crucified together.

The response we heard back from Berlin was like a shockwave. There was no way that Göring was going to be able to explain to the German people how twenty or more senior officers, many with the Knight's Cross or higher and many victories and years of battle, suddenly lost their nerve and avoided contact with the enemy. It was at this point, despite my previous dislike of him, that I truly hated that fat bastard. I heard from Galland that Hitler personally became involved. Then we had the Gestapo show up, wanting to speak to pilots about this, and many other things. They were trying to collect evidence to support hanging a scapegoat.

I always hated these guys. Well, several pilots were called in from every unit, and when they were from my unit, I demanded to be there. The Gestapo was less than enthusiastic about having me in the room. I guess they felt that their intimidation and coercion would get better results without me. I was there to support my pilots. This happened over two days. But there was nothing there, just a fishing trip.

One day I received a phone call from *Leutnant* Willy Kientsch, who had also called Werner Schroer from JG-27. Schroer told him to get me quickly. The Gestapo was there, and he wanted to warn me, as I thought they had left Sicily. I drove over fast because I knew that Edu Neumann had gone to Rome for a meeting with Galland, taking Rödel with him. As the senior-ranking officer in the area, I wanted to see what these guys were doing.

The Gestapo had already spoken to a few pilots, mostly asking the same tired questions about the failed bomber mission. Why did we not shoot down the bombers? What were their orders? That kind of thing. Then they left. However, these two Gestapo men were not the same guys who had been at the airfields for a couple of days. These were on a very different mission. My curiosity was high.

Then I was informed that they had called in Franz Stigler, whom I did not know very well, but we had spoken to each other several times over the years when he was a flight instructor, and I liked him. He was also there with us as Galland held court at Trapani with all the officers, and I had also known him from when I was in the advanced school. He was a good guy—older than the average fighter pilot like me, and a former flight instructor—and I did not want the Gestapo harming him, so I was there. I had no idea what this was about.

Well, I walked in and these two Gestapo clowns asked who I was and why I was there. I told them the same thing that I had told the previous men. I was there as the senior officer, even though I was only a *Major*. They reminded me that this was JG-27, not JG-77, and I had no business being there. I told them that I did not give a damn if it were the RAF, or what their concern was. A *Luftwaffe* officer was being interrogated and his senior officers were out of town, and I would be there to protect his interests.

This one Gestapo guy pulled out his credentials, as they were in civilian clothes, and introduced himself as a *Hauptsturmführer* [captain], and the other man was a junior noncommissioned Gestapo agent. They could see that I was not very impressed. The senior man told me that this was a private meeting and that I should leave. I reminded him that the last I recalled, a *Major* outranked even a *Hauptsturmführer* of the SS or Gestapo. I also reminded him that there were a couple of hundred *Luftwaffe* men within earshot, and he may want to remember that he was outnumbered. I could see him glaring at me. He was angry and I did not care. I folded my arms and leaned back against the wall behind Stigler and said, "Get on with it. I have things to do."

They asked Stigler about his brother, who had been killed as a bomber pilot, I learned. His brother had been in contact with, if not involved with, the White Rose group. This was the Catholic student group in Munich. They were caught and executed, but the Gestapo was casting a wide net. Stigler was guilty by association if nothing else. He told the men that he had no idea what they were talking about, and he did not have any idea as to what his brother did or did not do, or whom he knew. He was, after all, in North Africa and had little contact with him, even up to the day he was killed.

The *Hauptsturmführer* asked him about some of the Catholic Church's leadership and other clergymen who were known not to be sympathetic to the Nazis. Stigler admitted that he knew of the opinions and writing of Bishop [later Cardinal Clemens August Graf von] Galen, Dietrich Bonhoeffer, and others. He made me smile when he said, "you had to be dead" not to know who they were. Stigler was reminded of the laws that meant a death sentence for any written or spoken communication that undermined the war effort. We were all aware of it. Well, they were apparently satisfied with his answers, and they left. Good riddance, I said, and it was over. I went back to my airfield, and as they left, I shook Stigler's hand. I told him not to be a stranger and call me if he needed me. Later, we would fly jets together with Galland in JV-44.

Soon we were fighting against the new Spitfires, very dangerous aircraft that did not suffer the earlier problem of stalling in a dive. They still were not fuel injected, but they did have a two-stage supercharger. I was shot down by one and had to belly-land, during which I injured my back. The Spitfire had turned tight into me, and he had me good. Only the protective armor plate behind my head kept me from being killed by a 20mm. I used to inspect all of the aircraft, as some men would take this plate out. It reduced rearward visibility by about twenty percent, so they removed it. I ordered all the plates replaced, and I made it clear I would court-martial any man who disobeyed. Three more of my pilots had a similar experience, and they were believers.

Well, the Allies invaded in July, and we fought the entire month but were being pushed north. We were completely exhausted, sometimes unable even to stand. Our younger new pilots were not surviving, and we had heavy losses. Then we had the order to fly the men and aircraft to Italy. We stripped the armor plate and radios out, packed two and three men into the fuselage, and flew across the Strait. There were not enough transport aircraft to get everyone out. We had not just been robbing Peter to pay Paul, so to speak; given our limited resources, as Freiberg had said before he went missing, "we turned all the disciples upside down and shook the money out of them."

Soon after we lost Sicily, everyone fled across the Straits of Messina, and we were stationed in Foggia, Italy. There were no doubts that the Allies were coming at some point. The best we could do was just shoot down aircraft. That was our job. But there were more and more of them all the time—and fewer of us, I can say.

Then you also had the long-range fighter escorts, which made life difficult, until we flew the Me-262 jets armed with four 30mm cannon and twenty-four R4M rockets. Then we could blast huge holes in even the tightest bomber formation from outside the range of their defensive fire, inflict damage, then come around and finish off the cripples with cannon fire. We were really hard to kill in the jet as long as you did not try and dogfight with the enemy fighters, or get caught in the intersecting defensive fire of the bomber boxes. We had more to fear from our own flak most of the time, or on landing or taking off, of course. But that was much later in the war.

While in Italy we had a lot of combat, and our airfields were hit all the time. We were getting hit from the enemy bases in Sicily once we lost it, and then they established airfields in southern Italy. That was when the air war began to be really dangerous. We were outnumbered over a hundred to one every time we went up. These were days of great adventures. I remember hearing about the black American pilots for the first time, and I was intrigued and surprised. I never really thought very much of this racial superiority rubbish. No intelligent man could, and I was interested in the parallels between the racial segregation in America just as we had in Germany.

That was why we were amazed that black Americans were flying fighters. Once we realized which unit they were, with red tails, I realized that I had fought against them. They were not idiots; in fact, one of them shot me down almost immediately after takeoff. I managed to make it back to my field, but the engine was ruined. Good pilots. Brave. Later, Galland and I would have a series of chats with Neumann and Rödel, the senior commanders in Italy, about these black pilots.

There were many opportunities to engage the newest American fighters. We had flown against the P-40s, and they were only dangerous if you attacked them head-on. The same was true with the P-38. It had massive firepower in a head-on attack—all the American fighters did. Only the Mustang was a problem in a dogfight, and we lost most of our pilots to that fighter. I was able to meet with several captured pilots who flew all of these different fighters. I would say that the P-47 was also a bad animal to fight with, as it had massive guns, eight .50-calibers, and it could take more damage than anything I ever encountered. And of course, the air raids kept coming.

Once I was test flying a Me-109G with my aide near our base at Foggia. I had just received a refurbished 109G with a new engine, everything. The paint was even fresh. It was a nice fighter. This was before I had been exiled from Germany, during my first tour as *Kommodore* of JG-77. We were attacked at low level by a flight of P-38 Lightnings, about one hundred American fighters in all, but the two of us figured, why not attack? We had just taken off. We turned into them, and I flew through their formation going in the opposite direction, getting good strikes on a couple of them. I poured a good burst into this P-38 and the pilot rolled it over, and I saw him bail out. I had this on gun camera also.

Well, he was picked up and made a POW, and I invited him to my tent for a drink and dinner as well as to spend the night. We drank some of the local wine . . . and drank and drank. I thought to myself, "What am I going to do with this guy?" Well, it was long after midnight, so I lay down in my tent and stretched my legs so I could reach his head. He woke up and said, "Don't worry, I won't run away. You have my word as an officer and a gentleman. Besides, you got me too drunk." We slept, he kept his word, and I never placed a guard on him. It worked very well, you know. He was a very likable man, and I was very pleased to have the victory, but as I told him, I was even more pleased to see him uninjured and safe.

I was asked to write a report on the enemy fighters I had engaged. The Allies, especially the Americans, had such a variety of great fighter aircraft. The Lightning was a fast, low-profiled, fantastic fighter and a real danger when it was above you. It was only vulnerable if you were behind it, a little below and closing fast, or turning into it, but on the attack it was a tremendous aircraft. One shot me down from long range in 1944. It had .50-caliber and 20mm guns, and we all knew that no one should ever go head to head against one. The P-51 Mustang was deadly because of its long range and maneuverability, as it could cover any air base in Europe. This made things difficult, especially later when flying the jets. Mustangs used to hang around our airfields, catching us taking off and landing.

The Thunderbolt was very dangerous. It had a great roll rate and could out-dive anything but the jet, and its climb rate was also good, but not as good as the 190D or 109G. It could take as much damage as a bomber. I spoke with guys who emptied their cannon and machine guns into them, and sometimes they still flew for a while. The Thunderbolt pilot was well protected, with excellent armor plate around the cockpit. We had a special location where some of us flew captured aircraft so that we could be familiar with them. Rall, Walther Dahl, Heinz Bär, Anton Hackl, and I flew some of these together in 1944; they were excellent aircraft and very well built. The American fighters had three times the instrumentation that ours did. The number of gauges was almost overwhelming. One thing that I found amazing was the amount of ammunition storage the American fighters had. This was especially true of the P-47. Those were a lot of heavy bullets to deal with.

Following the latest meeting with Galland and the others, I had just been only a few days with *Kommando Nowotny* learning to fly the Me-262 when I learned that I would take command of the first *Staffel* and then the first *Gruppe* for a while—even though I was an *Oberstleutnant* and Nowotny—as a *Major*—was the *Kommodore*. There was some controversy about his being chosen with his rank. Some believed that he was chosen because he had the Diamonds, which made sense, and others said he was chosen because he was an Austrian, as was Hitler, as a way to try to persuade Hitler over to the fighters' side of the argument in getting the jets.

I outranked him, but he had more flying time in the jets and more victories, and I was only there to learn, not yet command. We worked well together during my early training, which was only three days long. I did not really get to know him since he was killed a couple of days after I arrived. I still had to return to Italy after my transition training. Nowotny was younger than I was, only twenty-three, I think, and he was a really great fighter pilot. He was also a good man.

Well, I had just been back with JG-77 when I received a call from Galland. I had to come to Berlin for a meeting, and I flew my 109 from Italy. After a few stops to refuel and eat, I finally landed at Tempelhof and called Galland. He was heading to a meeting that was supposed to be about something very secret. I called his office, and he said that I needed to go to Wannsee. Trautloft had a house there, which was his office also. This was in late November. I arrived. I entered and there were several men there, including Edu Neumann, Günther Lützow, Trautloft, Rödel, Ihlefeld, and others.

The atmosphere was grim, gloomy, I can say. Galland then closed the door and had a man standing outside. He then asked me if I had spoken to Göring or heard from him. I had not, and I told him this. Galland then said that I would very soon. He then suggested I take a seat. He told the others and me that Göring knew about the American Negro pilots.

One or two had been captured, or so we were told. Then he said that Göring was going to order that all of these black men be handed over to the SS, rather than going into the *Luftwaffe* prison camps. I asked him why, and Galland just made his hand into the shape of a pistol and pulled his middle finger. "He wants them to disappear."

I could not believe what I was hearing. I remembered the Gestapo investigation into our two pilots in JG-52, which resulted in nothing, because they were believed to have been Jewish. I told him, "We cannot just kill prisoners." He agreed and asked me, "If you get that order, Steinhoff, what will you do?" I did not hesitate, and I said, "That fat bastard is out of his goddamned mind. I will never issue that order." Galland smiled, and said, "I thought so. I told him that as General of the Fighters that I would never issue that order, either."

Well, I felt uneasy at the entire conversation. Neumann spoke and said, "Why would he even think that we would do this?" Before anyone could say anything, Rödel spoke up and said, "Because he is a true Nazi bastard, that's why. I know what is going on now. I suspected for some time. I heard it from Marseille; so did *Oberst* Neumann." Edu Neumann nodded his head and said, "Yes, that is true. He told me when he came back from meeting Hitler in 1942. He overheard some SS generals talking about a camp in Poland. He told several of us. That explained why he was so protective of his friend Mathias. I know you heard that story." We all nodded our heads. It was actually a great story.

Galland then poured us all a glass of wine, I think a Riesling, and he sat down. He said, "Look, Hannes here has more information that I think you should all hear," and he looked at Trautloft. I had known Trautloft longer than anyone except Galland. He was always an honest man and an excellent officer. He was also a great friend, so I was curious as to what he had to say.

Trautloft stood up and drank his glass empty in one swallow. I knew this had to be serious, because he was not really a drinker. He said that he spent two weeks the last month on an inspection tour, checking out facilities that manufactured things for the *Luftwaffe*, places making parachutes, uniforms, ammunition—things that were sometimes hit by Allied bombing. He had to submit a report to Galland. He had been in the Ruhr, Rhineland, and Weimar, and in Weimar he went to a factory that had been untouched by the bombing. He had his driver stop the car when he saw a large camp.

He went to the gate, and this SS guard stopped him and asked him why he was there. Trautloft told him that he was appointed by the General of the Fighters to write a report for the *Reichsmarschall* on the problems with receiving *Luftwaffe* supplies. The news was that the bombing raids had stopped the manufacturing and supplies. Then he told us that he saw all of these men. Hundreds of them were in prison clothes, but he was not aware of a prison being there. He knew that it could not be a prisoner of war camp, at least not one from the *Luftwaffe*. He turned to walk away when someone called out to him in German. He turned around and it was an American airman, so he said.

This prisoner said there were over a hundred airmen in the camp, and they were going to be executed by the SS. Trautloft came closer and was speaking to him, and three other men came forward also, but they did not speak German. At that time, one of the guards yelled at the men and pointed his rifle at them and told them to get away. Trautloft told the guard to shut up, and he continued speaking with the

American. This was a bomber crewman, and he said they had been shot down and taken prisoner by some people and handed over to the SS.

Trautloft wrote some information down, and then the man pointed to the chimney and said that they were killing people there. Trautloft then asked to speak to the commandant. The officer came out and Trautloft asked him about these Americans, what in the hell was going on. The commandant said that they were criminals and not military prisoners. He said that the crematoria was to burn the dead so that disease was not a problem. Well, it made sense perhaps, but then an American prisoner said that they were killing prisoners and then burning them, and most prisoners were Jews.

The popular term then for enemy bomber pilots was *Terrorflieger*, or terror flyers, and Trautloft told us that he cited the Geneva Convention and that any enemy airmen were property of the *Luftwaffe*. The SS officer was having none of it, but Trautloft forced his way in. He went straight into the commandant's office, took the phone, and called Galland and told him what he found. Galland apparently told him to get the hell out of there and come back to Berlin immediately, but to get the names and ranks. We had heard of some things happening to enemy aircrew after they were captured when civilians caught them, bad things. This was something different.

Trautloft told the commandant, a *Hauptsturmführer*, that he would be back, and he had better hope that nothing happened to those prisoners or he would be very unhappy. I do not remember the exact words he used, but it made us all smile. The next day, Trautloft was with Galland in [*Generalfeldmarschall* Erhard] Milch's office, telling him what Trautloft had found. Galland told Milch that he wanted those men in a proper *Luftwaffe* camp. Milch said that he could put nothing in writing for Trautloft but that he would make a call and see to it.

Well, Trautloft then told us that he sent one of his officers to oversee the transfer, and he received a call that the prisoners, well over a hundred men, had been sent to a proper camp, but he did not remember which camp it was at that time. Trautloft said that he called the camp and verified that the men were there the very same day that I arrived. He had just found out. Milch had made good on his promise. They had discussed what could happen to German pilots and crews in enemy camps if this kind of thing ever happened and it became known. That made good sense, but it was also basic human decency.

We now know what the SS and Gestapo did in the camps, and that is tragic. That dishonored every German who was decent and who had to fight for his country.

That was also another uneasy moment, when Galland got into the main reason for our meeting. The reason was to force Göring down as commander of the *Luftwaffe*. The silence was very clear at that moment. He said, "We have a couple of options, von Schleich and von Greim. We all know both men. They are good Germans and hate the Party. They are not very happy with Göring and Hitler. So, who do we choose?"

That was when Lützow said, "Why don't we just shoot the bastard—Hitler too while we are at it? It would be for the best anyway." Now, remember this was just four months after the bomb plot, when Stauffenberg and the others had tried to kill Hitler. I kept silent. I did not know what to think. The SS were still collecting people and placing them in camps or shooting them, even family members of those who were just suspected of being involved.

I spoke to Falck about this, as Stauffenberg was his wife's cousin or something. He was nervous. It was one thing to argue with Göring on facts, but it was something else to openly challenge his authority. That would get a man shot. Neumann suggested Schleich, and Galland said no—he thought Greim would be better. Both were anti-Nazis and both never hid it, although Schleich was less involved in the politics than Greim. Greim understood the politics, and that would be his advantage—or so Galland thought. Both men were well thought of by Hitler, and that was important. Well, we took a vote. Greim won.

I received orders to report to Achmer again in December, where *Kommando Nowotny* had been renamed JG-7. I was appointed as *Kommodore*, for a while. That only lasted a month, and then Theo Weissenberger from JG-5 came in. We had some of the greatest aces and pilots there: Walter Schuck, Heinrich Ehrler, and Theo Weissenberger from the "North Pole," as we called it [JG-5 "*Eismeer*"], Erich Rudorffer, Georg-Peter Eder, who was our great bomber killer, Rudi Sinner, Heinz Bär, Johannes Naumann, Erich Hohagen, Hermann Buchner, Wolfgang Späte, Karl Schnörrer, Rudolf Rademacher, and others.

This was a very aggressive and talented group of guys; most were high-ranking fighter pilots with many victories and high decorations. Galland had tried to get Hartmann to join us, but he decided to stay in our old home at JG-52. Galland even tried again to get him to join us in JV-44, but he declined. I respected his decision, but it cost him. Well, it cost me also, but I will get to that.

Well, after the death of Nowotny, I took over command of JG-7 in December 1944 as *Kommodore*, and that was when it was designated JG-7, after the jets were dispersed to individual *Gruppen*. We had no sooner buried Nowotny that we had our first big *Kommodoren* meeting with Göring. The entire purpose was for Galland, as General of the Fighters, to bring his most successful wing leaders and most highly decorated fighters to show solidarity in our cause. There were quite a few of the senior *Kommodoren* there: Neumann, myself, Rödel, Trautloft, Lützow, and a few others—mostly those of us fighting the American fighters and bombers. [Trautloft had been commodore of JG-54 "*Grunherz*" until Galland appointed him as Inspector of Day Fighters].

Galland's purpose was to convince Göring of several things. First, the fighters needed the jets, not the bombers, as we were in a defensive war fighting American bombers and *Blitzkrieg* was history. Second, cutting the training time for new fighter pilots was suicidal, and Galland left their deployment up to the *Geschwaderkommodoren*.

If the leaders felt comfortable sending a young boy up, then they could, but most did not until they had more airtime. This made Göring angry. He wanted numbers in the air, regardless of how competent the pilot was. Third, Galland wanted once again to impress upon him the need to discontinue all production of the 109. Keep building the Fw-190 Doras and focus the industry upon the Me-262. Fourth, keep the SS out of our business; they had been snooping around and trying to interfere with Galland. Hell, he even had a bodyguard, as I remember.

The bomber boys were also there: Peltz, [Werner] Baumbach, and Hajo Herrmann, who had created his *Wilde Sau* the previous year. He actually supported us. As usual, Göring tried to dominate the meeting. He started talking, pointing out our failures, blaming us again for the bombings, called the pilots cowards, unworthy of their rank and medals. Galland countered with a few good points of his own, and Göring told him, in front of us, that Hitler had said this or that, and he knew better. Galland then stood up and told him that what he just said was a lie. He had just spoken to Hitler a few days earlier, and what Hitler had told him was the exact opposite.

Göring was caught in several lies. Men twisted in their seats knowing that a fuse had been lit. Galland did not stop, and he told Göring that he should resign for the good of the service, if not for the greater good of Germany. That was it. Göring asked all of us sitting there, and we fighter pilots nodded. Göring asked each of us if we agreed with him. Everyone said, "Yes," and added his own comments.

I said, "Yes, *Herr Reichsmarschall*, we are losing too many young men who have no chance of surviving, and we also do not have enough fighters or enough 262s to do what you ask. Without qualified pilots and fighters, we can only respond with what we have." Let me just say that that meeting did not go so well. [The January 1945 meeting would be the final straw, and Galland would not be invited to attend.]

When I returned to JG-7, I chose various squadron leaders, such as Rudorffer, Barkhorn, Bär, and others. We reorganized into a more efficient unit—consolidated and streamlined everything from fuel and ammunition supplies to the rotation of the mechanics who kept the jets flying. Everything was a clock timed to the minute. I then found out that my presence was requested for another meeting with Göring, and this was December. I flew to the place Galland was staying at near Wannsee, and all the usual suspects were there.

I arrived and it was snowing, and colder than hell. I landed in my fighter and drove from the airfield to the house, a nice place really. I walked up, Trautloft welcomed me, and then

I saw the old gang: Galland, Ihlefeld, Henri von Maltzahn, Edu Neumann, Gustav Rödel, and Günther Lützow. We discussed the best course of action to take. Galland informed us that Göring had said that at this next meeting [January 1945], he was not to be present. He was later fired with a phone call [after the January revolt]. That was how the Fat One worked.

Well, we all decided and voted previously on whom we would ask to approach Hitler and demand Göring's removal. We had to choose someone the *Luftwaffe* would accept, and someone that Hitler respected. We also had to consider choosing someone who was not an insider, who could be swayed by Hitler. We definitely had to have someone who was not sympathetic to the Nazis. We also knew that our selection had to have the approval in the minds of the German people. Many people were supportive of Hitler and the Nazis to some degree before the war, but fewer were part of that support as the war went on. We also knew that the average German still had respect for the old aristocracy, and that had to be considered.

We were previously divided between von Greim and von Schleich. Schleich would have won the vote only because he was the farthest removed from the Berlin crowd and had the *Pour le Mérite*, like Greim, and a lot of credibility. He was also just a good, honest man. So was Greim, but we had word that his health was not good. We decided to approach Schleich first. If he said no, for whatever reason, then Greim was the second choice. Rödel said, "I could care less who replaces that fat bastard. In fact, we had a bear in our unit that had a better grasp on the daily condition than Göring. At least he never bit the hand that fed him." We laughed at that, and Neumann said, "That is true." That made us laugh even harder.

Some of us had been planning this coup against Göring for a long time, but we had to be careful. We knew what we were risking, and that also placed our families in danger. I did not tell my wife much because I thought that the less she knew, the safer she would be. I was, in fact, one of the few married men involved, which meant that I had far more to lose. After planning our move, just before Christmas I went with Galland, Lützow, Trautloft, Osterkamp, Rödel, Neumann, and others to Berlin to see *Generaloberst* [later *Generalfeldmarschall*] Robert *Ritter* von Greim, von Schleich, and even von Richthofen in order to have Göring removed and replaced, but this did not happen.

During another meeting, von Greim told us in January 1945, just before the revolt, that it was too late, and that Adolf Hitler would never remove one of his oldest and most loyal friends from his post. Well, all of us did have that previous meeting with Göring in November of 1944, if I am correct. We tried to explain to him the failures of his programs, the stupidity of not giving us the 262 for the fighters, and the even more stupid decision to reduce the training time and qualifications for fighter pilots.

I could not believe what I was hearing, and I was not alone. Our chief was telling us that we did not need the jets, since the bombers were going to strike the Allied airfields and destroy their air power on the ground. He also waved off any suggestion that young pilots needed any more than thirty or so hours flying time to go into combat. He had less than that in the First World War, when the aircraft and combat methods were far less involved and far less complicated.

I remember telling him, "Yes, *Herr Reichsmarshall*, but this is a very different war than the last one, and we are fighting far greater numbers of the enemy, and the aircraft are far more advanced and difficult to fly. Even Osterkamp and von Schleich said so. The training requirement for pilots is far more extensive that in the past." He did not want to hear any of this. I already disliked him, and now I personally hated him. The thought crossed my mind that if I were single and had no responsibilities, I could just shoot him and be done with him.

This was what eventually led to the Fighters' Revolt against Göring later [in January 1945]. Even Theo Osterkamp was with us, as he was Inspector of Ground Operations for the *Luftwaffe*. He even went head to head against Göring, telling him that he had better listen to us. We spoke for the entire fighter force, and his ideas were getting men killed for no reason. Göring fired him on the spot at the end of December. He told me what happened. He said to Göring, "I would rather resign with my honor than follow you into disaster." That was a real leader, and he spoke exactly what we were thinking.

First, I went back to JG-7 and had everything ready, so on New Year's Day I handed over the command to Weissenberger. This was also the day of Operation Bodenplatte, but I did not participate. I said my goodbyes to the men. You have to understand that for the guys in the unit, because we were so far removed from the normal *Luftwaffe*, things like rules and discipline were not as rigid as in the old days. They knew their jobs, and rather than have men waste time shining boots, I preferred them working on the fighters and working out tactical issues.

After Operation Bodenplatte I returned to Italy, and a couple of weeks later I received a call from Milch, telling me to get to Berlin immediately and bring Neumann and Rödel with me. I told them of the call. Normally we would receive a teletype with orders like that, rather than just a call. There was a reason, and I was worried that I knew what it was.

Once again, all of the usual guys were there. I asked them what was going on, and Galland said that we had another meeting with Göring, and this time Hitler ordered the meeting and chose all of the participants. Galland also gave us some good inside information. He told us so many things that my head was swimming. He said that Göring had tapped his telephone and there was a rumor, which he found credible, that Göring would try to have him killed and make it look like an accident. I had to speak, and I asked how did he know?

Well, Galland had always been on very good terms with many of the higher-ranking members of the other branches. The navy admired him for his work in 1942 during the *Scharnhorst* and *Gneisenau* operations. *Gruppenführer* Felix Steiner had always liked Galland, and it was through him that he confirmed what Albert Speer told Galland about the telephone taps, and Steiner said he was well aware of the assassination plot. Steiner was going to send him a personal handpicked man as a bodyguard.

Apparently, Steiner hated Göring as much as we did, perhaps even more. His *Waffen* SS troops had suffered badly when told to stay in place because the *Luftwaffe* transportation aircraft would drop supplies to help them continue fighting the Russians. The supplies never came, and Steiner's 5th SS Division was forced to fight a retreating battle, taking heavy casualties to break out of an encirclement, all because of the delays and promises by Göring. Steiner also later stated that he learned of the mass killings going on behind the lines. He had spoken with [*Obergruppenführer* Wilhelm] Bittrich about the policies they were given. Both men refused to follow those orders, much to their credit. They hated Himmler even more than Göring, and I later learned that they were at least aware of, if not involved in, in the bomb plot to kill Hitler. It was a crazy time.

Well, even without Galland, we still had the Fighters' Revolt. The next day we met with Göring again, and this meeting was just as worthless as the last. All of us were there except Galland. Trautloft was there with Lützow, who was the designated spokesman. Galland was apparently on the phone in the outer office, where Trautloft would give him information every so often as he went and gathered more files, which had been carefully staged so as to give him the excuse.

Göring gave the nod for Lützow to begin the briefing. I am not sure what Göring thought this meeting was about, but he quickly realized that it was something he did not want to hear. Lützow began discussing the aircraft and pilot shortages, and then the fuel and munitions. Göring waved his hand and said that he already knew about those problems. Lützow told him that if he interrupted and started his long, windy discussions then we would be wasting our time. Lützow also reminded him that Hitler had called the meeting, not him. This was the fighter pilots' day to be heard, not to be lectured.

Then Lützow began pointing out some great errors in judgment, and just very stupid decisions that Göring and others had made. He also brought up the ridiculous scapegoating of the fighter force. Lützow then made it very clear that he had to step down for the good of the service. Well, that did it, I can tell you. Göring then looked at me and asked if I agreed, and I told him that not only did I agree that he should step down, I told him that we should also be the people who chose his successor. Göring's face turned purple, deep red, and black. I thought he was going to explode from a heart attack or something. I was silently praying that would happen. Only Lützow could bring that kind of madness out of Göring. His sweat was pouring off of his fat cheeks and dripping onto the table. He was actually foaming at the mouth.

He screamed at Lützow that he would have him shot and also Galland as an example, and then he turned on me and said that he would see to it that I was fixed also. He banished me from Germany, back to Italy as a punishment. I was very happy to be there, and I enjoyed my exile for a while. Well, as you know, Göring was never replaced until later in the year, ironically by Greim, anyway. Göring threatened to court-martial me and told Lützow that he would be shot for treason.

Hitler ordered me, or rather banished me, to Italy for my own safety along with Lützow, and Trautloft was sent packing back to the East. Galland was replaced as *General der Jagdflieger* by *Oberst* Gordon Gollob, who was a competent fighter and leader but was a fervent supporter of Hitler and a nasty little man who was hated by almost everyone, including me. Needless to say, none of us *Kommodoren* were very enthusiastic about it, and we refused to accept it. All of the leaders remained loyal to Galland and stayed in contact with him, which infuriated Gollob and Göring, since it showed that the highest ranking and most decorated men in the fighter force were still going to do things their way.

I, of course, had been sent back to Italy and fired from my job with the jets at Achmer. Then Galland recalled me when he had permission from Hitler to create his own "Squadron of Experts," which was not the original intent, but this is the way it worked out. With Hitler's approval, Galland gave me full authorization to scrounge and recruit the best pilots possible. I went to every bar and recreation hall, even a few hospitals and forward units, until I had about seventeen or so volunteers, with more on the way. The list was impressive, and among this group were two or three inexperienced jet pilots, but they showed promise. I heard that Göring was never even informed.

Göring was a good, brilliant leader before the war started. He was a great ace from the first war, and he was very energetic and important in the buildup of the *Luftwaffe* in the 1930s, but during the Battle of Britain he became lazy. Göring started collecting artwork, diamonds, and precious stones and was no longer interested in the operation of the *Luftwaffe*. Toward the end of the war, he was a nuisance, and I personally hated him. Many pilots died needlessly because of him, killed before they were able to lead.

I must say that JV-44 was unique. Most of us had many kills. Nine of us had over 100 victories; a couple, such as [Heinz] Bär, had over 200; and Barkhorn had 301. Everyone, except a couple, had the Knight's Cross or higher decorations and hundreds of missions; and most of us were senior officers led by a squadron leader with the rank of lieutenant general. It was quite a unit, and I do not think there will ever be another one like it.

JV-44 and JG-7 were pretty much the same, I would say. The only significant difference was that in JV-44 we could create our own tactics on the spot to counter any new threat, whereas in conventional units you had to wait for a recommendation to be approved, and then the tactics had to be authorized, which wasted valuable time. We found that attacking from the flank, entering the enemy formation from the side, and attacking with rockets brought many good results. It was like blasting geese with a shotgun.

Attacking from the rear was also good, although at that angle targets offered a lower profile. When attacking from the side, we would lead the bombers a little, fire the rockets, then pull up or away and swing around for a rear pass on the survivors, where we fired our 30mm cannon. This would shred the bombers' wings or explode their bombs. Against fighters, one cannon shell was usually sufficient to bring it down.

I was angry as hell about these damned rockets. When they worked, they worked beautifully, but when they did not, then it was like carrying a few hundred pounds of rubbish, increasing my drag and reducing my speed and aerodynamic capabilities. I spoke with Galland about this, and he completely agreed, as did many others in JG-7 and JV-44.

Once we let the rockets go, we picked up an extra eighty to one hundred kilometers per hour, which was our life insurance against the American fighter escorts. However, if these damned things did not fire, you could not just jettison them as you would a bomb, and they would hang up [get stuck and not disengage] from time to time. One mission against the heavy bombers comes to mind in particular.

So here I am, going into a perfect three-quarter flank attack, lined up wonderfully, knowing that I have Mustangs and whatever else coming down on me. I know that when I fire I will hit or maybe even destroy something, and I can then pick up my air speed and climb away from the attack on my six o'clock. But then nothing happens, and I am going too fast to switch to guns at that time [from rockets]. This requires me to come around for another attack. This is bad, because now they not only know I am there, they know my intentions, and they know from which direction I will arrive.

I return to the attack and brace myself for the impact of .50-caliber bullets hitting my aircraft from the gunners on the bombers. Even with incidents like this, I did manage to get seven victories in the jet before I was out of the war.

Yet, even if we had built Me-262 in greater numbers, we did not have the trained pilots, or even the fuel, to take full advantage of them. It was too late in the war, and we could not win. However, if we had had the jets in 1943, things would have been different, I am sure, but that was not to be. It was only possible to use the jet airplane as a fighter [as opposed to Hitler's "Blitz Bomber"], as Galland was able to prove later in the war.

Then, of course, Himmler issued an order to have the jet program placed under the SS. It was an insane idea. It was nonsense; it was not possible. The training time required and the personnel made it unfeasible. Günther Lützow, Galland, Trautloft, and myself as well as many others were deeply involved. We were upset because the *Luftwaffe* was torn to pieces. Morale was poor, Galland was standing all alone, and the importance of the fighters was negligible [due to overwhelming Allied air superiority]. It was a very bad time.

I was shot down twelve times during the war. I only bailed out once. I never trusted the parachutes. I had always preferred landing my damaged planes, hoping not to get bounced on the way down when I lost power. I was wounded only once lightly, but never seriously until the thirteenth and last incident, when I almost died from the crash on takeoff. I almost did not make that mission.

Many writers have covered this crash, but hardly anyone has ever asked me about it, except for Raymond Toliver and Trevor Constable, so here is the true story. I was taking off in formation on April 18, 1945, for my nine hundredth mission.

Galland was leading the flight, which included Gerhard Barkhorn, Klaus Neumann, Krupinski, Eduard Schallmoser, Ernst Fährmann, a few others, and myself. We were to fly formation and engage an American bomber formation.

Our airfield had suffered some damage over the last several days due to Allied bombing and strafing attacks, and as my jet was picking up speed, the left undercarriage struck a poorly patched crater. I lost the wheel, and the plane jumped perhaps a meter into the air, so I tried to raise the remaining right wheel. I was too low to abort takeoff, and my speed had not increased enough to facilitate takeoff. I knew as I came toward the end of the runway that I was going to crash.

The 262 hit with a great thump, then a fire broke out in the cockpit as it skidded to a stop. I tried to unfasten my belts when an explosion rocked the plane, and I felt an intense heat. My twenty-four R4M rockets had exploded, and the fuel was burning me alive. I remember popping the canopy and jumping out, flames all around me, and I fell down and began to roll. The explosions continued, and the concussion was deafening, knocking me down as I tried to get up and run away. I cannot describe the pain. Men began pouring cold water on me, I remember, but that is all I recall until much later.

I remember lying there, wishing someone would end it all, and then Barkhorn was whispering in my ear. He reminded me that I had to live for Ursula and the children. He said I was strong, I would live, and the men would be with me. I also heard Punski saying something, but I do not know what it was. They thought I would die. Even the surgeons had no idea that I would survive, but I tricked them.

In 1969, a British doctor, a plastic surgeon, made new eyelids for me from the skin on my forearm. From the time of the crash until then, I could not close my eyes, so I wore dark glasses to protect them. I had dozens of surgeries over the years, and I recently had a heart [valve replacement] surgery, as you know, which delayed our new interview. I am now full of spare parts, you could say.

The strange thing about the war was that we pilots, from both sides, never really hated each other. I used to meet with Douglas Bader, Robert Stanford Tuck, and Johnny Johnson quite frequently, as well as many American aces such as Francis Gabreski, Hubert "Hub" Zemke, and others. We are all old men, wiser and appreciative that no one holds anyone to blame for anything. We are a small fraternity, and we are all good friends.

We never had any really bad fighter leaders, just a few who were much better than others were. You could not reach that position if you were not tested and deemed competent. Some of these men I flew with, and others I knew only by reputation. Some were better than others, such as Hrabak, who was outstanding, as was Neumann, for example. These were excellent administrators and leaders, as well as pilots. Joachim Müncheberg was also outstanding. Yes, he was a very good leader, very successful. He was killed when his Me-109 lost a wing in combat over Tunisia, fighting against the Americans. I took over the unit, which I had served in before. I became *Kommodore* of JG-77 not long after that.

Galland being fired and replaced by Gollob was a black day for the fighters. Losses soared under his leadership everywhere he went, much like Göring in the first war. He placed leaders in command of units not because of their competence but because of their loyalty to the Nazi Party, which was minimal in the *Jagdwaffe* [fighter arm].

Galland was an energetic man, a strong leader and great fighter, successful, loyal to his men, and a most honorable and honest gentleman, but a playboy. He was never awed by Hitler or swayed by Göring, and he always answered truthfully when they questioned him on any subject, regardless of how unpopular the truth might have been. Galland was a visionary who knew how to turn the tide in the air war and how to rebuild the fighter force, but his standing beside his pilots against Göring and Hitler, as well as many others, gave Hitler cause to replace him, which was a bad mistake. Honesty in Berlin was not always fashionable.

At the time of my crash, I had 176 victories, with 7 in the jet. I never thought I would serve in uniform again afterward. I spent two years in the hospital after the crash, and I was still in my bed when I was approached by Trautloft and others. They convinced me that I could do much more outside the hospital than inside, so I decided to once again wear a uniform. The Communist threat was still a large factor, and as years went by we saw the Cold War more clearly than you in America did. It was right next door to us.

I eventually became a NATO Air Commander and retired as a four-star general. As you may know, the F-104 argument was one of the things that should have killed my career. I was opposed to it, as was Hartmann, and those reasons are well known. We were also opposed to the entire *Luftwaffe* being managed by bomber types and, in most cases, men who had never flown combat. These were tense times, and the high leadership knew nothing about war. You Americans were a lot smarter, placing your combat leaders as command authorities later. That is the way it should always be. Later in life, I wrote my books, of course, and I enjoy painting and visiting my grandchildren in America.

I used to go on many speaking engagements, traveling to all of the seminars, speaking to young people and telling them about what we did. I like meeting young people. They are the future, and we should take care of them. I always enjoyed my time in America, both as a pilot and as a tourist. I wish we had your weather in California or Florida here in Germany.

I would tell the younger generations this: Love your country and fight for your country. Believe in truth, and that is enough.

A Leader of Aces

Generalmajor Dietrich Anton Hrabak
December 19, 1914–September 15, 1995
1,077 missions, 543 combats, 125 kills
Knight's Cross, Oak Leaves (Nr 337)

A YOUTHFUL INTEREST IN aviation and adventure led Dietrich "Dieter" Anton Hrabak to serve in two of the most successful *Jagdgeschwader*, or fighter wings, in the German *Luftwaffe*—JG-54 and JG-52—during World War II. He distinguished himself by his leadership and his fighting doctrine, which combined careful tactical evaluation with a philosophy of "hit first, hit hard, and bring your men home alive." His 125 aerial victories were a modest score by JG-52 standards, but that was partly because of his habit of giving credit for a disputed kill to the other pilot. In a 1993 interview with Colin D. Heaton, Dieter Hrabak—who died on September 15, 1995—described his flying career.

I was born on December 19, 1914, in a small village near Leipzig in Saxony. During the first four years of my life, my father was an infantryman, fighting in France during World War I. My mother, sister, and I lived on a farm, and my sister was a year older than I was. After the war, we had a very difficult time, as did everyone, and when my father returned he started his own business, a construction firm building homes. The terrible inflation and underemployment made it very hard on us. We continued on like this until I joined the service, and my father's business continued until the outbreak of World War II. As for me, I went to school, and after nine years in a public school I attended the Queen Carola Gymnasium in Leipzig, which is similar to your high school, until Easter of 1934. We studied Latin, Greek, and English.

I was about sixteen when I began to visit all the existing air bases near Leipzig, including Dessau, where the Junkers Company developed its famous airplanes, and I studied everything. My friends all wanted to be pilots, and most joined glider clubs, but I did not. That was how we trained later, before powered aircraft. I was always interested in following the aviation pioneers, like Lindbergh, rather than the military pilots. I wanted to be one of those.

The year before I finished gymnasium, in the summer of 1933, I tried to get a place in one of the two training centers for commercial pilots, but without success. There was no air force academy, as Germany was not allowed to have an air force in the years after the Great War. However, I did get a hint that there might be a buildup of a new air force in Germany in the future, and I was advised to contact the navy, or *Kriegsmarine*.

In April 1934, I started my military career as a naval officer candidate, and my next-door neighbor was another cadet named Johannes Steinhoff, and later in November 1935 I transferred to the new *Luftwaffe* and began my flight training in Ludwigslust again with Steinhoff. We have been close ever since. We also attended advanced flight and fighter training, with a few of the originals like Herbert Ihlefeld, Walter Oesau, Josef Priller, Heinz Bär, Walther Dahl, Adolf Galland, and others. I think everything went rather normally. I had two major accidents, however.

As a young *Leutnant*, I was stationed with a fighter group at Bernburg, with the Heinkel He-51, the older biplane. During a training mission, we encountered heavy ground fog, and due to a fuel shortage I was forced down into it, and I crashed into a building. The aircraft was totally destroyed, and I had a slight injury to my left eye that put me out of action for three months. Incidentally, Adolf Galland was with us as the technical officer, and he had crashed just two days before due to the same conditions, using the same type of aircraft.

This was the time when the operational fighter wing was created. Each wing had three *Gruppen*, sometimes four. Each *Gruppe* had three squadrons, or *Staffeln*, each with twelve to fifteen aircraft. Our *Geschwader* would be a "Group" in the American and British air forces.

My second accident occurred about two years later when I had my first flight in a Messerschmitt Me-109E, after having flown the Bf-109D model earlier. This was at Bernburg. The Daimler Benz engine was more powerful in the E type, and during takeoff I realized this rather suddenly—breaking the undercarriage away during a group loop. That was not a good start.

After about a half a year at Bernburg and another six months at Bad Aibling just southeast of Munich, I was transferred with the fighter group to Vienna in mid-March 1938.

Bad Aibling was a good place, and Hannes Trautloft was my squadron leader. This was before he and Galland joined the *Legion Kondor*. And Priller was there with us again, as well as Steinhoff. This was the Vienna *Jagdgruppe*, I./JG-138. I was made *Adjutant*. This unit was later changed to I./JG-76 during the Polish Campaign. It was changed again, becoming II./JG-54 in April 1940, just before the Battle for France started in May.

There we protected the Junker Ju-52/3m used by Adolf Hitler, flying escort. At Aspern, we were mixed together with Austrian *Jagdgeschwader* (JG) 2 and split into two groups. One stayed in Vienna; the other returned to Bad Aibling. At this time, I became *Adjutant* of the Vienna group, designated as a *Gruppe* of *Zerstörergeschwader* [destroyer wing or ZG] 76, until World War II broke out. On April 1, 1939, I took command of the first *Staffel* [*Jagd*], or 1(J)/ZG-76, which consisted mostly of Austrians. I was then an *Oberleutnant* and a squadron leader, or as we say, a *Staffelkapitän*. They were excellent, well-trained personnel.

Just before the war erupted, our unit moved to Upper Silesia, northeast of Breslau, which is now part of Poland and called Wrozlau. We flew our first missions in the campaign against Poland from an emergency airfield. The first two days of combat, we did not see a single enemy plane, but on the third day, while I was flying a four-plane fighter sweep, we received a radio call that Polish bombers were attacking German ground troops.

We flew to the area concerned and saw three PZL P-23s, and I immediately attacked the one in the center. However, I did this in a thoughtless, childish way, and before I could begin firing, the rear gunner shot my engine dead. The cockpit filled with smoke, forcing me to jettison the canopy and crash-land on the battlefield between the lines. I then ran away to hide in a nearby wood until our ground troops came and picked me up. So I learned my first lesson: "Think before you start an attack and use your head, not your muscles." I was shot down seven times in the war but never used my parachute. I was lucky that I was never badly wounded also.

My first victory was on May 12, 1940, in the French campaign, the third day after the invasion began. We took off from our base near Trier along the Mosel River. I was again flying in a four-ship formation over the Sedan region, where our mission was to protect the bridges spanning the Maas River. Here we encountered a Potez 63, a twin-engine, light reconnaissance plane. I was the first to attack, then the other three joined in. I fired and saw smoke coming from the left engine.

Well, the Potez belly-landed and the crew got out, near some of our own troops, but we wanted to see the aircraft burn, so after the crew was safe, we strafed the plane, setting it afire. We shot all our ammunition into this cripple. It seems that at that time I had forgotten my own advice of "use your head," because we were suddenly jumped by nine Curtiss P-36 [H-75A] fighters of the French air service. All we could do was open our throttles and run like hell for our home base.

It was stupid, but it's not only age, it's also gaining experience; you learn from each flight. Well, the war went on in France until June, but it was over Dunkirk that we faced the British Supermarine Spitfire for the first time. We were to protect our ground troops [who were] taking bridges and securing roads for the panzers. In the heavy air battle that followed, I lost two of my pilots—those were the first losses of my squadron—without any compensating success. This was also a learning experience, and it made me very cautious in future fights against Spitfires.

My second engagement against Spitfires was in the area north of Rouen, where I detected quite a large formation of Spitfires in a formation we called the "idiot snake"—one plane flying behind the other at a slightly lower altitude, weaving back and forth. I went to attack what I thought was the last plane, but another shot out my cooling system, which was a vulnerable part of the Me-109. I had to crash-land when my engine seized up.

After the French campaign ended, I was stationed near Rotterdam for a month to protect the oil refineries. On August 8, 1940, just five days before *Adler Tag* [an all-out *Luftwaffe* effort to eliminate the Royal Air Force], I transferred to an emergency field just south of Calais. This was still 1(J)ZG-76, yet we had been assigned to JG-2 and we flew missions against England until November 30, 1940. The fighting was very tough over the Channel, and we lost many pilots. Much of this was due to our orders coming from Göring. He wanted the fighters to stay with the bombers, to scare away the British fighters. The opposite happened.

The Hurricanes would go for the Dorniers and Heinkels, especially the Stukas, and the Spitfires would keep us busy. The only way to stay alive was to violate that stupid order. Some of the leaders, like Max Ibel and Galland, ignored the orders, and their pilots had great success. The RAF was a very professional group of pilots, and a couple of these fights were my toughest of the war in a one-on-one fight.

One fight I remember very well. In July 1940, my *Schwarm* was about two thousand meters above a Do-17 formation. We saw the Hurricanes climbing to attack and the Spitfires climbing to reach us. I told two of my pilots to engage the six

Hurricanes. My wingman, what we call a *Rottenflieger*, and I would take on the four Spitfires. We rolled over to attack as they climbed. I fired into one, and he was smoking; the Spitfire my wingman hit exploded. The other two flew past us, between us, and they turned around to dive on us. We then pulled up, using our diving speed to get more altitude.

I looked back and this Spitfire was only twenty meters behind me. I saw his guns flash. The vapor of his rounds went past my cockpit, and I heard a few thumps, but then my wingman shot him down. But then he, in turn, was shot down by the other Spitfire. I managed to roll away and shoot down the Spitfire who shot down my wingman. It sounds confusing, but that is how air fighting was. My two men who were shot down parachuted into the Channel and were picked up safely. I had one confirmed victory, one damaged and probable. Later, the second was confirmed by a bomber crew. Four of the Hurricanes were shot down and two were damaged. I had over a dozen holes in my fighter but nothing was seriously damaged, although my engine died and the landing gear was shot away. I slid into a nice landing.

This fight had been in the middle of August during a rejuvenation of all command position within fighter command proper, as ordered from Berlin. It was at this time that Hannes Trautloft became *Kommodore* of JG-54 "*Grunherz*" [Green Hearts], and I became *Gruppenkommandeur* of II./JG-54 in July 1940, so I knew him very well and held him in high esteem.

As a *Gruppenkommandeur*, to receive the Knight's Cross I had to have at least fifteen aerial victories. But this requirement would change as the war went on. I had already received the Iron Cross in both first and second classes. I received the Knight's Cross after my sixteenth victory—six in the Battle of France and ten in the Battle of Britain—and I was very proud to be the first pilot in JG-54 to receive the decoration. I had to drive all the way to *Reichsmarschall* Hermann Göring's command train, which at the time was stationed near Beauvais. With me was my very good friend and excellent fighter pilot named Josef Priller, whom we called "Fips" or "Pips." Priller ended the war with 101 victories, all flying against the Western Allies. At this time, he was a squadron leader in JG-26 "*Schlageter*" with Galland and others. He was getting his Knight's Cross also.

In 1940, Göring was a large, alert, and interested person, wanting details of the fighting and what we thought about enemy aircraft and our own new models. But this changed as the war went on, and he became lethargic, lazy, and disinterested in everything except himself. He became a joke to the fighter pilots, and some even said so to his face. But when I received my Knight's Cross, he asked detailed and interesting questions. I could see that he was keen to learn about the new war in the air from all the pilots he spoke with. My first impression of him was positive, but that would change later. I learned to detest him, to be honest.

I left the Channel on November 30, 1940, when JG-54 moved back to northern Germany. I then returned to France. We were in need of a serious replenishment of pilots and serviceable aircraft, as our losses had been high. We then returned to Germany again. The pilots and ground crews went on leave, and this was when I got married, which I guess would qualify as my next combat area, don't you think?

In the second half of January 1941, we were sent to Le Mans and Cherbourg in northwest France, but this was only until the war was carried into Yugoslavia in April 1941. We did not encounter any enemy aircraft. We flew ground attack missions and strafing missions, as well as reconnaissance, none of which was interesting to us fighter pilots. I do, however, remember hearing about a couple of pilots who encountered enemy-flown Messerschmitts that Germany had sold to them before the war—older [Me-109E-3] models. They did not have self-sealing fuel tanks or protective armor plating for the pilot, so it was easy to kill them.

After Yugoslavia was defeated, we handed over our aircraft to the fighter units continuing the war against Greece and Crete. II./JG-54 transferred by car and train to Stolp Reitz air base in northeast Germany, where we received our new Me-109Fs. I was promoted to *Hauptmann* and took charge of a *Gruppe*. I had great men under me, such as Hans Philipp. He was a character, as was Walter Nowotny, who had the Diamonds.

Before taking over JG-52, I had fought with JG-54 for over a year on the Leningrad Front, after the invasion of Russia on June 22, 1941 until October 1, 1942, when I was promoted to *Major* and took over command of JG-52 in the southern region from [Hubertus] von Bonin. This was where I again joined Steinhoff, I again met Krupinski, met Rall and many others who would become our greatest aces. This was where I also met Erich Hartmann, when he joined us later. Steinhoff, Graf, Barkhorn, Rall, and Krupinski had been with JG-52 during the Battles of Britain and France. Ihlefeld was there also, and he and Steinhoff both told us stories about Marseille, who had been with both of them. Marseille had become famous by then, the most famous pilot in Germany.

I would call the Leningrad Front rather quiet, static, since we were not required to continuously move from one base to another in order to fly our missions. In the south, however, it was a fast war. We flew at first from Kharkov to the

Stalingrad area in the north, then to the Caucasus Mountains and the Black Sea. My base was near the Caspian Sea. We were sort of a fire brigade, as the front was always moving back and forth, and we were expected to be at every spot that was burning—to put out the fire, so to speak. During my two years as *Kommodore* of JG-52, I flew from forty-seven different airfields.

There was a great difference between fighting the British and the Russians. I think the first and foremost thing to consider was the psychological factor: The British were a fair people and acted according to the rules of war under the Geneva and Hague conventions, especially concerning treatment of prisoners of war, the International Red Cross, et cetera. With the Soviets, however, we never knew if we would survive being down behind their lines or not, and history has proved that there was no such adherence to those regulations, or even the simple humane treatment of another warrior.

Well, I must say that the really experienced Russians who had been thoroughly trained in peacetime were killed off in the first three months of the invasion. Those who remained flew obsolete aircraft such as the Tupolev SB, which we called the "Martin Bomber," and the Ilyushin DB-3 bombers, as well as old Polikarpov I-15 and I-16 Rata fighters, and used no tactics whatsoever. Further, the Russians lacked the technical training and combat skill that the British had mastered early in the war. The Russians had no stomach for the prolonged dogfight, unlike the British. Later in the war, however, a new breed of Russian pilots emerged, flying excellent native aircraft. The best Russia had were placed in elite Red Banner fleets, and they claimed many German pilots.

Of my over one thousand missions, I can recall some Russian pilots with great clarity. My memories of fighting the Red Banner boys are the most vivid. We were flying in the south in a large formation. We had about fifty 109s in the air, from two *Gruppen*, on a massive fighter sweep to intercept Russian bombers attacking ground forces. We ran into about twenty bombers and over fifty enemy fighters. We were also relieving an Fw-190 unit that had already been fighting the bombers as they came in. We were to catch the bombers on their way home.

I led my squadron into a flight of Yaks, and we also saw a large number of LaGGs farther below, and the Pe-2s were heading east. The fight was incredible. Within two minutes, a dozen enemy aircraft were falling; parachutes were all over the sky. I shot down one and the pilot jumped, only to be struck by his wingman. The propeller tore into his body, and that pilot also had to get out. He also jumped, and I had to pull up to avoid hitting him—as did Krupinski, who was on my left.

Then we saw a 190 smoking, then catch fire. The pilot pulled up and safely left the fighter. His parachute opened, but then a Yak pilot flew right past us and shot that German pilot to pieces in his parachute. We were all shocked at this. Suddenly I heard Krupinski say "that bastard," and he rolled away from me. I called for him to return to the formation, but no response. I then followed him with the rest of the men. Krupi closed in and blew that Yak fighter apart, and then he seemed to go mad. He then threw himself into five other Yaks, shooting down another. Barkhorn was right behind him, covering him, and he had also shot down two Yaks on top of the previous LaGG kill he had made just a few minutes before.

I heard Hartmann call out a victory, then Rall, Steinhoff, Grislawski, Rossmann, and others. Everyone had a kill, but that was not on my mind. We finally broke contact. We did not shoot down a single bomber, but we had shot down about twenty enemy fighters, losing one pilot and fighter, with five fighters returning badly damaged. One 190 pilot managed to crash-land and climb out as the enemy strafed his fighter and tried to strafe him. He ran faster than anyone I ever saw to make it to the German soldiers, with the Russian soldiers chasing him and firing at him. The German soldiers held their fire until he was safe, and then they just opened up with machine guns and cut the thirty or so Russians down quickly, but there were many more behind them. Over a hundred would be my guess. There were too many of them.

Soon, both groups were in horrible hand-to-hand fighting. I ordered the men with me to cover our soldiers and strafe when safe to do so. We each made a pass and flew low, firing into the enemy. The scene was horrible, but it had to be done. Then my guns were silent. I was out of ammunition. Radio calls came in from the others. They were empty as well. I ordered the men to continue flying low, making passes. I thought that at least it would divert their attention. Then the low-fuel warnings came on. I told the men to return to our airfield. I thought at that time how happy I was not to be in the infantry.

Well, I landed and then ordered Krupinski to report to me with his *Abschuss*. The others were all writing theirs as well. Von Bonin was there as was Trautloft, who had just arrived that morning. Krupinski came in, and I chewed him out. Then I told him that I understood how he felt. The others and I saw what had happened. However, I explained to him that the moment a fighter pilot loses control of his emotions, he ceases to be clear-thinking and effective. I patted him on the shoulder and he apologized for breaking formation without permission. That was the end of it.

The air battles around Stalingrad from September 1942 into the next year were horrible. Graf was the best pilot during that time, and he received the Oak Leaves, Swords, and then the Diamonds after being the first pilot to shoot down two hundred airplanes. I saw many of his kills. He was a very good and aggressive pilot, but he was not really a dogfighter—more like an ambush hunter. The same with Krupinski and Hartmann; most of the great aces were like that. Barkhorn and Steinhoff were real exceptions. They were dogfighters.

Steinhoff, Barkhorn, Rossmann, and I all attacked this IL-2 once. We emptied every bullet and cannon round into this thing, and it still did not go down. We learned later that you had to either kill the pilot or hit the oil cooler. That would shut the engine down very quickly. Then I heard a voice over the radio telling me, "You cannot bite a porcupine in the ass." It was Hartmann, who watched, and had become very good at shooting them down.

I was informed that I was to receive the Oak Leaves, and I was quite pleased. Many of my pilots already had this award and even the Swords, and now I would join them. However, this news was somewhat darkened by another of the Gestapo visits. They wanted to speak to Rall. I was unaware of the reason, but I demanded to be there when they spoke with him. The two Gestapo men really had no problem with that.

Well, I called Rall in and he reported. He was always a good pilot, a great and honest man. Then they began asking him questions about his wife, Hertha, who had also been his doctor after he was shot down in November 1941. After almost a year, he recovered and came back to JG-52. Apparently, Hertha was being investigated for assisting

Jews, in Vienna as well as inside Germany, leave for Belgium, Denmark, or England for many years, even before the war. They wanted to know what Rall knew about this. I could tell by the look on his face that he knew nothing about it. He laughed and told them that they must be insane. How could they even come to this conclusion, and why would it even matter? After the war, we learned that it was true, and that she had never told him about any of that to protect him.

They were convinced that he knew nothing about any of this, and it was probably a mistake. I was sickened by the whole affair. I asked the men to leave, as their presence was not really a good thing for the pilots. I also remember telling them that this was becoming a bad habit.

Just afterward, I was ordered to Hitler's forward headquarters in Vinniza in the Ukraine in November 1943 for the award of the Oak Leaves to my Knight's Cross. When I landed my 109, I was informed that Hitler had already left and returned to the *Wolfschanze* [Wolf's Lair, his East Prussian headquarters]. Well, I left my fighter there and continued my journey in a courier plane, and of all people I met [Junker Ju-87 Stuka pilot] Hans-Ulrich Rudel, who, along with his gunner [*Stabsfeldwebel* Erwin] Hentschel, had been ordered there for the same reason.

He was the most highly decorated pilot Germany had during the war, winning the Knight's Cross with Oak Leaves, Swords, Diamonds, and Golden Oak Leaves with Diamonds. Rudel was a true fanatic up to the last day. We used to fly missions for his dive bombers, and just watching him you could see it. He brought along his gunner to meet Hitler. Rudel had requested that Hentschel be awarded the Knight's Cross, but it never arrived. [Hentschel drowned when Rudel was forced down in the Dnieper River in the winter of 1944.

They tried to swim across in sub-zero weather in a strong current, along with the crew from another crashed Ju-87.]

After we all had received our decorations, we had lunch with Hitler and several of his staff. He [Hitler] was very serious, hardly laughing or showing any humor, but this was after we had lost Stalingrad and the 6th Army—and the North African Front. I had also flown during the Battle of Kursk, and we lost that battle also, even though we had great success in the air. We had great numbers of victories, but we were far too outnumbered.

He asked us about our units, families, where we came from, and what our opinions were of the war at the front. I was very reserved, but Rudel discussed this issue as if it were a great crusade, amazing me. I was more amazed that Hitler seemed to enjoy the talk, as if defeat could be averted through this man. It was very interesting. I remembered what many of the others had said about Hitler after meeting him [regarding his delusion], and most were of the same opinion. After this, we had coffee with Hitler alone, and after some conversation, we left to return to our units.

I recall once that Hartmann had taken off in a new fighter, and then returned almost immediately. He claimed he detected a problem. I was skeptical and decided to take off in this fighter myself. I had just lifted off when the engine blew, and I landed. I never doubted him again. Then there was the time he was missing. We were sure that he had been captured. A few days later, I received a call from a *Waffen* SS officer telling me that Hartmann was with his men. That was good news because [Heinz] Mertens had gone off without permission to find him. I decided not to punish him when he came back. Mertens looked like a destroyed man. That kind of loyalty between men is what makes a great unit.

We also had Slovakian and Croatian pilots assigned to us in their 13th and 15th *Staffeln*. These were good pilots, but some defected to the Soviets, and after a couple of years, Hitler ordered that they were not to fly with us anymore. They were deemed untrustworthy, although most stayed with us until the end of the war. These were brave men, good pilots, and I felt sorry for them really. They had no real home to return to after the war. They were like isolated men, islands in the greater world.

Then we had another problem. These Gestapo types came to the field while we were in the Ukraine. They came to me as the commander and told me they were investigating two of my pilots. I told them they were insane, but do what they wished. Later, I was told that their car had been used as a lavatory and a dead dog had been placed in the back seat. I called the men in, and I knew that Steinhoff, Krupinski, and Rall were involved, but they admitted nothing. I was trying not to laugh as I recalled the looks on the Gestapo men's faces as they came to report the incident. I just told them they should leave while they could. They were getting a strong hint from my pilots.

I then took some weeks of leave, and when I returned to the front, the Russians had already overrun Vinniza. My transport aircraft, a Ju-52, flew low to avoid Russian fighters, but we were already in danger of partisan ground fire. My destination was Taganrog, where my unit had been reassigned. JG-52 had been having a very bad time. I scored some victories and had a couple of close calls, but my men protected me [in combat]—like mother hens, I think.

From Taganrog, we were forced to retreat by the Soviets, who were rolling over our ground troops by sheer weight of numbers. From the Crimean Peninsula, which we had abandoned in the spring of 1944, we went via Odessa to several bases in Romania, Hungary, and Poland, where I had my base headquarters at Krakow, leading a *Gruppe* in Hungary. Our wing had just celebrated its ten thousandth victory in October. We were the only unit to do so in the *Luftwaffe*—or the world, as far as I know.

This was when I handed over the command to *Oberstleutnant* Hermann Graf, and I transferred back to JG-54. Rall had transferred to the Western Front along with Krupinski; Steinhoff was commanding JG-77 in Italy; and Hartmann was with Graf, who was commanding the unit in Hungary from JG-52. Trautloft had been made Inspector of Day Fighters by Galland, and I was chosen to replace him as *Kommodore*.

This unit was at that time fighting in the Baltic region, and the military situation had changed completely. Three years before, when I was with JG-54, we had reached Lake Ladoga at Leningrad, cutting the city and its four million inhabitants off from the rest of the Soviet Union. Now our troops of Army Group North had been driven back through Latvia and Estonia, cutting them off from the rest of the German Reich. Just at the time I arrived, the unit was being equipped with the Focke-Wulf Fw-190D fighter, which had the inline engine, not the radial of the A series, which we flew against the Russians who had reached the Baltic Sea after driving through and separating East Prussia from Latvia. We still had the 109s, of course, as most of the 190s were used in ground-support missions.

Sometime during this period, around late April 1945, I learned about Steinhoff's jet crash and had the details from Galland personally. No one thought he would live. I was devastated. I had known and lost so many good friends, and now my best friend. I wrote Ursula a letter asking if there was anything that I could do. I had a letter back from her that just said, "Pray for him, and be safe." She has always been a very strong and wonderful lady. I also heard from Krupinski and Barkhorn, who wrote to me from his hospital bed. They were there when the crash happened along with Galland. We all knew the war had to end soon, as it was spring 1945. We had nothing left to fight with.

The *Luftwaffe* was very weak at this point. With two *Gruppen* of JG-54, it could never hope to gain air superiority against the mounting number of Russian aircraft. The Russians never defeated Army Group North, which held out until the last day of the war, surrendering about 210,000 Germans and Latvian volunteers to the Soviets in Kurland. Even though the surrender was signed on May 7, some of these isolated ground units fought well into May 9. They were not informed of the surrender, and there was another on May 8 with the Soviets also.

Well, not knowing any of this, on May 8, 1945, I received a telephone call ordering me to evacuate the remaining aircraft of JG-54 the next morning, weather permitting. We pilots ripped out all unnecessary equipment from our fighters, allowing us to take two men, your best friend and the first mechanic—one man crouching behind the seat after the armor plate and radio were removed and the other fitting into the fuselage. The war was over, but we did not know this. We were still fighting. I learned about this while I was in the air, and we thought that it was a rumor.

We were to fly to Flensburg on the Danish border; and since I maintained good relations with the German navy, mostly because I still had friends from the early days, they agreed to take as many of the ground personnel as possible by ship. For us, it became the last and longest flight of our lives, but at least ninety of my personnel escaped Russian capture. We did not know for sure the war had ended, but learned this fact after we landed and were taken prisoner by the British.

Because I held the rank of *Oberst*, I was sent to Belgium and placed in a special re-education camp until February 1946, when I was allowed to go home. I had decided that I would become an architect, and I applied at the University at Tubingen, but I was denied. I was also denied at all other schools. The reason was because I had been a professional officer, and they called us "militarists" and "war criminals," which I could not understand. The future looked bad for me. I worked a few years in the automotive and chemical industries, just trying to provide for my family. We knew that Graf, Hartmann, and many others were in Soviet prisons. We never believed that we would ever see them again. When they returned, especially Hartmann, it was wonderful, but Graf was a broken man, and remained that way for the rest of his life.

In 1953, I was asked by Chancellor Konrad Adenauer to join a group of former officers who were trying to make preparations for a new Federal German Air Force, or *Bundesluftwaffe*. The new forces were being built up, as you know, because of the Cold War. I joined this group, hoping to be able to fly again, and together with Steinhoff and Kurt Kuhlmey [a former Ju-87 pilot from North Africa and the Polar Front in Finland], we went for refresher training in the United States.

We went to Arizona, Florida, and California. I really liked America, and I always look forward to returning. We *Luftwaffe* fighter pilots became great friends with our former

American enemies. I guess that is the best part of being a professional pilot. When the war was over, there was not really much hostility between us, even the British, although I can't say the same where the Soviets are concerned. I have met a few over the years, and they really seem uncomfortable being around us. I was with Steinhoff, Rall, Krupinski, Trautloft, and others once when we were in a gathering with some former Russians. Steinhoff said, "Maybe we should put a note on the door to check your guns before entering." We all laughed at that. There were a couple of exceptions, though. However, remember, this was the Cold War also, and we were still the enemy.

In 1956, I commanded the Advanced Pilot Training Center at Fürstenfeldbruck. In 1962, I was in command of the air defense covering northern Germany and the Netherlands. In 1964, I became the NATO Chief of Air Defense/Central Europe. I was then placed as the special manager for the Lockheed F-104 Starfighter program. My last assignment was as the commander of the *Bundesluftwaffe* tactical fighter command. This situation became very controversial.

First, I must say that we had many problems with the F-104. We lost a lot of pilots and aircraft. There was a joke that we had strange weather in Germany—rain that fell like water, hail that fell like ice, snow that fell like flakes, and Starfighters that just fell everywhere. There were many investigations. Hartmann and Steinhoff were in the lead on that, as well as Rall. Rall was more open-minded, like I was, about the program.

However, Hartmann and Steinhoff were totally against us getting the fighter, unless we received much more money for pilot training and even more money for the high maintenance the airplanes required. Josef Kammhuber sided with them, and he carried a lot of credibility. Our government in Bonn was not as open-minded, and the new *Luftwaffe* was not being commanded by former wartime pilots, who understood such things. This would not change for a few years. Mostly the bomber men were in the high positions, or men who were *Luftwaffe* officers during the war but who had been staff officers, not combat pilots.

Hartmann then shot himself in the foot, as he was not one to back down from our superiors in voicing his opinion and calling things as he saw them, and he was positive that he would never become a general officer, but he did not really care. He was the only Diamonds holder from the fighters to return to the new air force, and he had the highest profile. I think that he intimidated the civilian leaders and weak-minded superior officers. There was also much jealousy against him—and also against Galland, I should say.

Erich's wife, Uschi, wanted him to retire anyway. She never wanted him to go back into uniform, but we all pushed him into it, so it was really our fault. I think that he just missed his old friends. He needed that camaraderie to heal his mind after ten years in the gulags.

After I retired, I stayed in contact with old comrades still on active duty, and I remained in the shadows as an advisor to an aircraft engine manufacturer until about 1973. I became president of a sport flying club until I had to stop flying due to serious illness in 1984. I still have many friends in America, and I enjoy the times when I can come. If you ask if I am happy to be retired, I must say yes. I spent more than thirty years in uniform, although I still watch with interest all the political and military developments going on all over the world.

I am of the opinion that there will never be another world war; but warlike situations exist in many places around the world today. Religion and economics are probably the greatest motivators for war. The United States has many worldwide obligations where peace is concerned and needs powerful forces, yet they should learn from Vietnam, Korea, Somalia, and now Yugoslavia. I hope that large wars will never happen again, where young men must give their lives for a useless cause.

The Third Man

Generalleutnant Günther Rall
March 10, 1918–October 4, 2009
621 sorties, 821 combats, 275 kills
Knight's Cross, Oak Leaves (Nr 134), Swords (Nr 34)
Wound Badge in Gold

FROM THE TIME THE *Luftwaffe* went to war on September 1, 1939, its fighter pilots immediately began to make their presence known. Slashing through the skies and inflicting enormous casualties, they amassed previously unimaginable scores of aerial victories. Very few of the great pilots survived the war, yet the fact that Germany's three leading aces did is testimony to their skill, determination, and luck.

Günther Rall served on the Eastern and Western fronts, rising to the rank of major and commanding fighter groups and entire squadrons. He finished World War II as the third-highest-scoring fighter ace of all time with 275 aerial victories. His final assignment was in the defense of the Reich itself, and his capture by the Americans was the beginning of a second career for him.

Continuing to rise in the *Bundesluftwaffe* [the postwar *Luftwaffe*], he trained in the United States and later commanded German jet fighter units in the 1960s. He is still good friends with many of his old *Luftwaffe* comrades, and he was reunited with many for the eightieth birthday celebration for General Johannes Steinhoff on September 15, 1993, shortly before Steinhoff's death.

After retiring from the new German Air Force, General Rall began working in an advisory capacity for several well-known companies, after which he enjoyed retirement, his family and his many grandchildren, and enjoyed corresponding with historians until his death. This is his story.

I was born on March 10, 1918, in Gaggenau, which is a small village in the Black Forest. My father was a merchant, and when I was born he was on operations during World War I. He first saw me when he came back. I have a sister who is still alive and lives in Stuttgart, which I consider my hometown. My family moved there when I was three years old, and I was brought up and educated in Stuttgart. I was in elementary school and high school, which we called gymnasium, where I was educated for nine years in Latin and five years in the old Greek, some English, with the education focused more on literature and such, not so much on science or mathematics. I took the final exam, which we call the *Abitur*. I graduated at the age of eighteen and became a cadet in an infantry regiment.

I never really thought about flying. I had been in the Christian Boy Scouts, part of the YMCA, before Hitler abolished this and created the Hitler Youth. I was a local champion sprinter, shot putter, and broad jumper. I liked track and field events. When Hitler became chancellor, there was no unemployment, no more Rhineland and Saar occupation by our old enemies, no more reparations to be paid, and he rebuilt the military. The Great Depression was really over for us long before the rest of the world. That was perhaps what really impressed us all.

When it came to his crazy speeches about Bolsheviks and Jews, I think most of us just thought that he was another politician trying to make points with the population. However, all of us for the most part knew very well that the Communists were a great threat. They had started a revolution in Germany as the Great War ended. I would meet Hitler several times during the war, and each time was a very strange and different event. We had mandatory military service, so I started my military life in the infantry as an officer cadet in 1936, and as a senior cadet I attended the Dresden *Kriegsschule*. I passed the rigorous officer's examinations, but after speaking with a friend of mine who was flying, and telling me how good life was there, I knew that the infantry was not what I really wanted to do.

I decided to become an air force officer. I thought that was a better life. Besides, I needed a job. I entered the flight-training program in 1938. During this time, we had a few years of crazy things going on. The political issues at the time, the purge of the SA, the *Kristallnacht*, and all of this was very confusing for many of us. I was confused.

I started flying as a senior cadet in the air force, as I had credits for my infantry time, and I went through to the final exam for promotion to *Leutnant*. In those days, the air force did not have the capacity to train all of its own cadets. And we took cadets from the navy and the army. I went to the air force and started flying in 1938 in Neubiberg, which is a suburb of Munich. I took to it naturally, and loved it. While I was there, Günther Lützow was my flight commander. I would get to know him much later also. This was at Werneuchen near Berlin. I graduated and was sent to II./JG-52.

I started flying patrols along the French border before the war started. We were forbidden to cross the border into their airspace. Sometimes German pilots would come across French reconnaissance planes crossing into our airspace, and sometimes ours crossed into theirs. Not often, but it happened, although not to me. I stayed there in the Stuttgart area from September 1939 until January 1940, then we went to Strasbourg and I was with 8. *Staffel*. Then we went to Mannheim, where the war with France started. I missed the Polish invasion.

The first combat that I experienced was at the age of twenty-one. I had my first victory on May 12, 1940. You know, most of the fighter pilots from all nations in the war were under the age of thirty. Many of our pilots started flying combat at age eighteen; some were even younger as the war went on. Well, this first victory happened because my flight was ordered to escort one of our reconnaissance aircraft coming back, and we saw twelve Curtiss P-36 fighters trying to attack it. This was at eight thousand meters over Diedenhoven. This first victory gave me a lot of self-confidence. This is important for a young fighter pilot.

We moved farther west as the army advanced, and we were finally stationed on the French coast near Calais. This was where our fighters were modified for flying over water. We had flotation vests, flare pistols, and inflatable dinghies in the cockpit should we go down. I was with the same unit as Krupinski, Barkhorn, Steinhoff, and some of the others. This was the only time I met [Hans-Joachim] Marseille, as he was under Steinhoff. He was very likable, but he had a bad reputation, and Barkhorn knew him from flight school. "Stay away from him, bad news," he told me. Later, Steinhoff fired him. That is another story altogether.

We would all later fly together in the Balkans and in Russia too, except for Marseille, who was sent to Africa. In France, we opposed the Royal Air Force and flew missions over the English Channel to the southern part of the British island. We were attacking convoys and things like that. Flights were short because of fuel; we could not fly any farther.

Then we started our missions to England. That was where the real fight was, and we were on a short leash in many ways. The British were outstanding. They were a well-trained and highly motivated force, with good equipment and good morale. They fought very well; it was almost like fighting against ourselves. I was in a wing that at that time was not very experienced, as it was newly formed. We learned our lessons over the British Channel, and we had tremendous losses against the Royal Air Force. I had the highest respect for them.

We had, unfortunately, been assigned to escort Junkers Ju-87B Stukas [dive bombers], which were very slow-flying aircraft. We had to fly close escort [in Messerschmitt Bf-109Es], giving up all of our superiority and speed to stick with them. So, we escorted them over the Channel where the Spitfires and Hurricanes waited upstairs for us, and we had tremendous losses. I lost my group commander, *Hauptmann* von Huwald, when I was with III./JG-52, of course. The *Adjutant* and all three squadron commanders, including my own, *Oberleutnant* Erich, were killed in a time span of about two weeks. I, as a young *Leutnant*, after only four missions, had to take over my 8th *Staffel* [squadron, or 8. III./JG-52] as commander at the age of twenty-two. I did this for three years with the exception of my nine months with a broken back.

The Spitfires were equal to our fighters; the Hurricane not so much. It was too slow, but it could turn inside us and had equal if not better armament. Our ammunition, especially the

20mm cannon later, was excellent. Our pilots were outstanding, and we had one officer to about four or five enlisted pilots. One *Luftwaffe Gruppe* was equal to a wing in the Royal Air Force, but three *Gruppen* made up a German fighter wing—a *Geschwader*, we called it. It is still the same today in the *Bundesluftwaffe*. A *Geschwader* was 120 fighters, 40 fighters per *Gruppe*, each *Gruppe* with 3 *Staffeln*, which were squadrons to the RAF, but we hardly ever had that many aircraft available. Later in Russia, sixty fighters would make up a *Geschwader* on a very good day.

Well, after Hitler stopped the invasion of Britain, we were withdrawn to Germany, near Berlin, where we trained new pilots, gathered new fighters—which were upgrades of the 109E model—and then we went to Romania. We were to protect the oil fields, harbors, industry, and the bridges over the Danube River down to Bulgaria. The strange thing was that Romania was still a neutral country. We were stationed near Bucharest, the capital of Romania. This was for only a short time, from December 1940 to March 1941. We spent much of that time training the Romanian fighter pilots, and they received 109s also.

What was also interesting was that the main hotel where we stayed had British, French, Russians, and Americans, and even though we were at war with the French and British, it was neutral territory. We spoke at great length with all of these people. We knew that Bucharest was a hotbed of spies, and we watched ourselves. We all went to the same nightclubs. When we moved into Bulgaria, the campaign in Yugoslavia and Greece was beginning. I also had operations over Crete in May 1941. We were staged in Athens, and I liked Greece very much. Later, we moved down to some of the islands where airfields had been made. This shortened our flight to Crete and gave us emergency airfields in case we were damaged. We also had air-sea rescue established to pick up pilots from both sides who landed in the water.

This was where I once again met Joachim Müncheberg. We shared a tent while at Athens, and we spent a lot of time talking. He was a well-educated and intelligent man, and I liked him very much. He took over JG-77 for a while, but he was killed and then Steinhoff took over in the last weeks of the war in Africa.

Crete was a grueling fight, supporting the paratroops. The paratroops would also have airdrops of ammunition and things, and each box had a German flag. They were to mark the safe areas with them so that we would not attack our own men. The British and South African pilots were damned good, and like against England, they were fighting a defensive battle. We were once again flying in the attack, which meant we were always lower on fuel than they were, and when they were shot down, they would not be captured and could fly again unless they were dead or wounded. It seemed like they were always waiting for us. I came back with the group from Romania when [the operation in] Crete was finished, and we were given a new airplane, the Messerschmitt Bf-109F, which was a much better aircraft.

It had round wingtips and a new Daimler Benz engine, the DB-603. This was really the best version of the 109 series, in my opinion. At that point, in June 1941, the war with Russia was just beginning. When the war alert was given, we were back in Romania. I was staying in this Gypsy village and the people were very nice to us. We were then ordered to Coustanza near the Black Sea on the second day of the war against Russia, June 24. In the first week, we shot down around forty-five to fifty Soviet bombers trying to hit Romanian targets. Ion Antonescu came to our unit and personally thanked us. The

Romanian people also thanked us. Then we had to move east as the army advanced, and we set up airfields just behind the front lines in southern Russia and the Ukraine.

Then we learned that the war there was not going to be over in a few weeks, like Hitler said. The winter came. I cannot tell you how cold it was, and we had no winter uniforms. We had no cold-weather clothing at all. We lit fires under the fighters to keep the oil from freezing.

I was doing well and had over thirty victories, until I was shot down and almost killed. This was November 28, 1941. I was flying between Taganrog and Rostov. In those days, it was very cold. We had temperatures of minus-forty degrees centigrade. That day, I flew an afternoon mission, what we would today call a fighter sweep, when my wingman and I ran into Russians, I-16 fighters. This was during the heavy fighting as our ground troops were taking the bridge at the Tirak River. It had just started getting dark, and I had a dogfight with a Russian, shooting him down in flames. In this late light, I was blinded a little bit. I was an idiot and I did not pay attention, since I watched that plane crash into the ground, and a Russian came in behind me. He shot my engine dead and it was over Russian territory, so certainly I moved and turned trying to reach the German lines—not a solid line, but I saw some German tanks.

To escape being captured, I was flying westward and I tried to make a belly-landing, but I saw where I was going to touch down, in what they call a *Baikal*. This was a little canyon just across my flight direction, and I touched the ground at too high a speed. The aircraft had no flap control so I could not slow down, and at high speed I hit the ground and the 109 jumped up again. I hit my head on the dash and gun sight as I bounced over a little canyon and pushed my stick forward. I bellied in and crashed on the other side. That was the last I knew, as I saw this wall coming against me, and in the big bang I was knocked out. The rest of the story I learned from my wingman, as he was circling over me and watching what happened.

When the battle and crash were over, my wings came off, my engine came off, and thank God these things came off so I did not catch fire. I was hanging in the wreckage, and nearby was a German tank. The crew jumped out and cut me out of the cockpit. I was unconscious, and I did not know how I got out. I learned about all of this long afterward. Later that night, I ended up in a burned-out school in Taganrog. This was a kind of aid station for the ambulance, and there was no medical treatment there—not for a serious case such as mine.

Well, I got a full body cast, later an extension cast, and when this was fixed after one week, I was transferred on a train, which took eight days to go through Romania and the Carpathian Mountains. We ended up in Vienna, and at night we came to the train station. The doctors came, and I had everything written on my chest as to what had happened to me. I was lucky. After I was x-rayed, I finally saw a neurologist, and the doctor told me, "Flying? You can forget it!" My back was broken in three places. Then they sent me home. That was when I met Hertha. She was a doctor working there, in orthopedics and recovery. I stayed there until after Christmas.

They took me to the hospital, and the next morning Hertha was the doctor who saw me, and afterward she became my wife. In the crash, I broke the eighth and ninth thoracic vertebrae and the fifth lumbar vertebra. I was paralyzed for a long time on the right side and in my right leg. I was out of the war for nine months. I spent three months in a body cast, and then I had to learn to walk again. The therapy took most of the time. As was usual, the attending physician and medical board had said that there was no more flying for me. Well, I was not going for that, you know?

Hertha knew of my desire to fly again. She spent most of her time working with me, making my legs and muscles strong again. This time was when we knew that we loved each other, and I proposed to her before I left to return to my unit. During my recovery, a friend of mine was commanding a flying school. He helped me ease back into flying old biplanes, after I finished a lot of physical therapy. This helped me get some of my skills back and regain confidence. I happened to be in an army hospital, not *Luftwaffe*, so I wondered what their regulations were. I found that they were less strict. Not being familiar with *Luftwaffe* regulations worked to my advantage. The attending doctor along with Hertha signed me off as fit for duty. This did not say flying duty, but that I was recovered. That was enough!

When I arrived back at JG-52 at Taganrog, they had a birthday party for me. It was not my birthday. This was a party we gave to every pilot who managed to survive a crash or situation that should have killed him. It was a way of saying you were reborn. By the end of September when I arrived, I had over sixty kills. I was back.

This was when I first met Erich Hartmann. He was assigned to 9. *Staffel*; I was with 8. *Staffel*, and later I was the *Gruppenkommandeur* and he became a *Staffelkapitän*, as did Friedrich Obleser and Krupinski. They were all under me. Funny thing was that I heard that Obleser did not believe Erich's victories, so he flew as wingman. He was convinced later. I already knew most of the others as we had been together for two years by that time. I have to admit that I was not very impressed with Erich at first. He looked like a child, and when I began flying with him, he took stupid chances. Erich was not really a good leader, but he was an excellent pilot. Like Marseille, he was a lone wolf type. But he never had a wingman killed, which says something.

Hartmann had many mentors. Paule Rossmann, Ernst Süss, Alfred Grislawski, and, of course, Krupinski worked with him. He became better, and soon he was shooting down Russians often. On my first mission with him, he was returning from a sweep and I was leading a flight to take over. He radioed me, gave me the coordinates and altitude of eight P-39s, and I shot down their leader, attacking from altitude out of the sun. Our radio people on the ground who knew Russian would listen in on the Russian radio channels, and we had great intelligence. The Russians spoke plain language, not [using] codes. Often we knew exactly whom we shot down, because the enemy pilots in the air would call the names out. [Germans used call signs, not pilots' names on the radios.]

Hartmann heard my "*Horrido*!" and congratulated me when I returned. He used to take off early in the morning, sometimes with a wingman, sometimes not. When he had his wingman, that pilot would often confirm a victory or two. I was getting suspicious, as were others. One day I asked him if I could go with him to his hunting ground, and he thought about it but said yes if I kept the secret. Hartmann flew as wingman to Grislawski often, but then Grislawski stepped on a mine at the beach and was badly injured. He was out for a while and Erich took over soon after.

We took off and flew to a Soviet airfield that I never knew existed. It was in a canyon, covered by a forest. You could never see it from the air. Erich told me that he found it by accident a few weeks before, when he followed a damaged fighter. The aircraft landed, and then he saw others. He decided to keep that to himself. I called him a greedy bastard, and he laughed at me.

We found the airfield, and the enemy would take off early in the morning; that was why Erich would take off before sunrise.

We circled overhead just as the sun was rising, and we caught four of them lifting off and then shot them down. That was what I called the fishing hole. We made quite a few trips there. I kept my promise and said nothing to anyone else, but somehow the word leaked out. One problem was that in the *Abschuss*, you had to give the coordinates and altitude of a victory. Erich was not even claiming some of these fighters, just to keep the secret.

The fighting over Stalingrad was insane. This was when Hermann Graf led all of us in the victory count. One thing about Graf, he earned the Diamonds eventually all for the air victories over Stalingrad. He was the first to get two hundred victories before the end of 1942. He shot down sixty-two in September before I arrived back. All were confirmed by many pilots. All of us were getting kills. There were just so many Russians in the air, and I believe that you could have thrown a stone blindfolded and hit one by accident. By the end of November, I had over a hundred kills—that was how busy it was. You really had to be there and see it. This was when I earned the Oak Leaves.

The greatest problem was avoiding collisions with either the enemy or your own fighters. It was at this time we learned that the Russians were using women fighter pilots. We found this unbelievable until one was captured by JG-51. We had the information, and we were shocked. We would never allow our women to fly combat.

The first time I met Hitler was in November 1942, when I received the Oak Leaves. Additional honors to the Knight's Cross, from the Oak Leaves onward, were presented by Hitler personally. I was there with Steinhoff—at that time it was *Hauptmann* Steinhoff and *Oberleutnant* Rall—with some others, like Nowotny; five of us in all. Certainly, we were impressed with his headquarters in East Prussia, at the *Wolfschanze* [Wolf's Lair] at Lotzen. We entered, he was standing there, and he handed over our decorations. We sat around the fireplace, and he asked each of us which units we came from, our battle experience, and so on. All questions such as this, quite normal.

Soon he started his own monologue, knowing that we would go back to our unit and repeat what he had told us and we would remark on what a great guy he was. Well, he started talking about the buildup of the antiaircraft defense and new communications systems in Russia, the railway system, and things like this. He talked about the width of the railroad tracks, how they needed to be made wider for standard German rail traffic and extended into the deeper regions.

This was to be the expansion of the Third Reich in the Middle East, the building of villages and towns, all of these very essential things, which was a program he had in mind, no doubt. Perhaps I was too courageous, but I interrupted him and asked, "Despite all of that, how long do you think this war will be? Because when we moved into Russia, the newspapers said that by the time the first snows came down we would be finished with the war in the east. Instead, we have suffered in the cold over there." So Hitler then said to me, "Well, I cannot tell you. This might be an open area. We have our settlements here, and when the enemy comes from the depths of the Asian steppe, then we will defend this area—just like in the days of Genghis Khan." I thought he was mad, and so did the others.

Remember that this was before the collapse of Stalingrad and before El Alamein. This was the apex of his war. He had these great ideas as to how he was going to still defeat the

Soviets, even though we were also technically at war with America and the rest of the world. I just do not think he understood the magnitude of what that meant.

Nowotny looked at me, as did Steinhoff also. I could see that they were thinking the same thing as I was. Was he serious? Did he really believe this? Did he really know what the situation was at the front? I was stunned when he said that with another three thousand fighters we could eliminate the Russian air force. Nowotny asked, "*Mein Führer*, where are these fighters coming from? We have only five hundred in the northern and central sectors, and half of those need parts that we cannot get, and fuel and ammunition as well."

Hitler took a deep breath and leaned back in his leather chair. He looked down and then said something like, "I have given the orders to have them built and delivered by next summer." Then Nowotny said, "That would only replace losses, and would all of these go to Russia? Would some go to Africa or the west?" Hitler seemed to become a little annoyed at the questions, and he changed the subject. He began talking about our successes up to that point in the war, the armies we had destroyed, all of this. He was living in the past. He could not clearly see the future, but then again perhaps none of us could.

Well, Hitler continued talking on and on about the problems in North Africa; the U-boat war was not going well, not like before, but he was taking care of that also. He also said that the military was going to get new and better weapons, guns, tanks, things like that. He also said that he had ordered a new uniform to replace the old field gray. He also mentioned crazy numbers of divisions that were being raised and trained. I wondered where he was getting the manpower. We finished with Hitler after a few hours, and I had some leave so I went to see Hertha and my mother. Then I had to return. This was when I married Hertha.

The units 8. and 9. *Staffeln* then moved to Rostov after leaving our fighters with II *Gruppe* under Hrabak. We had more of our men coming up from the Caucasus in Soldatskaya. We had to go by car, and the roads were terrible. 7. *Staffel* rejoined us in February 1943, and Hartmann was with them at that time. During this time, I shot down my 116th enemy, and it was number 5,000 for JG-52, so we had this great celebration. Our III *Gruppe* had over 2,500 kills at this time. We had learned a lot in the first year of the war in Russia. We had captured many Soviet fighters. Most did not have radios or gun sights. They had a painted ring on the windscreen. Many fighters did not even have altimeters of air speed indicators. Incredible.

The year 1943 was the beginning of the end for us. We had lost the 6th Army and Stalingrad that February, as well as El Alamein before in 1942 and the front in North Africa in May 1943. Then we had the great battle around Kursk, where we flew the most missions in four days than at any time dur ing the war. We were in the Crimea, Kuban, Novorossiysk, the Caucasus, everywhere. It was at Krupskaya where I shot down my first Spitfire flown by a Russian, but I shot down many more. They had many American and British aircraft. There were French and British officers and units assigned in the Soviet Union also as advisors. You never knew if you were fighting a Western European or a Russian in those fighters.

I landed and filed my report, and Obleser was my wingman; he confirmed the kill and the fighter type. I typed my report and handed it to von Bonin. He read it and laughed. "Rall, I think you are mad! Spitfires in Russia! You are crazy." But Obleser told him it was so. Two days later, we flew into a whole squadron of Spitfires with red stars and red noses. This was a guards unit, and they were very good. I got one victory, and I think we had seven total victories while losing only one fighter. I was vindicated.

The man I shot down was an interesting case. His tail came off and he crash-landed. He was brought to our field, which was close by, and he seemed to be badly injured. We had a man from Kharkov in our unit translate—this special guy who defected to us and who fixed everything. I offered the major a cigarette and some tea, but he thought they were poisoned. I lit a smoke and drank some of the tea to prove it was safe. He was not interested. This pilot had a lot of medals, too.

Well, we had to send him off in a Ju-52. When the plane landed later, this major somehow just walked off the plane and disappeared. We had taken his personal papers. We knew that he was from Leningrad, and his letters from his wife told him that the political types were eating and living well, while thousands of the regular citizens starved to death every day. I thought that was interesting.

Sometime around this period, I was flying with Joachim Birkner as my wingman. We were attacked and we scrambled, and within five minutes we were in a big fight with a lot of Yaks, and suddenly there was a great explosion in my cockpit. The canopy shattered; I lost most of my joystick control. Birkner saw flames and told me to bail out. I said "no" because I was just five hundred meters high and I crash-landed. The oxygen bottle had blown up, shattering the armor plate behind my head, opening my skull a little. There was blood all in the cockpit, but I was not seriously injured. I flew again in a few days.

I was appointed *Gruppenkommandeur* of III./JG-52 on July 6, 1943, during Kursk. This was a great, crazy battle, and the most dangerous situation for me was a collision in the air with a Russian fighter. I was flying with my *Adjutant* later in the day, flying from west to east. The sun was starting to set behind us, and in front of us was a huge cumulous cloud rising perhaps six thousand meters. As the war went on, we continued to be greatly outnumbered. In 1941, it was perhaps ten to one after most of the Soviet air forces were destroyed. By 1943, it was twenty to one. By the time I left in 1944, it was more like fifty to one.

We then saw two small dots on the horizon, easy to see against the cloud reflecting the sunlight. I could only see the silhouettes, but we saw that the fighters had radial engines. Now this could be a LaGG, or even one of our Fw-190s; it was hard to tell. I told my wingman, "Jesus Christ, they may be 190s. Be careful." We did not want to shoot down our own men. Well, we closed on them head-on and I did not fire, since I was not sure. So I pulled up and looked down as they passed by us.

Then I saw the red stars. I was still in the climb, at ninety degrees right wing up and vulnerable, so I rolled and did a dive to gain speed. When I did this, the LaGG pulled up and my propeller cut his fighter in half at the wing root, and his propeller cut my 109 in half behind the cockpit. The Russian went down in a spiral and crashed. I was still flying, but I had this terrible vibration. I thought the engine would fall off or the tail would fall away. My wingman had scored a victory and I asked him to assess the damage, and the response was, "You are all screwed up, sir." That did not make me feel very good, and I made sure that my parachute harness was tight in case I had to leave the fighter.

Well, I managed to land, and after I jumped out I saw the damage. The propeller had cut into the fuselage almost all the way. The steel spars connecting the tail from the armor plate was all that was still intact. That was the toughest victory I have ever had, I can tell you. Several of the other pilots heard what had happened over the radio, and they came to see my 109. Hrabak walked over and said, "You were very lucky, my friend." And I said, "Yes, more lucky than the other guy." I was certain that this Russian rammed me on purpose. I had seen this happen before, which was something that we Germans could not really comprehend.

I remember when Hartmann went down. Later, we learned that his fighter was damaged from the pieces of the victory he shot down. Everyone was depressed; he was like the little brother, you know? Then after he arrived, I think it was I who was shot down again. I had been in combat and shot down two Yaks when two others got me. I landed in this forest just beyond the Dnieper River—but on our side, as far as I knew. I had seen Russian soldiers all around, and I jumped out and took out my Walther pistol. The first guy I saw was wearing this leather coat and cap with a Red Star. I almost shot him until I found out that he was a Czech officer on our side.

Once, I was in this really long fight in the Caucasus, after I had returned from my injury. I was following this guy through the canyons. He was good, and he was fast in this Yak, but I got good shots into him. Obleser was my wingman. We ended up flying only a couple of meters above the ground. The Russian was trying to shake me. Then I fired and I hit him. His fighter hit the ground and did not explode; it disintegrated, rubbish flying all up in the air, and I flew right through it. I made it back but had to have a new windscreen and propeller.

Also during this time, I was with my *Adjutant*, and we encountered these P-39 Airacobras. The Russians loved that fighter, which had a rear engine and heavy weapons in front. I pulled lead on him and he just exploded. The flash was so bright, I lost my vision for a minute. I pulled up to make sure that I did not fly through the rubbish in the air. My *Adjutant* was laughing because he said that I had just pulled up and over the P-39 pilot that he had shot down; otherwise, I would have hit his parachute. I never even saw him until I banked over. That way I could confirm his victory.

Another mission that really stays clear in my mind was the support mission for *Stukageschwader* 2. This was Rudel's "*Immelmann Wing*," and they had changed their Stukas from dive bombers into tank destroyers. They had 30mm under-wing cannons, and this was how he became so famous. He destroyed over five hundred tanks this way. We would fly above them to keep away the enemy fighters, and they would dive in and attack the enemy tanks.

I saw this one Stuka, really hitting these T-34s and blowing up a couple, when a Yak came in fast and shot at him. The Yak had fired wide and missed, but he was coming back. I heard Hartmann say, "I have him," but I also heard Steinhoff, Obleser, Hrabak, and others say the same thing. And I was already on this guy. I closed in as he turned left to get back on the Stuka. I fired a deflection shot, but then he blew up. There were not even pieces to fall to the ground. I heard four others scream "*Horrido*!"

The Stuka pilot and his rear gunner waved at me as I passed by. I was looking them over, and they seemed fine. I remembered the markings on the Stuka. Later I found out it was Rudel, and he and I would later be roommates in England as prisoners. We received a nice telegram from Rudel the next day, thanking us for saving them on that mission. I do not believe that they even lost one aircraft during that sortie once we arrived. Then I saw Krupinski destroy three T-34 tanks. After that, we told him that he should transfer to the Stukas—they could use him.

We landed and then tried to figure out who would get the kill. We had all hit the Yak at the same time, so the kill went to the unit, not to any one of us. We did not share victories like the Allies did. The funny thing was that most of the fighters we fought were LaGGs, with just a few Yaks from July 4 and 5. We also had a couple of captured pilots who had bailed out. We also had an IL-2 crew. We liked speaking with these men, when we had a translator. It was always interesting to get their side of the war. However, our discussions were not usually as friendly as with the Americans or British. They hated us for the most part, although most of the Ukrainians we met hated the Russian Communists even more.

You must understand that in these combats, you really need your wingman. That is because you cannot have any distractions; you must be completely focused upon what you are doing. You get tunnel vision, pinpoint focus. That is dangerous, especially in a big fight with many fighters around you. Those of us who could aim and shoot quickly and then roll away, dive, or climb out of any possible danger were those who survived, but much of it was just luck.

The Russians used to fly over almost every night, dropping bombs. These were just to keep us awake. One group was called the Night Witches, women pilots. One night, Krupinski and I were lying on our cots with a transport pilot waiting to leave the next day. We heard the engines overhead, then the bombs fell. One exploded right next to our tent. The tent was gone; so was the tree line where we had set up. The transport pilot slept through it all, and we thought he was dead. We awakened him and saw that a large bomb fragment had lodged in his pillow, just two inches maybe from his head. We gave him a birthday party. Willi Batz was nearby, and he came running when he saw what had happened. Then more bombs. His tent took a direct hit. Had he been inside, he would be dead. Such is luck.

On August 7, 1943, I shot down my 150th victory and was told I would receive the Swords, with the two hundreds on August 28 at Makiefka and another forty aircraft in October 1943. Only [Walter] Nowotny had more victories than I did at that time. However, destroying all of these aircraft made little difference. There were ten to replace every one we shot down. From that point on, we went backward. Hrabak came to me and he said that I was exhausted, and he was giving me home leave. I had to go see Hitler again anyway.

Well then, it was nine months after having the Oak Leaves, and I had to come back again to receive my Swords from Hitler. He looked as if he had shrunk a few centimeters. He did not look the same. We stood in formation to receive our decorations, had the usual lunch, and then Hitler again asked his questions. He started with the usual things: how were our families, how was morale at our units, what improvements could be made that we observed—that sort of thing.

You know, at that time we had a hell of a time with the submarine war, which he again mentioned, as well as his new weapons. I again thought he was mad, yet this was now a very different Hitler. He was no longer talking about tangible facts. He was talking about, "I see the deep valley . . . I see the strip on the horizon," and it was all nonsense. He was speaking about magical figures of manpower and production, a fantasyland. We saw this man as infirm. Although I was pleased to have my medals, I was even happier to leave that world. I had a few days to see my wife and family, and I had secret thoughts about my future, and that of Germany, that I did not discuss with them.

After this meeting, I was called to see Göring, who had accused my wife of helping enemies of the Reich escape Germany. This was the same questioning that the Gestapo idiots had with me in Russia. I had asked Hertha about this some months before, after that visit. She had never told me anything. But, when I asked her again [after the war], she told me that she had been doing this since 1936 or so. She had many academic and professional friends who were Jews, and especially after the *Kristallnacht*, she helped forge papers and make contacts with people. She wanted to get these people and their families out. She was not sure where Hitler was going with his stupidity, but her highly educated mind knew that it would not be good.

Göring told me to sit down. He congratulated me on my Swords, but said that he had some serious issues with my wife. He told me that the Gestapo were going to arrest her, and possibly me, for what she had been doing. I asked him if there was any evidence of this. He said, "No, but they are putting the case together against her." I told him that when they had something that looked like proof to let me know. Otherwise, I told him that it would be very difficult to arrest the wife of a national hero, or even me, without raising unpleasant questions.

You must understand that I did not know anything about the concentration camps and the "Jewish problem." That was kept top-secret, and I guess the reasons were obvious. However, Hertha suspected, and she had information and she told me what she thought. I told her that this was crazy, that no one would do anything like that. I did tell her that I was aware of Hitler's Commissar Order, and we pilots had often discussed this. This was a violation of the Geneva Convention. Unless people were caught as partisans, they could not be just shot upon capture.

Göring told me that the issue with Hertha had started with [Reinhard] Heydrich. He was the SD [*Sicherheitsdienst*] leader investigating. He worked under Himmler, who had approved of the investigation. They had also come to our unit and were investigating two of our JG-52 pilots for being Jewish. I never met Heydrich, and he was killed anyway in 1942, but I had met Himmler. I despised him in all ways, as much as I despised Göring. He was a very strange man. Göring said that he would see to it that the matter was dropped, that I should just tell my wife to stop what she was doing, if she was doing anything.

I learned about the Jewish killings after the war, and it astonished me. I was able to travel to England much later, and even to America and other countries to where the people she saved were living. They had children and grandchildren, and many times we were invited to Jewish holidays with them. They were very fine people. I think there were more than fifty people she smuggled out before the war, and about half that during the war. She was quite busy.

Well, after the meeting with Göring, I wanted to call Hertha, but I thought that the phones were tapped, so I had a few days and just told her about the meeting and what Göring had said. She just smiled and said that she would think about it. Speaking to her in person was important, as the telephones were not safe and all letters were censored. After my home leave of two weeks, I returned to the unit and flew again. It felt good to be in the air, but I arrived in the Crimea, near Sevastopol, and we were ordered to evacuate. From then until 1944, I was in the southern part of Russia, moving down through the Caucasus and on to Dnepropetrovsk, the areas south of Stalingrad—all of the important names. This was a fast-moving war, contrary to the northern part of the Russian Front, which was more stationary.

The southern front in the Soviet Union was a very dangerous place. Hrabak, who was my *Kommodore*, gave me my orders. I was promoted to *Major*, and I was to take over a new command. In the spring, I came back to Germany to the Home Defense [*Reichsverteidigung*], flying high-altitude fighters against the 8th Air Force, as you know, against all the North American P-51 Mustang, Lockheed P-38 Lightning, and Republic P-47 Thunderbolt fighters and the heavy bombers. We even had occasional encounters with Spitfires, but not too often.

I flew the Messerschmitt Bf-109 in all of the different marks [variants]: the E, F, G, and the K model, and, of course, the Focke-Wulf Fw-190, but I liked the 109 most because I was most familiar with it. Certainly I flew the 190, but only the D model long-nosed version, toward the end of the war in some missions. I also flew the Me-262, but not in combat.

I can tell you that all the characters you may name are, and were, good friends of mine, such as Johannes Steinhoff, Adolf Galland, Hannes Trautloft, Werner Mölders, and Dieter Hrabak. Hrabak was my wing leader at one time, and he is one of my closest friends now. I respect him as a fighter leader and as a person. In the war, I served with JG-52 exclusively on the Eastern Front. Steinhoff and Krupinski also have their special place, as do Hartmann and Barkhorn.

Werner Mölders was a great character and fighter leader, and he was a strong Catholic. In those days, he had his own rules and personality. He was a great man, creating new tactics, leading his men into combat, and being concerned for them and caring for them in the air, as well as on the ground. This was, I think, the real Werner Mölders. Despite his young age, he was known as "Daddy Mölders." It was because of his experience in Spain and his leadership that he was given the nickname.

I met most of the big heads in the Nazi Party. I did not think very much of Hitler or Himmler and the others. You could not like Göring. He was perhaps a capable man before the war. He was a great organizer, helping to build the air force after the First World War. Also, he was a great fighter pilot in World War I. As you also know, he was injured in 1923 when Hitler started the Putsch in Munich, and he had a very difficult injury. He had to take morphine for the pain and became addicted. It might have changed his character.

At the time I became acquainted with him, I was cold to him. He was a big, fat man, a very pompous man, and not only I but also my comrades felt that he was out of touch with reality. He was certainly not respected as an air force leader. Actually, he did not lead the air force at all; it was somebody else, but not Göring. Hermann Göring would make silly statements to Hitler. Hitler said, "You are the leader of the air force," and Göring made a long statement about the Battle of Britain, you know, that he would triumph over the Royal Air Force, which was wrong, as we had tremendous losses in our fighter fleet from which we never recovered during the war. He said, "We can support Stalingrad—the air force can do it," which he was not able to do. It was a costly statement.

Many times, Göring would have his pilots join him for hunting adventures at Carinhall. This was his great estate. He also had all of these titles, like Hunting Meister, and all kinds of things. He saw himself as this great hunter, a hero from the First War. I do not know of anyone who actually liked him personally.

Göring also had his favorites, those who thought like him or at least agreed with him. If you disagreed with him, you were the enemy. Ask Galland about that one. Göring thought a lot of Erich Hartmann, but I think that was because Erich was not a threat to him. He was just a young pilot without any close contact to the high leaders in the Reich. He also favored Gordon Gollob and Hans-Ulrich Rudel, Werner Baumbach and Dietrich Peltz. But challenging Göring was dangerous. He was a mean-spirited and angry man.

The third time I saw Hitler was January 12, 1944, when I was summoned to receive my documentation for my Oak Leaves and another for the Oak Leaves and Swords. They were engraved, gilded, and beautifully made with a lovely skirt, frame, and so on. They were later stolen in Vienna, most likely by the Russians. There are some of them still available, but not mine. I gave them to my wife and told her to keep them safe and place them in the bunker in the city of Vienna. When we came back a couple of years later, they were gone and nothing was left.

At that time [of the awards in 1944], there were only sixteen or so [who had been so honored] remaining, with names such as Adolf Galland, Helmut Lent, Walter Nowotny, as they were all still alive. Lent and Nowotny died before the war ended. They had the Diamonds. Walter Oesau, Dietrich Peltz, Heinz Bär, Walter Nowotny, Adolf Galland, Gustav Rödel, Heinz-Wolfgang Schnaufer, Egon Mayer, Emil Lang,

Toni Hackl, Herbert Ihlefeld, Prince Heinrich zu Sayn Wittgenstein, Hartmann, and I were present, about sixteen of us total, when Hitler awarded these certificates. Then we had lunch with him. The main subject of his speech was the pending Allied invasion. This was in January 1944. I then was officially transferred to the Western Front, Defense of the Reich, where I took over JG-11 on April 19 for a while. Krupinski was there, with some others.

Later, I had to see Hitler again one last time, and Göring was there. This was in April 1944, when I was in a meeting with other Western Front and Home Defense fighter leaders. Galland, Walter Oesau, Josef Priller, Günther Lützow, Heinz Bär, Eduard Neumann, Gustav Rödel, Hannes Trautloft, Herbert Ihlefeld, and my old friend Steinhoff, all now on staff or flying in the west or in Home Defense, were all there that day. Everybody expected the invasion all along the Channel coast, wondering when it was coming and how they were coming and so on. At that time, Hitler developed his ideas, and you could see that he was hopping around, very uncertain. He seemed to be distracted and occupied in his mind.

One thing that was typical of him was his stating how the British were always having problems with their opposition parties—the Labor Party, the labor unions, and so on. He also mentioned that the Americans and British would soon see the threat of Stalin and change sides. It was clear to me that this man was a little out of his mind. Hitler did not have a clear, serious concept of the situation. Whatever their problems, the British came together during the war as one nation.

Finally, we got down to the business as to the locations and numbers of fighters, the training of new pilots, and other matters about equipment and such. It was not long after this that Galland appointed Trautloft Inspector of Day Fighters, because we really had no one inspecting and checking on these details.

My last mission where I scored a victory was also when I had my thumb shot off. I was the *Gruppenkommandeur* of II./JG-11, which was at the time on *Reichsverteidigung* [Home Defense] duties against the 8th Air Force. This victory was May 12 while flying a mission, and I did succeed in destroying two Thunderbolts of this unit [56th Fighter Group]. But I lost my thumb.

This mission was terrible. We took seventy-five fighters, about fifty 190s to attack the bombers, and the rest of my 109s to take on the fighters. The 8th Air Force had sent eight hundred bombers with a thousand fighters. And here we were with seventy-five aircraft. I was flying one group, and Toni Hackl had the Fw-190s. I was at eleven thousand meters, and it was cold as hell. We did not have the pressurized cockpits in the 109s. Well, I was in this dogfight. I shot up three P-47s, but I could confirm only one kill before I was caught and shot up.

My left thumb was gone, and the fighter was falling apart. I pulled up and climbed, knowing that the P-47s could not follow me up. I climbed until I stalled, and then I rolled it over, lost the canopy, and fell out. I was very worried about hitting the tail section, as had happened to many pilots, including Hans-Joachim Marseille. I also had a fear that with my old back injury, crash-landing would hurt me badly. Well, I managed to stabilize myself, open the parachute, and land in a tree north of Frankfurt. I then slipped out and fell about three meters down a slope. I tumbled, but I was okay. I was bleeding badly from where the thumb used to be.

I was in the hospital during Operation Bodenplatte [January 1, 1945] because the wound to my hand was still open and I had an infection. I listened in on the higher staff, so this was how I learned about Bodenplatte. We did not have access to penicillin as the Allies did, and many of our men died from simple infections.

Hertha came to be near me, and she followed up on all of the medical procedures. My mother was also very worried, but that is what all mothers do, you know? There was also the fear that they may have had to amputate my hand if the infection spread.

We lost many of our most experienced unit leaders, irreplaceable losses, during Bodenplatte. A total of fifty-eight unit leaders were lost in that operation, I believe. These were some of the most experienced men in the *Luftwaffe*, with years of training and combat experience. I then became the commander of the Fighter Leaders School while I healed. Galland and I spoke about Bodenplatte later. He was extremely angry about how it was conducted. He was not in on the planning because Göring was angry with him.

After I was released from the hospital, I was for a short time on Galland's staff, until I became the commander of the German Fighter Leaders School for about four months or so. Here is where I again was with Nowotny, as he was also commanding the school when I was leaving. At that time, we had formed a squadron with captured enemy aircraft, and we flew them—the P-38, P-47, P-51, as well as some Spitfires. There was also a B-17 that we were able to fly, and that was a bonus for us. We were really able to study this bomber closely.

Some of these aircraft were flown with our markings in deception missions. I did not fly these missions, but a few others did. My left hand was still in bandages, but I was flying all of these aircraft as I was very eager to learn about and evaluate them. I had a very good impression of the P-51 Mustang, where the big difference was the engine. When we received these aircraft, we flew about three hundred hours in them. You see, previously we did not know anything about how they flew, their characteristics, or anything.

In the P-51, there was no oil or coolant leak; the same was true of the P-47. This was one of the many things that impressed me, but I was also very interested in the electrical starting switches, which we did not have in the 109. This made it difficult to start our engines in the Russian winter. We had the inertia starter. The cockpits of all of these enemy aircraft were much more comfortable. You could not fly the 109 for seven hours; the cockpit was too tight, too narrow. The P-51 [cockpit] was for me a great room, just fantastic. The P-38 with two engines was great, but I think the best airplane was the P-51.

Certainly, the Spitfire was excellent, but it didn't have the endurance of the P-51. I think this was the decisive factor. The P-51s flew for seven hours, and we [in 109s] flew for one hour and twenty minutes. Compared to the Mustang, we were really screwed. You would have to get down because you were short on fuel, then look for the nearest air base, and they still had fuel for three hours more. Usually they were hanging around our air bases. During this time, I also trained on the Me-262.

The first time I sat in it, I was most surprised about the silence. If you are sitting in a standard piston-powered aircraft, you have a hell of a noise in the radio headset—background noise and static and such—which I did not experience in the Me-262. It was absolutely clear. With radio from the ground, they controlled the flight. They gave me my orders, such as, "Now accelerate your engines, build your rpm." It was totally clear. One other thing was that you had to advance the throttles very slowly. If you went forward too fast, you might overheat and set the engines on fire.

Also, if you were up to eight thousand rpm, or whatever it was, you released the brakes and you were taxiing. Unlike the Bf-109, which had no front wheel and was a tail dragger, the Me-262 had a tricycle landing gear. It was a new sensation, beautiful visibility. You could go down the runway and see straight forward. This was, however, also a weak moment for the Me-262. The aircraft at this point was a little bit stiff and slow during landing and takeoff, but fine when coming up to speed gradually. It was absolutely superior to the old aircraft.

I never did get to shoot the 262 weapons because when I had about fifteen or twenty hours in the jet, I left JG-11 and I became commander of the JG-300 in late February or early March 1945, which was then equipped with Bf-109s. I only made some training flights, but never flew the jet in combat. This was no longer a wing, just a ruin of the former wing because one of its three groups was in the north. A wing has to have three groups to be a wing.

JG-300 had been started by Hajo Herrmann as a *Wilde Sau* unit in July 1943, as a night fighter group. Then it became a day bomber interceptor unit. That was early on, and that time had passed. It did not usually work well. Now we had normal fighter missions. In February 1945, there were no normal fighter missions left, you know. We were merely looking for targets of opportunity. We had no idea where the enemy was at any time. We were totally in the dark.

In the meantime, the Americans got to the Elbe River, cutting this northern *Gruppe* of JG-300 off, and some managed to escape to the south. I had only two rudimentary groups, and I will tell you something that was typical: When I arrived at the wing to take over, I came by jeep because I had no aircraft. While I was commander of the Fighter Leaders School, they sent me a jeep and said, "You are going up to Plattling in Bavaria to take over as commander of JG-300." When I approached the base, I saw that some airplanes were standing out on the apron, and my driver said, "Oops, we are being attacked!" We stopped and ran off the road. It was an attack by P-38 Lightnings, and when I finally arrived, there were fifteen of our aircraft in flames.

This was my introduction to the wing. The next day we were transferred to the south, and from there on we had no solid operations. We had no radar, no air situation. We had only narrow contact to higher authority in the division, so we relocated to the area south of Munich. On the way to Salzburg, I dissolved the wing, as the war was over, and told the group commanders, "This thing is over and you had better go home." We pilots gave all that we had, including our food, to the airmen and ground personnel. Then we gave a final salute, and everyone went away on his own.

As you can imagine, at that time there was no solid warfare. Even the higher ranks came to my headquarters and asked if they could stay there because they wanted to get through it [the end of the war]. You could only get out using your feet in a normal unit. So, this was a very bad time, and there were no firmly planned or controlled missions. The main fight for me was to try to get fuel for the aircraft. Without it, we could not fly, naturally. Every day we found out that wing so-and-so dissolved at the hands of the Americans; it was because of this situation that you were alone and on your own.

The war changed over time. At the beginning of the war, we flew short-range missions and encountered Spitfires, which were superior. And do not forget the Hurricanes. I think that the Supermarine Spitfire was the most dangerous early on. I flew the Spitfire myself, and it was a very, very good aircraft. It was maneuverable with good climbing potential. Then in Russia, the first aircraft we encountered were obsolete. But they got better.

The Russians lost about seven thousand aircraft in the first three to four months of the war, but they learned their lessons and began building better aircraft—the MiGs, Yaks, and the La-5. Developed by Semyon A. Lavochkin and Mikhail I. Gudkov from their earlier, unsuccessful La-3 with an in-line, water-cooled engine, the La-5 came out in 1943 and had a big radial engine. It was a powerful, excellent aircraft and served as the basis for even better versions: the La-5FN and the La-7.

The Soviets did have great fighters, like the La-5 and 7, the Yaks, and others. The La-7 was excellent. I remember once I chased a Lavochkin a great distance at full throttle, and I still could not get him. He was damned fast. Then by way of foreign aid, particularly in the south around the Caucasus where I was fighting, they brought in Spitfires and the Bell P-39 Airacobra, which I liked and the Russians liked, but which was inferior to the Bf-109 as its engine was behind the cockpit.

The big thing in the Home Defense as far as problems went was the P-51. The P-51 was a damned good airplane and it had tremendous endurance, which for us was a new dimension. The P-47, which as you know shot me down, we knew right away that it had tremendous diving speed and could run up to 1,400 kilometers per hour, where the Bf-109 was limited to 1,000 kilometers. I learned this quickly when they chased me. The structural layout design of the P-47 was much stronger. It had eight heavy machine guns, a more powerful hit, yet I consider the P-51 the best battle horse you had of all the fighter escorts.

I was at Ainring near Salzburg when we finished the war. I told my group commanders to take whatever they could use and go to the Americans and surrender. I walked with my staff, retreating at night, and with my group we went to the Americans, who did not care too much for us. It was almost as if they were not interested. So at daylight, we decided to try and go home. At Lake Chiemsee, we could not go any farther and were captured. The Americans took me back to Salzburg and put me in prison. I was sent from Salzburg to Neu-Ulm, then to Heilbronn, and there the CIC [Counter Intelligence Corps] saw me. They knew my name, and they said that all air force officers should report, and they took me very quickly to interrogation. Then seven of us were taken to England.

Hundreds of us were there, and we began to hear our names being called. "Rall," "Bär," "Steinhoff," "Krupinski," like that. Well, Steinhoff was in the hospital, and many other names they called out were dead. They had a list somehow, of all of us who had flown the Me-262. These guys really wanted to have a serious chat with us. This was what the Americans called Operation Paperclip. They were gathering together jet and rocket pilots, scientists, all the technical experts, before the Russians could get them.

They took us to Heidelberg, which was in the British zone, and we had fresh vegetables, meat, real coffee, and even beer. We had not seen these things in a long time. We were treated like honored guests. Then we went to Wiesbaden, then to England. I was there in Bowington Camp 7 with

Galland, Bär, Krupinski, Barkhorn, and all the high-ranking and high-scoring pilots who had flown the jets. I was paired with [Hans-Ulrich] Rudel; well, he was a bit of a maniac. I flew with him as his fighter escort for his group several times. After the war, I was a fellow prisoner with him in France, as guests of the Americans.

Rudel and I were then sent to Tangmere in the same camp, and later we were borrowed by the Royal Air Force. I was sent to the British Fighter Leaders School at Tangmere. This was for interrogation, which lasted three weeks. I was there with Rudel as well, and we slept in the same room. Living very close together, you get acquainted, and you come to understand the thinking of such a man, even though I had known him personally before that. I was surprised at his egocentrism; he was the greatest in his own mind. It was a little disgusting to me.

There was a situation that I will never forget. There was a Mr. Reed, at least that was the name he gave me—his CIC name anyway. He knew everything about my life and career. I was surprised. When he came to pick me up, he asked me, "*Major*, I understand that you flew the 262," and I answered, "Yes, I did." He knew more about me and what I had done than I knew myself. Then he asked, "Are you willing to assist us in building up a jet force?" Well, the war was over, so I said, "Yes, sure." He also wanted to know if I was willing to go to England and then to America. I went to England for interrogation. His last question was, "Would you be willing to fly with us against the Japanese?" Well, here I said, "No," and he asked me why not. I told him that they were former allies, and I could not do that.

I was able to meet all of the British aces when I was at Tangmere. We were greeted by Wing Commander Robert

Stanford Tuck. Saluting, the first thing he asked was, "Have you gentlemen had lunch?" I said, "Not for the past three months." He said, "Well, we shall remedy that right now. Follow me." This was the first time I had been treated with respect in as many months. Tuck called us "gentlemen." This was a surprise. As was the lunch with beer, the hot baths, and clean blankets in the rooms.

I had been transferred with Rudel, and we became roommates again. He received a lot of attention due to the Golden Oak Leaves, Swords, and Diamonds. They put us in prison, really a barracks, but they left the door open and there were no guards. I thought that this was strange, and Rudel said that this was a good sign. I told him that was because they knew that we had no place to go. Tangmere was where I became friends with Bob Tuck, Douglas Bader, and many others. We were also visited by many senior Americans, too. Being pilots, there is always a great interest in speaking with the enemy. We met our British intelligence interrogator, a very nice man, and I became friends with him and his wife after the war. When they were finished with us, they put us on a ship to France.

We arrived in Cherbourg, and I was with my old friend Krupinski, when suddenly a French soldier reached for Krupinski's Knight's Cross and Oak Leaves. Another French soldier raised his rifle and struck him in the head. Blood went everywhere, and then we German officers went for the Frenchmen. The British officer and guards who were with us then pointed their weapons at their allies and told them to stay away. Krupinski was carried away, and I would not see him again for several years.

We had physicals, of course, and I told the British doctor about my wounds and the problems I was having. I was shot down eight times. I was always lucky, except that I was seriously wounded three times. The first time it was my back. I was then shot and hit right in the face and in my hand, and the third time I jumped out and a P-47 Thunderbolt shot my left thumb off.

I asked if I could go home to be with Hertha, who was a doctor. He said yes and signed my medical release papers. Like that, I was going home. I needed to spend some time with Hertha. She had been pregnant four times, but lost all the babies during Allied bombings, and I knew that disturbed her. We met in Vienna, and we started all over again with nothing. This was right before the Russians came and occupied the city. But she finally told me the entire story about her activities [when Rall was released from captivity], and we went to England in 1948 and spent Christmas and Hanukkah with some friends of her friends, some of the people she saved. It was very moving for me. The rest of their families, left behind in Europe, had disappeared.

We then left, and started over where I wanted to go to the university and study medicine, but after the war those career paths were closed to us officers. The strange thing was that we regular officers were forbidden from joining political parties; we were considered criminals. So, I started working in a textile mill until they learned who I was, when I was fired. Then I started a woodcutting business while Hertha tried to start her medical practice. I then worked for Siemens until 1953. I was able to work with Prince Georg Wilhelm of Hanover, as Hertha had taken a position as house physician at the Salem School on Lake Constance. I had been able to join her full-time when I was offered the job where he was the headmaster until 1955, when Steinhoff, Trautloft, and Hrabak said, "You must come with us. We are starting a new *Luftwaffe*."

I knew that they were creating a new air force. Steinhoff and Dieter Hrabak were already preparing this. I was in industry with Siemens and at the Salem School, where my wife was a doctor, and I was in the organization. My old friends sent me letters saying, "You have to come," and so on. The first of January 1956, I went to Bonn and there I joined the air force again at the rank of *Major*. From there on, I underwent the refresher training on the T-33 at Landsburg, Germany, and later we went to train in the Republic F-84 [Thunderjet] and F-86 [Sabre] in the United States. This was at Luke Air Force Base in Arizona, and from then on I spent quite a lot of time in your country. Then we learned to fly the F-100, F-101, F-102, and F-104.

It was a beautiful time. It looked different than it does today. Luke Air Force Base and the whole Arizona area was just beginning to build up. It was not as extensive as it is today. Phoenix was not as big a city as it is now, and it was beautiful. All we did was fly, and then I came back. General Kuhlman asked me if I wanted to fly the F-104. Of course, I said yes. I was appointed to a staff [position], and then I became the project officer for the F-104, which took me again to the States.

The F-104G version had the replacement of the American ejection seat with the British Martin Baker seat. I qualified in the F-104 and other jets since they were starting to send the Starfighter to Germany. In 1961, I qualified in the F-104G at Palmdale, where all NATO nations sent their pilots. I also had to go to Japan and Canada on occasion. The F-104G was an excellent and very fast aircraft, but dangerous. It was unforgiving. You could not recover from a flat spin, and ejecting was apparently impossible, hence using the Baker system. We called it the "flying coffin" and the "widow maker."

I was in Palmdale and Edwards Air Force Base in California, Nellis Air Force Base in Nevada, and many other places. I later became general and division commander. Then I became chief of staff of the 4th Allied Tactical Air Force, and then I became commander of German Air Force Command and the chief of that later. From January 1, 1971 to March 31, 1973, I was *Inspekteur der Luftwaffe Bundeswehr*, and from April 1, 1974, to October 13, 1975, I was a NATO. At the end of 1975, I retired.

Regarding the F-104 problem, I understood where Steinhoff and Hartmann were coming from. I supported them to a point, in that more funding for training was needed. I disagreed that we did not need the fighter. Also, I had to fight like hell for Erich to get promoted to *Oberst*. He had angered a lot of people, and many thought that he was too high-profile, being the only Diamonds holder in the new air force. There were some who did not trust him because he was with the Russians for ten years, but that was bullshit and I said so. We all knew that Erich would never be a general because of these kinds of politics.

My wife died [in 1985]. I have two daughters, Francesca and Felicita. Francie lives in Paris, France, and is married to a Frenchman. She is an art restorer at the Louvre. She has a good career, and she has two children: Clement and Anna Louise. My other daughter is married and lives in Munich with her husband. My son-in-law is a designer with BMW, and my daughter is also a designer. They also have two children, girls. My second daughter, Felicita, and my son-in-law studied for one year in Pasadena, California.

When I retired, I went into industry, and I was on different boards in an advisory capacity. I am still involved with companies such as BMW. I do quite a bit of traveling in the

States. There is a great interest in some galleries, as in signing all these paintings [aviation prints] and in giving autographs. This is a good chance to get in close contact with some of my former opponents. I am very close friends now with Colonel Hub Zemke; it was his wing that shot off my thumb [56th Fighter Group], and we know exactly who got me. I have a lot of friends in the United States I was always asked to do these television documentaries such as *The World at War* and the *Wings of the Luftwaffe* series, and be interviewed by historians such as you, but you must buy the beer.

Bibliography

Articles

Heaton, Colin D. "Colonel Hajo Herrmann: Master of the Wild Boars," *World War II*, vol. 15, no. 2 (July 2000), pp. 30–36, 78–80.

________. "The Count: Luftwaffe Ace Walter Krupinski," *Military History*, vol. 15, no. 2 (June 1998), pp. 62–68.

________. "Interview: Luftwaffe General Adolf Galland," *Eyewitness to War* (Special Edition, 2003), pp. 26–33, 86.

________. "Luftwaffe Ace Adolf Galland's Last Interview," *World War II*, vol. 15, no. 5 (January 1997), pp. 46–52.

________. "Luftwaffe Ace Günther Rall Remembers," *World War II*, vol. 9, no. 6 (March 1995), pp. 34–40, 77–78.

________. "Luftwaffe Eagle Johannes Steinhoff," *World War II*, vol. 13, no. 1 (May 1998), pp. 28–34, 74.

________. "Luftwaffe's Father of the Night Fighters," *Military History*, vol. 16, no. 6 (February 2000), pp. 42–48.

________. "The Man Who Downed Nowotny: Interview with Colonel Edward R. Haydon," *Aviation History*, vol. 13, no. 1 (September 2002), pp. 22–27.

________. "Wolfpack Ace Robert S. Johnson," *Military History*, vol. 13, no. 3 (August 1996), pp. 26–32.

________. "Jimmy Doolittle and the Emergence of American Air Power," *World War II*, vol. 18, no. 1 (May 2003), pp. 46–52, 78.

Books/Secondary Sources

Amadio, Jill. *Günther Ral l: A Memoir*. Santa Ana, Calif.: Seven Locks Press, 2002.

Andrews, Allen. *The Air Marshals*. New York: William Morrow, 1970.

Arnold, Henry. *Global Mission*. New York: Harper & Bros., 1949.

Barnett, Correlli, ed. *Hitler's Generals*. New York: Weidenfeld & Nicholson, 1989.

Baumbach, Werner. *The Life and Death of the Luftwaffe*. New York: Coward-McCann, 1960.

Bekker, Cajus. *The Luftwaffe War Diaries*. London: Macdonald, 1966.

Bender, Roger James. *The Luftwaffe*. Mountain View, Pa.: R. James Bender, 1972.

Bond, Brian. *Liddell-Hart: A Study of His Military Thought*. London: Cassell, 1977.

Boog, Horst. *The Conduct of the Air War in the Second World War: An International Comparison*. New York: Oxford University Press, 1991.

Bowman, Martin W. *The Reich Intruders*. Somerset, U.K.: Patrick Stephens, 1997.

Bowman, Martin W., with Theo Boiten. *Raiders of the Reich: Air Battle Western Europe: 1942–1945*. Osceola, Wis.: Motorbooks International, 1996.

Bowyer, Chaz. *History of the RAF*. London: Bison Books, 1977.

Boyne, Walter J. *Clash of Wings: World War II in the Air*. New York: Simon & Schuster, 1994.

Brooks, Andrew J. *Photo Reconnaissance*. London: Ian Allen, 1975.

Brown, Eric. *Wings of the Luftwaffe*. London: MacDonald & James, 1977.

Brütting, Georg. *Das Warren die Deutschen Kampfflieger-Asse 1939–1945*. Stuttgart: Motorbuch Verlag, 1975.

Brunswig, Hans. *Feuerstürm über Hanburg: Die Luftangriffe auf Hamburg im Zweiten Weltkrieg und Ihre Folgen*. Stuttgart: Motorbuch Verlag, 1978.

Buchner, Hermann. *Stormbird: One of the Luftwaffe's Highest Scoring Me 262 Aces*. Manchester: Crecy, 2009.

Busch, Hans, Lance C. Frickensmith, and Trevor James Constable. *The Last of the Few: An Me.262 Pilot Remembers*. Bement, Ill.: World War 2 Books & Video, 2009.

Cooper, Alan W. *Bombers over Berlin: The RAF Offensive November 1943–March 1944*. London: William Kimber, 1985.

Cooper, Matthew. *The German Air Force 1922–1945: An Anatomy of Failure*. London: MacDonald & James, 1981.

Crandall, Jerry & Judy. *Wolfgang Falck, The Happy Falcon: An Autobiography by the Father of the Night Fighters*. Hamilton, Mont.: Eagle Editions, 2002.

Cross, Robin. *The Bombers*. New York: Macmillan, 1987.

Deichmann, Paul. *German Air Force Operations in Support of the Army*. USAF Historical Study No. 163. Maxwell Air Force Base: Air University Press, 1962.

Dierich, Wolfgang. *Die Verbände der Luftwaffe*. Stuttgart: Motorbuch Verlag, 1976.

Divine, David. *The Broken Wing: A Study in the British Exercise in Air Power*. London: Hutchinson, 1966.

Doolittle, James H., with Carroll V. Glines. *I Could Never Be So Lucky Again*. Atglen, Pa.: Schiffer Publishing, 1991.

Ethell, Jeffrey. *Bomber Command*. Osceoloa, Wisc: Motorbooks International, 1994.

Ethell, Jeffrey, and Alfred Price. *Target Berlin Mission 250: 6 March 1944*. New York: Jane's, 1982.

Faber, Harold, ed. *The Luftwaffe: A History*. New York: Quadrangle Books/The New York Times Book Co., Inc., 1977.

Fischer, Wolfgang, and John Weal. *Luftwaffe Fighter Pilot: Defending the Reich Against the RAF and USAAF*. London: Grub Street Publishing, 2010.

Forsyth, Robert, and Jim Laurier. *Luftwaffe Viermot Aces 1942–45*. New York: Osprey Publishing, 2011.

______. *Fw 190 Stürmbocke vs B-17 Flying Fortress: Europe 1944–45*. New York: Osprey Publishing, 2009.

Frank, Howard. *The Conquest of the Air*. New York: Random House, 1972.

Freeman, Roger A., Alan Crouchman and Vic Maslen. *The Mighty Eighth War Diary*. Minneapolis: Motorbooks International, 1990.

Galland, Adolf. *The First and the Last*. New York: Bantam, 1978.

Galland, Adolf, Karl Ries, R. Ahnert, and David Mondey, eds. *The Luftwaffe at War, 1939–1945*. Chicago: Henry Regnert/Ian Allen, 1972.

Hannig, Norbert, and John Weal. *Luftwaffe Fighter Ace*. London: Grub Street Publishing, 2004.

Heaton, Colin D, and Anne-Marie Lewis. *The German Aces Speak: World War II Through the Eyes of Four of the Luftwaffe's Most Important Commanders*. Minneapolis: Zenith Press, 2011.

_______. *The Me-262 Stormbird: From the Pilots Who Flew, Fought and Survived It*. Minneapolis: Zenith/MBI Publishing, 2012.

_______. *Night Fighters: Luftwaffe and RAF Air Combat over Europe 1939–1945*. Annapolis, Md.: Naval Institute Press, 2008.

Herrmann, Hajo. *Eagle's Wings*. Osceola, Wis.: Motorbooks International, 1991.

Hinchliffe, Peter. *The Other Battle: Luftwaffe Night Aces Versus Bomber Command*. Book Sales, 2001.

Jablonski, Edward. *Air War*, vols. 1–4. New York: Doubleday, 1971.

Johnen, Wilhelm. *Battling the Bombers*. New York: Ace Books, 1958.

Killen, John. *The Luftwaffe: A History*. London: Muller, 1967.

Knoke, Heinz, John Ewing (trans.). *I Flew for the Fuhrer: The Story of a German Fighter Pilot*. New York: Henry Holt, 1953–54.

Lipfert, Helmut, and Werner Girbig. *The War Diary of Hauptmann Helmut Lipfert*. Atglen, Pa.: Schiffer Publishing, 1992.

Longmate, Norman. *The Bombers: The RAF Offensive Against Germany, 1939–1945*. London: Hutchinson, 1983.

Lyall, Gavin, ed. *The War in the Air: The Royal Air Force in World War II*. New York: William Morrow, 1968.

Macksey, Kenneth. *Technology in War*. London: Arms & Armour Press, 1986.

Mason, Herbert Malloy, Jr. *Duel for the Sky*. Garden City, N.J.: Doubleday, 1985.

Maloney, Edward T. *Luftwaffe Aircraft and Aces*. Toronto: The Air Museum, Inc., 1969.

Messenger, Charles. *Bomber Harris and the Strategic Bomber Offensive, 1939–1945*. London: Arms & Armour Press, 1984.

Michie, Allan A. *The Air Offensive against Germany*. New York: Henry Holt, 1943.

Middlebrook, Martin. *The Battle of Hamburg*. London: Allen Lane, 1980.

________. *The Nuremberg Raid*. London: Allen Lane, 1973.

Milward, Alan S. *The German Economy at War*. Atlantic Highlands, NJ: Humanities Press, 1965.

Mosely, Leonard. *The Reich Marshal*. Garden City, N.J.: Doubleday, 1974.

Obermeier, Ernst. *Die Ritterkreuzträger der Luftwaffe*. Mainz: Verlag Dieter Hoffmann, 1966.

Overy, Richard. *The Air War, 1939–1945*. London: Europa Publications, 1980.

Price, Alfred. *Battle Over the Reich*. New York: Charles Scribner & Sons, 1973.

________. *The Last Year of the Luftwaffe*. London: Arms & Armour Press, 1991.

________. *Luftwaffe: Birth, Life and Death of an Air Force*. New York: Ballantine Books, 1971.

________. *The Luftwaffe Data Book*. London: Greenhill Books, 1997.

Probert, H. A. *The Rise and Fall of the German Air Force, 1933–1945*. London: Arms & Armour Press, 1983.

Reschke, Willi. *Jagdgeschwader 301/302 "Wilde Sau": In Defense of the Reich with the Bf 109, Fw 190 and Ta 152*. Atglen, Pa.: Schiffer Publishing, 2004.

Richards, Dennis. *The Hardest Victory: RAF Bomber Command in the Second World War*. New York: W. W. Norton, 1995.

Rigg, Bryan Mark. *Hitler's Jewish Soldiers: The Untold Story of Nazi Racial Laws and the Men of Jewish Descent in the German Military*. Lawrence: University Press of Kansas, 2002.

Robertson, Scott. *The Development of RAF Strategic Bombing Doctrine, 1919–1939*. Westport, Conn.: Praeger Publishers, 1997.

Rumpf, Hans. *The Bombing of Germany*. Munich: Holt, Rinehart & Winston, 1961.

Saundby, Air Marshal Sir Roger. *Air Bombardment: The Story of Its Development*. London: Chatto & Windus, 1962.

Schuck, Walter. *Luftwaffe Eagle: 206 Combat Victories in the Me 109 and Me 262*. Crowborough, U.K.: Hikoki Publications, 2009.

Smith, J. Richard, and Eddie J. Creek. *Focke-Wulf FW190: Volume One 1938–1943*. London: Ian Allan Publishing, 2012.

________. *Focke-Wulf FW-190: Volume Two 1943–1944*. London: Ian Allan Publishing, 2012.

Smith, Starr. *Jimmy Stewart: Bomber Pilot*. Minneapolis: Zenith/MBI Publishing, 2005.

Späte, Wolfgang. *Top Secret Bird*. Missoula, Mont.: Pictorial Histories Publishing, 1989.

Spick, Mike. *Luftwaffe Fighter Aces: The Jagdflieger and Their Combat Tactics and Techniques*. London: Greenhill Books/ Lionel Leventhal, 1996.

Steinhoff, Johannes. *The Final Hours: The Luftwaffe Plot Against Göring*. Dulles, Va.: Potomac Books, 2005.

Stokesbury, James. *A Short History of Air Power*. New York: William Morrow, 1986.

Suchenwirth, Richard. *Command and Leadership in the German Air Force*. USAF Historical Study No. 174. New York: Arno Press, 1968.

________. *The Development of the German Air Force, 1919–1939*. USAF Historical Study No. 160. New York: Arno Press, 1968.

Taylor, John W. R., and Kenneth Munson. *History of Aviation*. London: Crown Publishing, 1977.

Taylor, John W. R. *A History of Aerial Warfare*. London: Hamlyn Publishing Group, 1974.

Terraine, John. *A Time for Courage: The Royal Air Force in the European War, 1939–1945*. New York: Macmillan, 1985.

Time-Life Books. *The Air War in Europe*. New York: Time-Life, 1992.

Toliver, Raymond F., and Trevor J. Constable. *Fighter General: The Life of Adolf Galland*. Zephyr Cove, Pa.: AmPress Publishing, 1986.

________. *Fighter Aces of the Luftwaffe*. Atglen, Pa.: Schiffer Publishing, 1996.

Verrier, Anthony. *The Bomber Offensive*. London: B. T. Batsford, 1968.

Völker, Karl-Heinz. *Die Deutsche Luftwaffe, 1939–1945*. Stuttgart: Deutsche Verlags-Anhalt, 1967.

Weal, John. *Fw 190 Defence of the Reich Aces*. London/New York: Osprey Publishing, 2011.

Wells, Mark K. *Courage and Air Warfare: The Allied Aircrew Experience in the Second World War*. London: Frank Cass Publishers, 1995.

Zaloga, Stephen J. *Defense of the Third Reich 1941–45*. London/New York: Osprey Publishing, 2012.

Research Papers, Dissertations and Theses

Carroll, Major James J. "Physiological Problems of Bomber Crews in the Eighth Air Force During WWII." AU/ACSC/0609D/97-03. The Research Department, Air Command and Staff College. March 1997. Located at http://www.dtic.mil/cgi-bin/GetTRDoc?AD=ADA398044.

Reichert, Capt. David, USAF. *Schweinfurt—The Battle Within the Battle for the U.S. 8th Air Force*. March 10, 2004. Located at http://www.airpower.maxwell.af.mil/airchronicles/cc/reichert.html.

Rigole, Julius A. "The Strategic Bombing Campaign Against Germany During World War II." Louisiana State University and Agricultural and Mechanical College. May 2002. Located at http://etd.lsu.edu/docs/available/etd-0413102-132317/unrestricted/Rigole_thesis.pdf.

British Archives Public Record Office

76. BA/MA, RL 2 III/1194, Genst. Gen. Qu. (6. Abt), "Flugzeugunfälle und Verluste bei den fliegenden Verbänden."

77. BA/MA, RL 2 III/1025, Genst. 6. Abt., "Front-Flugzeug-Verluste im Oktober 1943." Part of the confusion undoubtedly lies in exactly how German records were compiled and for what purposes. Unit leaders issued reports and requests at the *Geschwader* level, yet all reports were filed in Berlin under higher *Fliegerkorps* categories. After action reports were filed separately from asset requests according to *Staffel.*

78. Based on the figures of fighter pilot strength and losses in the tables in BA/MA, RL 2 III/722, 723, 724, 725, Genst. Gen. Qu.6. Abt. (I), "Übersicht über Soll, Istbestand, Einsatzbereitschaft, Verluste und Reserven der fliegenden Verbände."

88. BA/MA, RL 3/62, "Stenographische Niederschrift der Besprechung beim Reichsmarschall am 23.11.43. in Karinhall."

89. BA/MA, RL 3/61, "Stenographische Niederschrift der Besprechung beim Reichsmarschall am 28.11.43. in Karinhall," p. 88.

90. USSBS, ESBGWE, Appendix Table 102, p. 277.

91. "Alliierte Luftangriffe im Jahre 1943 auf Werke der deutschen Flugzeugindustrie," AFSHRC: K 113.312-2, v. 3.

92. BA/MA, RL 2 II/365, Der Oberbefehlshaber der Luftwaffe, Führungsstab Ic, Nr. 32487/43, 5.10.43., "Luftlagebericht West, Stand: 1. Oktober 1943."

93. BA/MA, RL 2 II/365, Der Oberbefehlshaber der Luftwaffe, Führungsstab Ic, Nr. 4222/43, 2.11.43, "Luftlagebericht West, Stand: 1. November 1943."

94. BA/MA, RL 2 II/365, Der Oberbefehlshaber der Luftwaffe, Führungsstab Ic., Nr 4611/43, 3.12.43., "Luftlagebericht West, Stand: 1.12.1943."

95. BA/MA, RL 2 II/320, "USA Fliegertruppe, die schweren amerikanischen Kampfverbände, Stand: Dezember 1943," Luftwaffenführungsstab, Ic/Fremde Luftwaffen West.

99. BA/MA, RL 8/92, "Besprechung beim Bef. Mitte am

6.11.43., 15.00 Uhr in Berlin-Dahlem."

100. BA/MA, RL 8/92, "Besprechung beim Bef. Mitte am 6.11.43. 17.45 Uhr in Berlin-Dahlem."

101. BA/MA, RL 8/92, "Besprechung beim Bef. Mitte am 7.11.43. 10.30 Uhr in Berlin, Reichssportfeld."

102. BA/MA, RL 8/92, "Besprechung am 8.11.43. 13.00 Uhr aufdem Gefechtsstand De Beul."

103. BA/MA, RL 8/92, "Besprechung in Stade am 16.11.43."

109. BA/MA, RL 2 III/726, 727, 728, Gen. Qu. 6. Abt. (I), "Übersicht" über Soll, Istbestand, Einsatzbereitschaft, Verluste und Reserven der fliegenden Verbände.

122. BA/MA, RL 2 III/1025, Generalstab 6. Abt. (III A), Front-Flugzeug-Verluste, January-June 1944.

125. BA/MA, RL 2 III/1025, Generalstab 6. Abt. (III A), Front-Flugzeug-Verluste, January-June 1944.

126. BA/MA , RL 8/93, 1 Jagdkorps, "Niederschrift über die Divisionskommandeur-Besprechung am 25.1.44. um 12.30 Uhr in De Breul."

152. BA/MA, RL 7/521, Besprechungspunkte Oberst i. G. Kless am 17.6.43. in Robinson 4 mit Generaloberst Jeschonnek.

157. BA/MA, RL 2 II/5, Reichsmarschall, 21.11.43., An Lft. Kdo, 4, Chef d. Genst., Lft. Kdo, 6, Generaloberst. Gen. d. Kampfflieger, Generalmajor Dietrich Peltz.

158. BA/MA, RL 10/257, Kriegstagebuch Nr. 8 des Zerstörergeschwaders "Horst Wessel" Nr 26 vom 1.1.-30.9.44.

159. BA/MA, RL 10/544, Leistungsbuch, Leutnant Elmar Boersch, 3./K.G. General Wever.

160. BA/MA, RL 10/639, "Notizen zur Traditionsgeschichte der III. Gruppe des Jagdgeschwaders Udet, (Quellen: Kriegstagebücher der III./e)."

161. BA/MA, RL 10/639, "Notizen zur Traditionsgeschichte der III. Gruppe des Jagdgeschwaders Udet (Quellen: Kriegstagebucher der III./e)."

162. BA/MA, RL 10/639, Notizen zur Traditionsgeschichte der III. Gruppe des Jagdgeschwaders Udet.

163. BA/MA, RL 2 II/329, Luftwaffenführungsstab Ic Nr 13/44

(III A), 2.1.44., "Luftlage West Nr. 1 vom 31.12 und Nacht zum 1.1.44."

164. BA/MA, RL 2 II/329, Luftwaffenführungsstab Ic, Fremde Luftwaffen West, Nr 1193/44, 18.3.44. "Luftlage West Nr. 32."

165. BA/MA, RL 2 II/5, Luftwaffenführungsstab, Ia op Nr. 8865/43, 9.11.43., Anlage: "Kurze Studie: Kampfgegen die russische Rüstungsindustrie."

166. BA/MA, RL 2 III/722, 723, 724, 725, 726, 727, 728, Gen. Qu. 6. Abt. (1)., "Übersicht" über Soll, Istbestand, Einsatzbereitschaft, Verluste und Reserven der fliegenden Verbände.

167. BA/MA, RL 2 III/722, 723, 724, 725, 726, 727, 728, Gen. Qu. 6. Abt. (I) Übersicht über Soll, Istbestand, Einsatzbereitschaft, Verluste und Reserven der fliegenden Verbände.

168. BA/MA, RL 2 III/725, 726, Genst. Gen. Qu. 6.Abt. (1), "Übersicht über Soll, Istbestand, Einsatzbereitschaft, Verluste und Reserven der fliegenden Verbände," July, August, September 1943.

169. BA/MA, RL 2 III/728, 729, Genst. Gen. Qu. 6. Abt. (I), "Übersicht über Soll, Istbestand, Einsatzbereitschaft, Verluste und Reserven der fliegenden Verbände."

170. BA/MA, RL 2 III/728-731, Gen. Qu. 6. Abt. (I), Übersicht über Soll, Istbestand, Einsatzbereitschaft, Verluste und Reserven der fliegenden Verbände.

171. BA/MA, RL 2 III/1025, Genst. 6. Abt. (III A), Front-Flugzeug-Verluste, reports for November and December.

172. BA/MA, RL 2 III/1025, Genst. 6. Abt. (III A), Front-Flugzeug-Verluste, and RL 2 III/729, Übersicht über Soll, Istbestand, Einsatzbereitschaft, Verluste und Reserven der fliegenden Verbände.

173. BA/MA, RL 3/1, "Stenografische Niederschrift der Besprechungen während des 'Untemehmens Hubertus' v. F.-11.3.44."

174. BA/MA, RL 3/1, "Stenographischer Bericht über die Jägerstabs-Besprechung am 4. Marz 1944 im RLM."

175. BA/MA, RL 3/61, "Stenographische Niederschrift der Besprechung des Reichsmarschalls mit GL and Industrierat am 14.10.43. in der neuen Reichskanzlei, Berchtesgaden."

176. BA/MA, RL 3/62, "Stenographische Niederschrift über Besprechung unter dem Vorsitz des Reichsmarschalls am 28.11.43. in Neuenhazen bei Berlin."

177. BA/MA, RL 7/51, Der Chef der Luftflotte 6, Br. B. Nr. 241/43, 12.6.43., Bert. Bekämpfung der sow. russ. Kriegswirtschaft.

178. BA/MA, RL 8/91, I Jagdkorps, "Kommandeurbesprechung am 29.9.43. im Zeist."

179. BA/MA, RL 8/92, "Niederschrift über Divisionkommandeur-Besprechung am 4.11.43., 14.00 Uhr in De Breul."

180. BA/MA, RL 8/93, "Niederschrift über die Divisionskommandeur-Besprechung am 29.12.1943."

181. BA/MA, RL 8/93, I Jagdkorps, "Niederschrift über die Divisionskommand eur-besprechung am 29.12.43.

182. Based on the figures in BA/MA, RL 2 III/1193, 1194, 1195, Genst. Gen. Qu. (6. Abt.), "Flugzeugunfälle und Verluste bei den fliegenden Verbänden."

183. Based on loss tables in BA/MA, RL 2 III/1025, Genst. 6. Abt. (III A), Front-Flugzeug-Verluste; and BA/MA, RL 2 II/728, Gen. Qu. 6. Abt. (1), Übersicht über Soll, Istbestand, Einsatzbereitschaft, Verluste und Reserven der fliegenden Verbände.

184. PRO AIR/20.5815.

185. PRO AIR 14/3489, Probable Reconstruction of German Night Fighter Reaction, Raid on Nuremberg 30/31.3.44.

186. PRO AIR 22/203, "War Room Manual of Bomber Command Ops 1939/1945," compiled by Air Ministry War Room (Statistical Section).

187. PRO AIR 22/203, War Room Manual of Bomber Command Ops, 1939-1945, Air Ministry War Room (Statistical Section).

188. "Statistical Summary of Eighth Air Force Operations, European Theater, 17 August 1942-8 May 1945," AFSHRC.

Index

www.ingramcontent.com/pod-product-compliance
Lightning Source LLC
LaVergne TN
LVHW010604100826
845148LV00014B/2840

* 9 7 8 0 7 6 0 3 6 1 5 5 9 *